ASIAN FRONTIER NATIONALISM:

Owen Lattimore and the American Policy Debate

James Cotton

Studies on East Asia

MANCHESTER
UNIVERSITY PRESS

First published in 1989 in Great Britain by
Manchester University Press
Oxford Road
Manchester M13 9PL, UK

Copyright © James Cotton 1989

Editorial responsibility for *Studies on East Asia* rests with the Northumbria
Universities Joint East Asia Centre, University of Newcastle upon Tyne and
University of Durham, England, which promotes publications on the individual
countries and culture of east Asia, as well as on the region as a whole.

British Library cataloguing in publication data
Cotton, James
   Asian frontier nationalism : Owen Lattimore and the
   American policy debate.–(Studies on East Asia)
   1. Asia. Nationalism related to foreign relations between
   Asia & United States, 1945–1975
   2. United States. Foreign relations with Asia, 1945–1975
   related to nationalism in Asia
   I. Title   II. Series
   320.5'4'095

ISBN 0–7190–2585–0 *hardback*

Printed in Great Britain by
Billings and Son Ltd, Worcester

Contents

Preface

This book was researched over a number of years while I was a member of the East Asia Centre and the Politics Department of the University of Newcastle upon Tyne. As I have incurred many debts to individuals and institutions during this time I should like here to thank: the British Academy and Newcastle University for timely grants to facilitate travel in connection with my research, David S G Goodman for his continued encouragement and welcome advice, and Charles Bawden, Urgunge Onon, Judith Nordby, Tom Ewing, Don Rimington, Fujiko Isono, Caroline Humphrey, Michael Oakeshott, Keith Pratt, John Gardner, Mark Elvin, John Cayley, A Doak Barnett, Robert P Newman, Stanley I Kutler, and G L Ulmen for helpfully responding to written or personal enquiries or for providing suggestions for additional lines of research. The Inter-Library Loans Service at Newcastle University and the British Library have been of unfailing assistance in my quest for materials.

On 31 May 1989, after this book had gone to press, Owen Lattimore died in Providence, Rhode Island, aged 88. I would like to record here my enduring obligation to him for being kind enough to devote the better part of two days (in Cambridge in 1980 and again in 1982) to sharing with me his reflections on a long and eventful life.

Note on Romanisation

Although the scholarly preference now is to employ the *pinyin* system of transliteration in reference to Chinese place and personal names, as many of Lattimore's works are quoted using the earlier Wade-Giles system (sometimes with modifications) or local names then in currency these have been used throughout this text. However the *pinyin* equivalent has been added in parenthesis the first time a particular place or name occurs, and if the place is now known by a different name it is that name which is appended - thus, Kansu (Gansu); Ku Ch'eng-tze (Qitai). In the case of Mongol names, for the same reason the earlier transliteration system is generally employed (thus: Sukebator) except in cases where the most common usage encountered has been an alternative or later system (thus: Natsagdorj). Alternative transliterations are similarly appended, though in the case of mediaeval names there has been no systematic attempt to employ the most rigorous scholarly orthography (thus, Chinggis Khan rather than 'Činggis Qan').

Introduction

As a historical figure Owen Lattimore is best known for the part he played, albeit unwillingly, in the brief but prominent national career of Senator Joseph McCarthy in American politics. The involvement of Lattimore and State Department China specialists including John S Service, John Carter Vincent, and O Edmund Clubb in the rise of this unsavoury and opportunistic politician could well be considered as one of the great puzzles of modern American politics. McCarthy's charges prompted a search for those spies and traitors who had allegedly manipulated American policy so as to deliver China to the communists. Though careers were ruined (and the course of much subsequent US policy in Asia transformed as a result) none such could be found, and the focus of inquiry shifted to the academic community. It was now asserted that pro-communist values had been insinuated into the policy debate in the 1940s by communists and their sympathisers posing as scholarly commentators. Once again Lattimore became a key figure, this time as an influential member of the Institute of Pacific Relations and former editor of its journal, *Pacific Affairs*.

This major episode in American political history has received detailed scholarly treatment. Even at the time, the extensive documentation made available, as much as media and public attention, generated many studies and commentaries, Lattimore himself offering an exposé of McCarthy's methods in *Ordeal by Slander*. Materials obtained more recently with the new accessibility of US government records (including Lattimore's heretofore confidential FBI file) have facilitated a reexamination of past interpretations.

As an attempt to present the first full intellectual biography of Owen Lattimore this study includes a consideration of this phase of his life.[1] It is apparent that it had a major impact, not merely on Lattimore's academic and public career, but also on his thinking. The approach taken, however, will be to regard this episode as a less than fully enlightening phase in a long process of intellectual evolution, much of which is only intelligible with reference to biographical and intellectual developments in the 1930s. Although Lattimore was repeatedly cross-examined by members of two Senate committees as to his views and commitments in these years and later, his interrogators were preoccupied by the likely impact of his answers on contemporary political debate. Few had any real knowledge of China let alone Mongolia, whereas it will be argued here that by about 1934 or 1935 Lattimore had developed an emotional and intellectual identification with Mongol nationalism which has remained a dominant influence on all his subsequent activity. Indeed, it would not be too far fetched to compare his commitment to the Mongols with that of T E Lawrence to the Arabs. This commitment has been both a strength and a weakness in his work since it has afforded him insights into the world view of and pressures upon a poorly understood people while it has also provided him

1

with an often inappropriate yardstick by which to judge other peoples and situations.

It is necessary, therefore, to begin the story in the late 1920s and to follow carefully Lattimore's various attempts to organise and comprehend his experiences as he travelled in a period of change and upheaval in the frontier regions of China. Having tentatively identified these organising ideas this identification can be tested by tracing their influence in his subsequent work, from his writings on foreign policy in the 1940s to his later and more diverse work on topics ranging from Mongol civilisation to the role of frontiers in world history. It will be shown that at different times Lattimore has been an influential figure and something of an intellectual pioneer.

As this study aims to be both critical and historical some assessment will be offered on the coherence of his ideas and on the extent to which he has made a lasting contribution to scholarship. In the long term Lattimore's greatest achievement is likely to be seen as the central hypotheses of his great synthesising historical geography of the Chinese periphery, *Inner Asian Frontiers of China*. But the vocabulary of modern politics will be long indebted to Lattimore since he seems to have been the first to use the term 'satellite' to connote a political and ideological dependent state, and one of the first to refer in the post-war world to the emergence of a 'Third World' of nations.

Note on the Introduction

1   For a brief outline of Lattimore's biography, see John G Hangin and Urgunge Onon, 'Professor Owen Lattimore - A Biographical Sketch', *The Mongolia Society. Occasional Papers* 8(1972), pp 7-9. Lattimore himself offers some autobiographical remarks in 'Preface', *Studies in Frontier History. Collected Papers 1928-58* (London: Oxford University Press, 1962), pp 11-31.

CHAPTER ONE

A Frontier Perspective

The China of Owen Lattimore's earlier years was a country in political, economic, and social flux. The collapse of the imperial system in 1911 had led to the complete erosion of central authority. At the beginning of the 1920s China was divided between cliques of contending warlords, the conflict between whom disrupted trade and engendered widespread social misery. After 1923 the growing power of the Kuomintang (Guomindang) and their new communist allies in the south threatened a wider conflict since with Soviet aid Sun Yat-sen (Sun Zhongshan) had pledged himself to the reunification of his country by means of a military Northern Expedition. On the economic front the old Western dominance was fading with the rise of Japan whose trading position greatly expanded during the First World War when European economic energies were otherwise absorbed. At the same time the growing world market system was drawing even the most far flung areas into its embrace. The old élite of landlord and gentry families acquired new economic roles, or were displaced by compradores and merchants prepared to adapt to the requirements of the times. A new Chinese self-assertiveness after the May Fourth movement of 1919 further portended an end to the era when foreigners and foreign enterprises in China could necessarily expect the privileges and protection due to them under the unequal treaties of the nineteenth century.

It is evident that Lattimore was more aware of the profound changes under way in China than many of his contemporaries. As he later recalled, doing business in the interior, far from the treaty ports where Western power was still concentrated, forced him to deal directly with the consequences of the breakdown of the old economic and political relations.[1] His employment also brought him into contact, albeit indirectly, with those frontier areas of China by then drawn into commercial relations through merchant intermediaries with the world economy. This chapter will deal with Lattimore's first explorations of the northeastern and northwestern frontiers of China. While it is clear that he was from the first taken with the antiquity of frontier trade he was also well aware of its contemporary significance, and soon came to be especially preoccupied with the impact of trading and of colonisation on the peoples of these regions.

Travel, Trade Routes and Geopolitics

Lattimore spent most of his infancy in North China with his parents, his father being a mission educator in Pao-ting (Baoding). Returning to China after schooling in Switzerland and England, Lattimore worked first for the *Peking-Tientsin Times* (edited by H G W Woodhead) before joining the trading firm of Arnhold & Co. Unhappy with the superficial life of the Treaty Ports he sought to develop a better understanding of China by study of the language, proficiency in which led him to conduct business for the firm in the provinces. For one fascinated from his youth by history (at school he wrote much epic poetry on historical themes[2]) a trip to Kuei-hua (Hohhot) and Pao-t'ou (Baotou) in 1925[3] to negotiate the release of a trainload of wool caught between the forces of contending warlords, was to prove, as he later expressed it, a 'turning point'.[4] Arnhold & Co were at the time major dealers in commodities ranging from fleeces and camel hair to dried egg powder, their buyers obtaining these goods from merchants trading with frontier regions including the northwest and Mongolia. Thus began for Lattimore a preoccupation with the connection between China and the interior.

To study the origins and conditions of the trade from Sinkiang (Xinjiang) to Kuei-hua Lattimore embarked on the northern or desert trading route from Kuei-hua to Ku Ch'eng-tze (Qitai) travelling for more than four months by camel to complete the journey in January 1927. This route was chosen partly because of its novelty from the point of view of exploration but also because the more northerly 'great' road was blocked by independent Mongolia, and that through Kansu (Gansu) by civil war and unrest. From this expedition several publications resulted, including his earliest book *The Desert Road to Turkestan* (1928). Although Lattimore has since criticised the work for its immaturity and condescension, by the standards of the time it is both lively and perceptive. He touched on areas traversed by Younghusband, Stein and various Russian explorers (including Prejevalsky)[5] but he was the first to cover the entire route. Moreover it was the manner of his travelling, attaching himself to trading caravans, and the fact that he was fluent in the language and even the dialect of the caravan men which was to give him insights missed by individuals more concerned with geography than the beliefs and mores of traders and the people with whom they had contact.

From the writings of this time several themes stand out. Although he had steeped himself in the works of the great travellers he had read little that could be described as more theoretical with the exception of the available works of Ellsworth Huntington. Consequently this author's *Pulse of Asia*, a work then very much in vogue (and employed in Toynbee's 1934 account of the achievement and predicament of nomads), is often alluded to,[6] and is the foundation for Lattimore's discussions of climatic desiccation and pulsation as the root cause of the nomadic historical cycle:

> A very slight climatic variation is enough to upset the economy of
> people who depend on the grazing to be found for their cattle; it is
> known that there have been such variations in Central Asia on the
> edge of our historical period, and it is arguable that most of the

migratory wars of the barbaric hordes originated in the necessity
so caused of finding new pastures.[7]

In the case of the Mongols this nomad cycle was brought to an end by the introduction of the 'artificial measure' of lama Buddhism which enervated the race and drained the society of its wealth.[8] But Lattimore was also absorbed by the geography of the Great Wall frontier, the relationship between the geography and the history of the area, and the mechanics, lore and determinants of trade and trading routes. And it is clear also that the parlous condition of the Mongols as a people Lattimore found both moving and also a puzzle. It is apparent that this experience is at the root of his lifelong quest to understand the mainsprings of the nomadic way of life, and to elucidate the relationship between nomads and the sedentary civilisations of the oases and China within the Great Wall.

In *Desert Road to Turkestan* the Mongols are described as a race who had come to a 'stand still' if they were not actually 'dying'. Lattimore contrasts the potential of the nomads with the narrow and squalid life of the Chinese frontier peasantry who were displacing them,[9] although he is also aware that the continuing encroachment of Chinese on Mongol lands though often organised by frontier officials was only possible with the connivance of the Mongol nobility who sold such titles as they possessed to their lands at the cost of the future of their people. Weakened in their own habitat the Mongols had become pawns in the struggle between China, Russia and Japan. As Lattimore explains in a popular article of the time, the Russians used Buryats to win over the Mongols and it still seemed possible that with Russian encouragement they might detach Mongol inhabited areas of the newly established Nanking (Nanjing) Republic from China.[10] Indeed, at this time Lattimore was inclined to see Russian machinations in other areas of Inner Asia, notably Tibet,[11] and growing Russian influence was one of the themes of his next group of writings which were devoted to the condition and prospects of Sinkiang.

His wife having joined him (after a series of frustrations and adventures) on the Soviet border at Chuguchak (Tacheng, Qoqck) Lattimore travelled in Sinkiang for most of 1927, visiting Turfan (Turpan) and Kulja (Yining, Gulja) before crossing into Ladakh in British India through the Karakoram pass. He then travelled to the United States, by way of Italy and Britain writing *High Tartary* (published in 1930) and several attendant pieces. There was already an extensive literature on Chinese and Russian Central Asia, and the geographical influences upon its history had recently been the subject of two lectures published by Sir Aurel Stein.[12] Lattimore restricted himself, therefore, to further explorations of some of the themes broached in *Desert Road to Turkestan*, but he did develop an analysis of the domination, precarious as it was, of Sinkiang by the Chinese, and the likely future role of Soviet Russia in this domination.

The influence of Huntington was still apparent in his treatment of migration and nomad conquest,[13] and Lattimore offers some remarks on the influence of geography on trade and on relations between the oasis and steppe peoples north and south of the Tien Shan (Tian Shan) in *High Tartary*. In an article published in 1928 on political conditions in this area Lattimore developed a perceptive interpretation of the strategy and consequences of Chinese rule. Whereas Chinese rule in Mongolia was inept and served chiefly to undermine the prosperity of the inhabitants their conduct in Sinkiang, which was assisted by the presence of capable and energetic rulers, had done much to improve the material condition of the subject peoples in a region where the proportion of Han Chinese, soldiers, traders and administrators alike, was always small.[14] The political strategy employed had been to keep Turki (Uygur), Kazaks, T'ung-kan (Hui) and Mongols apart, and to accept the several paper currencies which existed in the province, the administration only taking such revenue as would keep the loyalty of its functionaries. The price of this domination however was considerable. Sealing Sinkiang from contact with the rest of China kept the currencies stable, prevented exactions from central government, and avoided expensive and fruitless entanglements in warlord conflict, but the consequence was increasingly to draw the dominion into closer economic contact with Soviet Central Asia, contact facilitated particularly by railway building. Thus enters the 'geopolitical' theme of these writings, given further expression in an article on Chinese Turkestan written a little later (but published in 1933) and bemoaned by their author when writing his retrospective comments in 1973.

Although he now doubts that at that time he was even familiar with the term 'geopolitics'[15] Lattimore adopted the view in the late 1920s that conflict between a now reviving China and a resurgent Soviet Russia was bound to occur. Referring clearly to the establishing of the Nanking regime Lattimore believed that great changes had already 'broken down all the old social standards and political forms in China', and that portended an 'outward' surge which would bear upon all the frontiers of China and which must 'meet the thrust of the expanding Russian people':

> Frontiers that are now ... nothing but vague swaths of country will
> ... have to be narrowly defined. Already a thrust and counterthrust
> is bearing on them (as in Manchuria and Mongolia). It is a play of
> primal forces, far more significant than superficial considerations
> of politics.[16]

The geography of the frontier regions had thus not become obsolete since 'like causes ... produce like results'. Although Sinkiang was falling within the Soviet economic orbit the Chinese had made it clear when they were given an opportunity that they sought 'domination ... over every race that comes within the scope of Chinese action'.[17] Undermined economically and likely to be subverted by the new Chinese resurgence, the old order in Sinkiang was bound to crumble.

In the later article on Chinese Turkestan there is some development of Lattimore's position. There are signs that he is not so persuaded of the value of Huntington's environmental approach;[18] moreover Lattimore has begun to pay considerable attention to the views of the frontier inhabitants themselves. It had been their historical fate to 'face' China, consequently their history had been hitherto determined from that quarter, being 'an alternation of advance and retreat'. They could not be expected to play an active part in a coming Chinese expansion since this would have required them to partake of an alien style of life, and one which was increasingly to be seen as inferior to that enjoyed by peoples similar to themselves in Soviet Central Asia. If the Chinese continued to adopt Sinification as their chief frontier policy when the old order was finally swept aside it was to Russia that the people of Sinkiang were likely to turn given that many of them saw China then as a civilisation 'crumbling inward on its own center'.[19]

The next five years were to see changes in Lattimore's career almost as momentous as those wrought by his trip to Pao-t'ou in 1925. Completing the cycle of writings which derived from his expeditions of 1926 and 1927 he began to develop strong connections with the academic world. Writing and personal experience led him to seek a more intimate knowledge of the Mongols and their language, and in 1933 began his connection with the Institute of Pacific Relations, a connection which would enhance his scholarly standing but would be used by others to undermine his career and reputation.

Manchuria and the Struggle of Civilisations

Returning to the United States Lattimore was fortunate, despite his lack of formal academic qualifications, to secure Social Science Research Council support for work on Manchuria. Whilst his greatest interest was in Chinese colonisation, Japanese activity in the region gave the intended research great topicality. The Japanese already controlled the strategically vital South Manchuria Railway, and from their base at Lü-shun (Lushun, Port Arthur) were progressively extending their economic control of the region. In 1928 their endeavours to dominate Manchuria received a setback with the decision of the local warlord, Chang Hsüeh-liang (Zhang Xueliang), to throw in his lot with the now successful Kuomintang Northern Expedition after his father had been killed in an incident perpetrated by the local Japanese military. Chang's decision was ultimately to precipitate the 'Mukden Incident' of September 1931 which was engineered as the pretext for the occupation of the region by the Japanese Kwantung Army.

In order the better to prepare for the travel in Manchuria that he proposed Lattimore spent the academic year of 1928-29 working in the graduate division of the Harvard University department of anthropology. In 1930 Lattimore and his wife travelled extensively in Manchuria, completing

Manchuria, cradle of conflict shortly after the annexation of the region by the Japanese. A revised version of the book with two additional chapters considering the events of 1931, and the creation there in 1933 of the Japanese puppet state of Manchukuo (Manzhouguo), was published in 1935.

Manchuria is Lattimore's first attempt at sustained scholarly writing. Although he is critical, in his retrospective assessment of the book,[20] he does offer some extremely perceptive analyses of aspects of the recent history of the region and he develops further his conception of the frontier and its historical role. Indeed, it is best to consider the work as one on two levels, the first concerned with these more detailed analyses of historical and contemporary topics, the second with the altogether more 'portentous' (though sometimes insightful) struggle of powers and civilisations.

In the history of Manchuria Lattimore detects 'a well-defined historical process',[21] an alternation of barbarian invasions of China followed by Chinese attempts to extend their authority into barbarian territories, usually upon the overthrow of a conquest dynasty that has been enervated by Sinification. When barbarian dynasties from beyond the Great Wall controlled China, the northern frontier, which was a zone rather than a fixed line, constituted a 'reservoir', supplying officials as well as troops for the service of their kindred at the centre from whom they derived much in the way of rewards and honours, while protecting the rear of the state against those tribesmen farther off who did not participate in the creation of the dynasty. The performing of the latter function is confirmed by the presence of defensive walls far beyond the line of the Great Wall, the purpose of which was to protect the reservoir itself against northerly invasion. Although Lattimore clearly had in mind Manchu practice,[22] the remnants of which were still to be seen in his day in the form of the Banner (*ch'i, qi*) tribes of Inner Mongolia, he extends his analysis back to the fourth century. Thus the relationship between China and the frontier that persisted until the 1880s in the Manchu (Manzhou) Ch'ing (Qing) Empire can also be seen in the Wei, the early T'ang (Tang), the Liao, the Chin (Jin) and the Mongol Yuan dynasties. It follows, argues Lattimore, that the reservoir region should be regarded 'as the key to the sovereignty of North China - often of all China'.[23] Here we find a succinct statement of that theme that was to dominate much of Lattimore's historical writing, though he also believed it was an insight that could be applied to the present.

The history and mechanics of Chinese colonisation in the area are the subject of a careful analysis which continues to stand the test of time.[24] With the destruction of the old reservoir system the thinly inhabited frontier became for the Ch'ing dynasty not a strength but a weakness, since by the 1880s only a peopling of the area along conventional Chinese lines had come to be seen as the most effective check on Russian designs. Railways caused colonisation to take on a new form, permitting the rapid movement of colonists through intervening areas and putting newly opened areas into contact with a market denied to frontier cultivators whose only transport was the cart. Lattimore shows that in some more remote parts of Manchuria the cultivation of opium provided as much of a stimulus to settlement as the discovery of gold in America and Australia. But much of Manchuria was never virgin territory and thus settlement was only possible after the absorption or displacement of the original inhabitants.

Beyond the Chinese pale Manchuria may roughly be divided, argues Lattimore, into two regions. An easterly zone, much of it of forest, was occupied originally by Manchu and Tungus who engaged in both hunting and herding supplemented by agriculture. In the west and northwest this zone shades over into a habitat akin to that found in Inner Mongolia peopled in the main by Mongols practising pastoral nomadism and organised, since the Ch'ing period, for the most part in Banners under hereditary princes and nobles. Lattimore contrasts the means by which the two zones had been or were being absorbed in the march of Chinese settlement.[25] In the Manchu regions much squatting had already taken place and since there was a general understanding here that the land was held by the state it was a relatively easy matter to turn the land over either to an owner who would negotiate with the squatters or who, in farther flung areas, would bring in colonists himself. All such transactions were arranged by local officials who stood to gain in the first instance by arrangement with the new owners, and thereafter because of the increased taxation to be levied on newly settled land. Many 'tribal' areas were thus absorbed, a singular example of which Lattimore found in the case of the Goldi or 'Fishkin Tatars' of the lower Sungari (Songhua) river, a people who were also the subject of a separate anthropological study published in 1933.[26] Having the status of Bannermen and known as 'New Manchus' the Goldi, who were already a non-nomadic people living in scattered villages by fishing and hunting, were given title to their lands by the Manchu government after the opening of the river to steamer traffic in 1904. Already much attached to Chinese wares and ways the Goldi were no match for the Chinese who rapidly came into possession of most of their lands. Lattimore reported that the Goldi were reduced to the status of a depressed class though there was little animosity between the two peoples, and much intermarriage between Chinese men and local women.

The process and consequences of colonisation in Mongol areas were both very different. Land passed from public to private ownership and was then subjected to conventional forms of administration but only by ignoring Mongol tradition and practice. Mobility was as great a value in the Mongol way of life as permanent occupation or tillage of any site was repugnant. Manchu elevation of the Mongol nobility and sponsorship of the lama Buddhist clergy and their establishments effected inroads into that way of life, but to treat the princes and the church as the actual and personal owners of Mongol land was a gross violation of tradition. This was the mechanism by which individuals or land or grain companies, abetted by officials and railway interests, came into possession of many areas in Manchuria hitherto the exclusive preserve of the Mongols. Compensation was usually paid to the former owner in the form of rent, but the bulk of the people were often faced with the stark alternatives of 'withdrawal' and the complete displacement of their culture, or what amounted to 'gradual extermination'. The co-operation of the princes in this destruction of their people is accounted for by Lattimore in terms of their increasingly anomalous position. They were driven to look only to their own interests, for to identify with Outer Mongolia was to invite the extinction of their class which had already occurred there, while identification with China made them little more than 'subsidised figureheads' and mere 'tools of Chinese policy'.[27].

Once again an interest in the frontier had led Lattimore to contemplate the predicament of the Mongol nomads. It is clear, from an account written much later that this contemplation was the product of disturbing personal experience:

> Among the places that we visited [in 1929-30] was a Chinese colonisation project in the western part of Liaoning Province, the Xingan (Hsingan) Tun Ken Chu, a modern version of an ancient Chinese practice in the margin of contact between Chinese farmers and Mongol herdsmen, a military garrison settlement (*tun*), supporting itself by agriculture (*ken*). This colonisation was brutally carried out: the Mongols were evicted at the point of a bayonet and Chinese colonists planted on their land. If any Mongols resisted, they were dealt with as 'bandits'.[28]

It is when the second level of *Manchuria* is examined that Lattimore's argument becomes more speculative, though in the longer term he does offer some perceptive views on the character of Chinese modernisation and the coming crisis in East Asia.

Drawing upon his analysis of the historical function of the 'reservoir' Lattimore was of the view that this mechanism may still come to operate in contemporary China. The Manchurian colonist was not a frontiersman in the mould of the American West, he was the bearer of an immense historical legacy, the chief burden of which was that civilisation is only found within the Great Wall beyond which is only barbarism:

> ... the colonists are less pioneers, carrying with them a young and confident tradition, than refugees, looking over their shoulders at a homeland unwillingly abandoned.[29]

Such a population along with its leadership was inclined to face inwards rather than outwards, the power of leaders beyond the Great Wall to interfere in the affairs of metropolitan China being enlarged by the presence of railways. The local warlord Chang Tso-lin (Zhang Zuolin) thus exercised power at the centre in accordance with his 'historic "reservoir" position', and so far the Republic had been fortunate that his son and successor Chang Hsüeh-liang being familiar with the challenge of the west had been more inclined to guard the northern frontiers than meddle in internal politics.[30]

Similar leverage or potential leverage was exercised upon China (though not upon the external frontiers) by military figures in the north and northwest, whereas in Ssuch'uan (Sichuan) the pressure of a Tibetan population gradually encroaching upon Chinese areas had no consequences whatsoever for the politics of metropolitan China.[31] And the growing power of Russia in the north constituted something of the order of an 'extra-reservoir' which 'transmits *cumulating* pressures southward, but *diminishing* pressures northward',[32] pressures which had been present since Manchu times but which now assumed a new form.

It is clear that Lattimore believed that an old pattern of Chinese civilisation was to be detected in these events. That is that the north and the north-west were the heartlands of the civilisation and the key to Chinese sovereignty, and that for the civilisation as a whole expansion towards the south had brought success, whereas expansion to the north had usually brought danger if not disaster. This view Lattimore now attributes to the influence of Spengler, the first volume of whose *Decline of the West* he took with him during his travels of 1929-30.[33] Hitherto the greatest intellectual influence on Lattimore had been Huntington, but there are clear signs in the writings of this period that he found Huntington's stark environmentalism no longer convincing. The extent to which Spengler had displaced Huntington may be judged in Lattimore's remarks on the likely causes of the nomadic migrations of the past: climate may have provided an impetus but the evolution of the Mongols into a conquering people 'must have been in the main a spiritual phenomenon'.[34]

For Spengler and for Lattimore at this time then, China was an example of a 'late' culture: having passed through those prior phases found in the history of every civilisation, youth and maturity, it had 'long ago fulfilled and matured every potentiality of growth inherent in its own powers'.[35] The original edition of *Manchuria* closed with the following peroration which similarly captures the spirit of this new influence:

> The underlying struggle in Manchuria is, and will be throughout our century, caused by the conflicting migration of cultures and peoples, and the effort of cultures to assert themselves over peoples. In such a struggle, generals and statesmen are the accidents of history; tradition, the way of life, the effort of race and region to assert themselves in the face of culture and nation, and the effort of nation and culture to impose themselves on race and region, are history itself.[36]

Yet there was much in contemporary Manchuria to support such a view. On the one hand the tide of Chinese civilisation was sweeping before it other cultures and ways of life with which no compromise seemed possible. On the other, this tide had been impelled originally by the irruption of civilisations with which the Chinese could not deal and from which they could only learn with difficulty. Moreover the expansion of China into the frontier, producing an 'artificial' colonisation, seemed likely to touch off a struggle with external powers which would be highly unequal. In his assessment of the internal tensions within China as well as her external predicament Lattimore's choice of a mentor had not been entirely infelicitous.

As a late culture the tactic most readily resorted to by the Chinese was passivity, and China had great difficulty in adopting the techniques of the West for her own uses. The railway was an alien instrument which made colonisation possible but in the process threw the traditional civilisation out of balance, since southern rather than northern expansion had been the historical pattern, and since the areas thus colonised threatened to exercise the old northern military domination. And it was in the imperfect adaptation of Western technology and ideas that Lattimore perceived the greatest threat to the society as a whole. The very difficulties of adaptation may stimulate a movement which abandons altogether any hopes of piecemeal change:

> If the conflict between east and west should end in such a catastrophe, the nation that would at last emerge might be a China dominated and exploited by the west, or it might be something totally different; but it certainly would not be either an 'evolved' nation like Japan, in which the old currents have been turned into new channels, or a nation vigorously preserving in all its integrity the old civilisation of China, fortified externally by borrowed western methods.[37]

But previous attempts to adapt the West to China had manifestly failed, and the intellectual class, those most familiar with Western ideas, were then at the mercy of 'the man of action', militarists and their followers. Lattimore places some hope if hope was to be found in the 'Chinese Renascence'[38] but in the longer view these observations are singularly prescient. Chinese Communism was indeed to prove 'the embodiment of the danger that all alternatives of adaptation may be abandoned and swept away'[39]; military men were to master the men of ideas of the May Fourth generation who were then personally to receive treatment as summary as that given to their views.

Lattimore then combines the insights he owes to the inspiration of Spengler with what he knows of the historical and political geography of Manchuria and its environs, thereby broaching a theme which was to be restated in his writing for a decade. A contest between Russia and Japan in East Asia was almost inevitable. Both occupied strategic positions of an 'imperative' nature which compelled them to exert growing pressure on Manchuria,[40] an area which for historical as well as contemporary reasons was subject to strong centrifugal forces. Despite advances in the race for colonisation Chinese civilisation could not match the power of her neighbours. Japan possessed the vigour of a nation which had recently and successfully employed her old energies in a wholesale borrowing of Western standards and techniques. Russia with a similar though more selective history of Westernisation also represented a rising force. In terms borrowed from Spengler, Russia was the only modern nation sufficiently 'young' to possess 'men of destiny'. Moreover the Russians had inherited a tradition of administration (emblematic of the syncretic nature of a 'young' culture) in the east which 'spreads control *through* a local population, rather than exercising it *over* them',[41] making it possible for them as an Asian land power to exercise the old 'reservoir' control of China by way of her northern territories. By contrast the Japanese like their Western mentors were mere 'sea barbarians' whose attempt at leadership over the peoples of Manchuria would at best reproduce the colonial tutelage to be found in India and Korea.[42] The unfamiliarity of a challenge from the sea to that traditional element in the Chinese outlook, however, renders this challenge the more threatening of the two.

In 1935 Lattimore published a second edition of *Manchuria* offering a revised opinion of the likely role of the region in world politics. But his new viewpoint was to a significant extent the product of research and personal experience in the intervening years during which his involvement in the Mongol problem increased, and he became more preoccupied with the international ramifications of East Asian affairs.

Notes to Chapter One

1 Preface to *Studies in Frontier History* (London: Oxford University Press, 1962), pp 13-14.

2 cf 'Gosforth Cross', *The Mitre* (St Bees School) vol 1, no 9 (July 1919).

3 *The Desert Road to Turkestan*, (London: Methuen, 1928), pp 7 ff.

4 Preface to *Studies in Frontier History*, p 14.

5 'Caravan Routes of Inner Asia' [1928], *Studies in Frontier History*, pp 45, 56, n 3; N Prejevalsky, *Mongolia, The Tangut Country, and the Solitudes of Northern Tibet*, 2 vols (London: Sampson Low, 1876): N Prejevalsky, *From Kulja, Across the Tian Shan to Lob Nor* (London: Sampson Low, 1879).

6 On Lattimore's reading at the time, see 'Preface', *Studies in Frontier History*, pp 15, 18; Ellsworth Huntington, *The Pulse of Asia* (Boston: Houghton Mifflin, 1907); Arnold Toynbee, *A Study of History* vol III, 2nd edition (Oxford: Oxford University Press, 1935), pp 7-8.

7 *The Desert Road to Turkestan*, p 48; cf 'Caravan Routes of Inner Asia', *Studies in Frontier History*, p 62.

8 'Caravan Routes of Inner Asia', *Studies in Frontier History*, p 63.

9 *The Desert Road to Turkestan*, p 85.

10 'Now the Mongols are Pawns in a Game', *New York Times Magazine* 2 September 1928, pp 4-5, 19.

11 'Strife over the Last Forbidden Land', *New York Times Magazine* 23 September 1928, pp 10-11, 16.

12 Sir Aurel Stein, 'Innermost Asia: Its Geography as a Factor in History', *The Geographical Journal* LXV(1925), pp 377-403, 473-501.

13 *High Tartary* (Boston: Little Brown, 1930), pp 110, 147, 157.

14 'The Chinese as a Dominant Race' [1928], *Studies in Frontier History*, pp 200-217. Andrew Forbes argues, however, that though the economy of Sinkiang appeared to be more orderly than that of the remainder of republican China, in fact the policies of the Chinese governor, Yang Tseng-hsin (Yang Zengxin) were 'bleeding Sinkiang to death'. Andrew D W Forbes, *Warlords and Muslims in Chinese Central Asia: A Political History of Republican Sinkiang 1911-1949* (Cambridge: Cambridge University Press, 1986), p 31.

15 'Introduction to the AMS Edition', *High Tartary* (New York: AMS Press reprint, 1975).

16 *High Tartary*, p 227.

17 'The Chinese as a Dominant Race', *Studies in Frontier History*, p 217.

18 'Chinese Turkestan' [1933] *Studies in Frontier History*, p 193.

19 'Chinese Turkestan' *Studies in Frontier History*, pp 196, 198.

20 'Introduction to the AMS Edition', *Manchuria, cradle of conflict*, revised edition [1935] (New York: AMS Press reprint, 1975), iii.

21 *Manchuria, cradle of conflict*, p 36.

22 Although Lattimore notes that he has employed the standard Ch'ing works on Manchuria, he adds that he has done so in order 'to check, as far as possible, my own conclusions formed in the course of travel and from previous reading'. (*Manchuria, cradle of conflict*, xiii).

23 *Manchuria, cradle of conflict*, p 41.

24 *Manchuria, cradle of conflict*, pp 119 ff, 178 ff, 209 ff.

25 *Manchuria, cradle of conflict*, pp 119 ff.

26 'The Gold Tribe, "Fishkin Tatars", of the Lower Sungari' [1933], *Studies in Frontier History*, pp 339-402.

27 *Manchuria, cradle of conflict*, pp 126, 128.

28 *The Diluv Khutagt. Memoirs and Autobiography of a Mongol Buddhist Reincarnation in Religion and Revolution*, Asiatische Forschungen, 74 (Wiesbaden: Harrassowitz, 1982), p 2. On the supposed advantages of Chinese colonisation of frontier lands, see Chang Yin-t'ang, *The Economic Development and Prospects of Inner Mongolia* (Shanghai: The Commercial Press, 1933), pp 172 ff.

29 *Manchuria, cradle of conflict*, p 100.

30 *Manchuria, cradle of conflict*, pp 288-9, cf 31-2.

31 *Manchuria, cradle of conflict*, p 282.

32 *Manchuria, cradle of conflict*, p 107.

33 *Manchuria, cradle of conflict*, iii, v; 'Preface', *Studies in Frontier History*, pp 27-8; cf 'Spengler and Toynbee', *Atlantic Monthly* 181 (April 1948), pp 104-5. Here Lattimore refers to the impact of reading a review of Spengler by Toynbee in the *Times Literary Supplement* ('Europe in the Valley of Death' no 926, 24 June 1920, p 390). Much later Lattimore was to observe that his reading while a schoolboy of Winwood Reade's *The Martyrdom of Man* (1872) 'prepared' him 'for the influence of Spengler': 'Preface', *Studies in Frontier History*, p 27.

34 *Manchuria, cradle of conflict*, p 74.

35 *Manchuria, cradle of conflict*, p 79, cf 96.

36 *Manchuria, cradle of conflict*, p 301.

37 *Manchuria, cradle of conflict*, p 97.

38 *Manchuria, cradle of conflict*, pp 287, 289-90.

39 *Manchuria, cradle of conflict*, p 97.

40 *Manchuria, cradle of conflict*, pp 4-5.

41 *Manchuria, cradle of conflict*, p 245.

42 *Manchuria, cradle of conflict*, p 291 n 1.

CHAPTER TWO

Frontier Society and Mongol Nationalism

From what he knew of Inner Mongolia, and from what he had seen in his travels of 1929-30 Lattimore was aware that the pressures upon the Mongols and their way of life were eliciting a variety of responses from the people themselves. In order to understand the political and social dimensions of these responses and perhaps as a result of his excursions in anthropology[1] Lattimore, in addition to studying written Chinese, took on the study of Mongol. This decision was to shape all of Lattimore's subsequent career.

The Mongol Predicament

In Manchuria, endeavouring to come to some assessment of the policies of provincial and local authorities towards the Mongols - he found that troop commanders expropriating their lands were acquiring large sums of money in the resulting land transfers - Lattimore met Kuo Tao-fu (Guo Daofu) a Daghor (Daghur) from Hailar whose Mongol name was Merse. According to Lattimore's much later recollection Merse who had until recently been a member of the Inner Mongolian Kuomintang (Guomindang) had been involved in the Pan-Mongolian nationalist movement of 1920, Japanese sponsorship of which had subsequently blighted his political career with the Chinese authorities. Possibly as a means of controlling his activities, when Lattimore met him in Mukden (Shenyang) Merse had been placed in charge of a school for the training of Mongols as bureaucrats. Lattimore several times adverts to the impact of meeting this well educated and informed spokesman of his people,[2] and to his tragic political murder following the Japanese invasion of Manchuria. To understand the confused political currents at work amongst the Mongols Lattimore explained that he needed to master their language; this evidently struck a responsive chord in Merse who introduced him to Bügegesig, a teacher at the Mongol-Tibetan school in Peking (Beijing).

Though both of these Mongols spoke Chinese and were involved in the Chinese administrative machine they were also staunch nationalists. Bügegesig, as well as giving Lattimore his first lessons in Mongol, drew him into what he later was to call the 'labyrinth' of Mongol nationalism by introducing him to Sain Bayar. Through Sain Bayar who had been a leader of the Inner Mongolian Kuomintang Lattimore met in 1931 the Dilowa Khutukhtu (Diluv, Dilov Khutagt) and then the Prince Demchukdonggrub (Demchugdongrov) whose Chinese title was Te Wang (De Wang, De Van).[3] These two acquaintances were to prove among the most important of Lattimore's entire career. The former was a leading incarnation in the

17

Mongolian Buddhist church before fleeing the anti-religious policies of the Mongolian People's Revolutionary Party regime to take up residence in China in 1931. He became a life-long friend as well as 'godfather' to his son, Lattimore partly as an act of homage to his deceased friend publishing an annotated edition of his memoirs and biography in 1982. The latter, the leading figure of Inner Mongolian nationalism, became the source of many of Lattimore's contacts in the nationalist movement and the subject of a number of his subsequent writings. Two of Te Wang's associates were later brought to the United States by Lattimore, the group then to do much to develop Mongol studies there and later in Britain. Moreover, in the lives of both of these men, the learned and saintly priest and the aristocratic man of action was embodied much of the tragedy of their people, Lattimore's reaction to which lay behind most of his writing and research in the next five or so years. In order to follow this phase of his career, however, it is necessary first to outline something of the history of Inner Mongolian nationalism.

It was the fate of the national aspirations of the Mongols to be caught in the complex of relations between Russia, China and Japan. Following Chinese and White Russian invasions the creation of a national regime in Outer Mongolia had only been possible with the military and political support given to the Mongolian People's Party by the new Soviet state in 1921. A Pan-Mongolian movement to unite all Mongols under a single regime which had received backing from the Japanese military had come to nothing,[4] and the Inner Mongolian areas had fallen under the control of provincial warlords who sought to extend to them Chinese style administration and colonisation by Chinese settlers. The failure of many of the Mongol nobility and clergy to defend their people against Chinese encroachments had undermined the old leadership structure and caused many Mongols to seek more radical alternatives.[5] But the most prominent of the new nationalists remained men of aristocratic birth and Chinese education. Thus in the 1920s appeared the group known as the Young Mongols of which Te Wang was a leading member. Similarly the most important political faction of this decade, the Inner Mongolian Kuomintang, was also led chiefly by men of noble backgrounds.

In the era of Kuomintang-Communist co-operation which began in 1923 Sun Yat-sen's movement from its base in Canton sought to orchestrate a national anti-imperialist upsurge to unify China, with Russian assistance. In these, the closing years of his life, Sun had come to place greater emphasis on the struggle against imperialism; he also promised an equality of the nationalities in a new Kuomintang China. In these circumstances common cause with the Mongols appeared possible; accordingly the Mongolian People's Revolutionary Party sent a delegation to Canton from Urga where they met Pai Yun-t'i (Buyantai), the most prominent Mongol in Sun's entourage. After discussions which touched on co-operation between the Kuomintang and the Mongolian People's Revolutionary Party, and the possibility of eventual unification of the Mongols, Sun gave his approval for the formation of an Inner Mongolian Kuomintang. With the assistance of the warlord Feng Yü-hsiang (Feng Yuxiang) then in control of Peking and in receipt of substantial Russian aid, the First Congress of the new Party was held in Kalgan (Zhangjiakou) in October 1925. The regime in Outer Mongolia, now the Mongolian People's Republic, sent several delegates, and the Congress declared its support for the freedom and development of the Mongol people as a whole.[6] The present feudal order was to be overthrown and the prosperity of the Mongols was to be provided in a new federated Chinese Republic to be established in close collaboration with the Chinese Kuomintang.

But no sooner had this alliance been formed than its elements began to separate. Feng Yü-hsiang was defeated in his struggle with Chang Tso-lin and forced to withdraw from the scene, spending more than a month in Ulan Bator (Ulaan Baatar, Urga) in March-April 1926[7] before travelling on to the Soviet Union. The Comintern began to take a different view of Mongolian development,[8] and the tensions in the Kuomintang-Communist alliance caused it to fall apart in April 1927. Similar fissures appeared in the Inner Mongolian movement. First Pai Yun-t'i and then other leaders including Merse had taken refuge in the Mongolian People's Republic following Feng Yü-hsiang's defeat. Pai Yun-t'i however chose to throw in his lot with Chiang Kai-shek in late 1927 after disagreements with his confederates. The Inner Mongolian Kuomintang was formally merged with the parent organisation, now based in Nanking, where Pai Yun-t'i was given nominal state office. But his former colleagues in the Mongolian People's Republic entertained a different vision of the Mongol future. In August 1928 Merse led the 'Young Barga' revolt the aims of which were, with help from the Mongolian People's Republic, to detach the Barga region from Manchuria and bring it within the fold of the new Mongol state. The revolt was defeated by Chang Hsüeh-liang, and Merse and his accomplices along with Pai Yun-t'i were branded as renegades by the Soviets.[9] It was shortly after this debacle that Merse was to meet Owen Lattimore.

Though Pai Yun-t'i possessed high office in Nanking this did not result in any advance for the Mongol cause. In August 1928, soon after its foundation the Kuomintang government proposed the reorganisation into regular provinces of the Mongolian special districts of Jehol (Rehe), Chahar, Suiyuan, and Ninghsia (Ningxia), a move that brought protesting Mongol petitioners to Peking. With the formation in the capital of the Mongolian-Tibetan Affairs Commission Yen Hsi-shan (Yan Xishan), whose regime in Shansi (Shanxi) had done so much to promote the rapid colonisation of former Mongol lands, was appointed Chairman. The Mongols were clearly being denied the position held out to minorities in the ideology of the now canonised Sun Yat-sen, and their disaffection grew accordingly. The need for a concerted Mongol response came to a head with two further developments. Immediately following the Japanese occupation of Manchuria, a significant area of which was populated by Mongols, the Kuomintang published a draft plan (in October 1931) to further reorganise the four frontier provinces created in 1928 in a way that would extend Chinese administration into those Mongol tribal areas which were still largely self-governed.[10]   Then the Japanese army occupied Jehol, and a Mongol 'province' of Hsingan (Xingan) was created in the west within the boundaries of the puppet state of Manchukuo. Japanese military pressure continued, the Japanese occupying part of Chahar province before a truce was agreed with Nanking.

It now became clear that Nanking was not prepared to uphold its authority in the frontier region nor would it protect the Mongols against the Japanese. Te Wang who held office in the government of Chahar province led a delegation to Nanking in 1932 seeking reform and assistance which was largely ignored, the government responding only belatedly by appointing him a Defence Commissioner in the area.[11] But the Kuomintang response to the Japanese military encroachments of 1933 was to abandon plans to improve the military preparedness of the Mongols.   In Pailingmiao (Bailingmiao, Batkhaalagh monastery) in Suiyuan province a number of meetings of Mongol princes and intellectuals began in May 1933 in an attempt to formulate a concerted Mongol strategy.[12] It is apparent that at these meetings a variety of arguments was aired by the nobles and intellectuals present. Although many sought a defence against Japan, from subsequent events it can be conjectured that there was some ambiguity in the Mongol view. Even before the Japanese militarists had become interested in the Mongols Japan had been a model for the reforming Prince Gungsangnorbu who had been impressed by the results of the Meiji reforms when he had visited Japan in 1903.[13] Gungsangnorbu had been particularly energetic in seeking to build a modern Mongol system of education and Pai Yun-t'i had been one of his pupils. Following the creation of Hsingan province the Japanese began to contact the old ruling princes in Inner Mongolia in the hope of securing their support, and agents began to make forays into Chahar and Suiyuan. In these circumstances the Mongols had at the very least acquired the possibility of political leverage in their dealings with Nanking.

The Pailingmiao meetings initiated a long period of negotiation with Nanking.   Initially the response from the Chinese side was adjudged insufficient, and on 14 August the ruling princes of Western Inner Mongolia declared that it was their intention to establish an autonomous government, such a regime actually being founded in October despite protests and blandishments from Nanking. At this stage Te Wang began to receive overtures from the Japanese and by threatening to align his movement with Japan and the soon-to-be-enthroned Emperor of Manchukuo, the last Ch'ing ruler Pu-yi (Puyi), he finally forced a measure of official recognition. The Mongolian Local Autonomous Political Council of the Nanking government with Te Wang as the director of the Political Affairs Bureau was in existence by May 1934, but it was almost immediately frustrated in its purpose. The funds provided by Nanking were insufficient for its civil and military responsibilities, and in attempting to raise revenue by taxing the trade of the area the council was opposed by the local warlord Fu Tso-i (Fu Zuoyi) who also prevented attempts to extend its administrative authority to areas of Inner Mongolia under his control.[14]

These frustrations generated tensions within the autonomy movement which were exploited by the Japanese, and by Fu Tso-i and his overlord Yen Hsi-shan. Some time in 1935, with growing military pressure being placed on Chahar by Manchukuo and the Japanese, and with an apparent lack of resolution by Nanking to defend north China, Te Wang finally threw in his lot with the Japanese. When he did so is difficult to determine but by February 1936 the autonomy movement split, with a rival pro-Chinese Mongol council being established under Fu Tso-i (with Yen Hsi-shan as 'adviser') in Kweisui. Te Wang removed his supporters to Tehua (Dehua, Jabsar)[15] where he established in June an Inner Mongolian Government.

1936 marks the end of the autonomy movement since Te Wang's fortunes thereafter rose and fell with those of the Japanese. A joint Mongol-Manchukuo invasion of Suiyuan in November 1936 was beaten back by Fu Tso-i but with the outbreak of the Sino-Japanese war in July 1937 the area was soon overrun. The Japanese then sponsored several Mongolian 'governments', Te Wang heading one based at Kweisui in 1938, moving to Kalgan in 1939. According to Lawrence Shyu (whose opinion on this question is noteworthy given his Kuomintang sympathies), of all the client governments established by the Japanese on Chinese territory:

> only the Inner Mongolian regime under Teh Wang achieved some
> degree of stability and prestige because of the greater autonomy it
> enjoyed and the attraction of pan-Mongolism to ethnic Mongols in
> the region.[16]

The true Japanese attitude towards the Mongolian Federated Autonomous Government was revealed however in 1940 with the creation of the puppet Nanking regime of Wang Ching-wei (Wang Jingwei) when Inner Mongolia was brought under such authority as it possessed. Ever in pursuit of the goal of Mongol autonomy Te Wang attempted to change his allegiance in 1945 but received no encouragement from Chiang Kai-shek. Between 1945 and 1948 he lived in Peking under house arrest while most of his people fell under communist control. Even in the crisis year of 1948 he was still unable to secure Kuomintang support for his final stand in the Alashan (Alxa) region, and from 1949 he was imprisoned by the communists first in Ulan Bator and later in China.

The Failure of Inner Mongolian Nationalism

Returning from his travels in Manchuria Lattimore spent the years 1930 to 1933 based in Peking. Fellowships from the Harvard-Yenching Institute and the John Simon Guggenheim Memorial Foundation, and assistance from the American Geographical Society allowed him to devote his time to writing and study and he also began to make forays travelling by camel in the Mongol style in Inner Mongolia with his companion Arash. On his return to America in 1933 Lattimore began his association with the Institute of Pacific Relations. Following his attendance at the Institute conference of 1933 held in Banff, Canada, he was invited to become editor of the journal *Pacific Affairs*, published by the Institute from New York. It was agreed that he could reside in Peking where he would devote half his time to his editorial duties; thus Lattimore was able to continue his work in China (broken only by travel to Europe and the Soviet Union) until the outbreak of the Sino-Japanese war in 1937.

Increasing familiarity with the predicament of the Mongols led Lattimore to produce a number of writings on this theme. This in turn led him both backwards and forwards in time. He sought the historical basis of the relationship between Mongols and Chinese, and since that relationship in his own time was having and was likely to have significant international repercussions he explored further the nature of the tensions that were soon to produce war in East Asia. He began work also on successive drafts of *The Inner Asian Frontiers of China*. In these years Lattimore's increasing facility in the Mongol language, and his friendship with and knowledge of an extremely diverse group of Mongols gave him an unrivalled insight into these questions. From aristocrats and lamas he was able to learn something of the character of the old order and its response to the twentieth century; from herdsmen and traders he was to acquire a wealth of folklore and tradition as well as direct personal understanding of their social and material conditions.

The lengthiest work of this period is *The Mongols of Manchuria* published in 1934. Although the contemporary importance of the region provided the impulse for the book, most of it is concerned with the historical organisation of the Mongols as ordained by their Manchu overlords, and with the erosion of this organisation under the pressures of colonisation and frontier rivalry in the nineteenth century. Lattimore draws on a number of Mongol and Chinese works particularly the nineteenth century *Records of the Mongol Pastures*;[17] he also pays tribute to the pioneering research on this subject by Lieutenant G C Binstead which itself was based on a Russian translation of the latter work.[18] In the more contemporary chapters of this book as well as in a number of articles written at the time Lattimore returns repeatedly to several themes which will now be considered. These themes remain remarkably constant with the exception of Lattimore's estimate of the role of the Inner Mongolian nationalist movement. Like many Mongols he was initially hopeful that it would rescue them from oblivion and render them equal partners in a revivified and reformed Chinese republic; by 1936 he came round to the view that the movement would henceforth be a prisoner of the Japanese largely as a result of Kuomintang ineptitude and irresolution, and the greed of frontier élites, Chinese and Mongol alike.

Lattimore's development of an interest in the Mongols coincided with events which, in his view, enhanced their political importance since their future allegiance could well provide the key to the outcome of the struggle of the powers in the Far East. The first edition of *Manchuria* had sketched the context for that struggle. Having rejected Huntington in favour of Spengler, Lattimore now began to emphasise the geopolitical factors at work, finding less and less plausible Spengler's belief in:

> the logic of history as a form, the idea that cultures and
> civilizations are organic bodies, subject to the laws of youth and
> age, growth and decay.[19]

The history of East Asia was a history of land powers and after a century in which this pattern had been disrupted by the irruption of new forces from the sea it was reasserting itself.[20] In this observation Lattimore felt himself to be on firm historical ground: the history of China was largely a record of barbarian conquerors becoming assimilated over time to the values of Chinese civilisation in a way that was impossible for the sea-going barbarians. Although the international position of East Asia had for a time been determined by an order sea-going in its inspiration, the 'Open Door', this order was being eroded by the recrudescence of Russian land-based power. Indeed it could even be claimed that the balance of power in world politics was shifting towards continental as opposed to maritime nations.[21]

But if an old pattern was re-emerging it did contain, in Lattimore's view, some new features. The character of the frontier would continue to be an important determinant in Chinese history but changes in Chinese society and the employment of Western arms and technology offered the possibility of a new form of Chinese mastery of the frontier. The position of Japan in this coming age of land power was somewhat anomalous. Japan had turned the maritime order to her own advantage in East Asia, but with the diminishing returns that the exercise of such power now offered was seeking to build a land empire in the region. On land the only effective check to Japanese expansion was the power of the Soviet Union, and were that check to be exercised the area between the Great Wall and Siberia would be crucial.

The new continental strategy of Japan led, according to Lattimore, to an 'inevitable opposition' between Japan and Russia. While world attention was focussed upon a likely confrontation on the Siberian-Manchukuo frontier, the flank position, that is those territories in Manchuria, China, Mongolia and the Soviet Union occupied by the Mongols, in a protracted war would prove far more important:

> The only flank which either nation could turn by a sweeping and
> decisive movement is the Outer Mongolian flank of Manchukuo.
> The problems of Vladivostok and the Ussuri-Amur frontier are
> local and tactical; the problem of Mongolia is one which allows
> room for strategy. ... Mongolia, therefore, of which the world
> knows less than it knows of China, Siberia or Manchukuo, is the
> key to the destiny of the whole Far East.[22]

This had accordingly transformed the position of the Mongols. From being a
degenerate and helpless people who could only choose extinction at the hands
of the Chinese, or drastic social revolution under Russian auspices, their
allegiance must now be courted, and they themselves would play an active
role.[23]

Between 1933 and 1935 when it appeared that the Mongols could be
independent actors in this conflict Lattimore considered in several written
pieces the alternatives open to them. Largely on the basis of his conversations
with refugees he formed the view that in Outer Mongolia though the influence
of Russia was considerable yet the regime was Mongol in character, led by a
young and energetic faction whose model for modernisation and sole source of
assistance was Soviet Russia. Their answer to the 'failure of the old order to
rise to the national emergency' was to effect a social revolution in which the
church in particular, the political prerogatives of its dignitaries and the
possessions of its monasteries, were afforded uncompromising treatment.[24]
The position in Inner Mongolia was that it stood as a repository of all that had
been uprooted in the new Mongolian republic, 'the old tradition, the power of
the princes, the sanctity of religion'. The encroachments of colonisation and
Chinese impatience with the Mongol way of life had stimulated the formation
of the 'Young Mongol' reformers, a group with varying prescriptions for
national regeneration though all opposed in some degree to the enormous
privileges of the lama church. The Japanese annexation of Manchuria,
followed by the creation of Hsingan province and the enthronement of the
Manchu emperor Pu-yi had given rise to divided loyalties. For now the
possibility was held out of national regeneration under princely tutelage since
the Japanese had employed the princes in their 'autonomous' provincial
regime, and particularly given the wide sentiment that existed in favour of
some reunification of the Mongol people. On the other hand some princely
leaders would have preferred a more independent role, using the threat of
alliance with the Japanese to enhance their power *vis-à-vis* the Chinese
republic. Lattimore was uncertain of the leverage possessed by the Chinese in
this situation, though he noted that such concessions as were offered by
Nanking were unwillingly granted and insufficient.[25] In the circumstances,
with the initiative on the side of the Japanese, Lattimore expected Japan to
pursue 'an active Mongol policy', one likely to stimulate a clash between
Inner and Outer Mongolia, political entities which were opposed
geographically and politically, in the name of Mongol reunification.[26]

But the Mongols were not to be permitted to grasp the opportunity which seemed to be theirs. The Japanese proved inept in their administration of Hsingan and thus alienated much Mongol support. Although their early Mongol 'experts' were often sympathetic to the Mongol predicament and with a good command of the language, Lattimore asserts that they were increasingly supplanted by a type of petty bureaucrat whose only concern was personal preferment. The regime thus rendered the princes into mere figureheads, and was only able to offer employment to educated Mongols as interpreters. And the reform of the Mongol herding economy, so essential if their distinct way of life was to continue, was similarly subordinated to the Japanese need for a cheap source of agricultural products and a quick return on their initial investments. The explanation for this failure to exploit Mongol nationalism is to be sought, according to Lattimore, in Japan and in Japan's international position. The rewards of empire had to be seen to be shared, and twentieth century empire building was a brutal business especially for a country in Japan's condition, short of capital and beset by the hostilities of the more successful imperial powers.[27] No national regeneration could be expected under the aegis of such a regime, and accordingly by 1937 there were open signs of disloyalty from Mongols under Japanese occupation.

Japanese ineptitude in failing to offer any independent role for the Mongols was matched by Chinese inability to come to terms with Te Wang's Inner Mongolian autonomy movement. Te Wang had originally sought separate provincial status for the Mongols and their recognition as a distinct people within a defensive alliance with Nanking. The essential prerequisite for such an alliance would have been the amalgamation of the various Mongol areas into a single entity, and the ending of Chinese colonisation therein. The Chinese, as Lattimore saw it, would thus have ceased to be competitors with the Japanese in the exploitation of the Mongols, and common interest would have made possible a common stand. But even though only a small group of frontier military and officials stood to lose the profits they made from colonisation and trade by their treatment of Mongols and Chinese alike, Nanking was without any of the statesmanship that the situation required; and this despite the presence of many Mongols from Manchuria among the supporters of Te Wang, a fact which was so demonstrative of the potential of his movement:

> The Mongol policy of the Nanking Government did not go beyond
> using Mongol pressure on the provinces in order to increase the
> Central Government's power of intervention in provincial
> politics.[28]

And the selfishness of the provincial authorities was little short of treasonable. Although the Mongols were given institutional recognition in 1934, Nanking did not grant them sufficient finances to render their organisation effective. They were, however, given the right to levy taxes in their region, but in attempting to raise revenue from the traffic across Inner Mongolia controlled by the opium monopoly of Shansi they came into conflict with Yen Hsi-shan. Nanking's adjudication of the dispute placed much of these revenues in the hands of Yen Hsi-shan who then had an obligation to disburse a proportion to the Mongols, though they were never to see any part of a share. Yen then succeeded in his manoeuvres to split the autonomy movement by creating a separate Council for Suiyuan whose members, according to Lattimore, were men heavily compromised by their association with Chinese colonisation. Lattimore's judgment on the reasons for Te Wang's change of allegiance is uncompromising:

> The Nanking Government finally indicated its abandonment of Te Wang by recognising this Council, and appointing as Chinese political adviser to it Yen Hsi-shan himself, the man who from the beginning had most openly obstructed Te Wang's movement. As for Te Wang, he has not 'gone over' to Japan; he has been tied hand and foot and thrown to the Japanese.[29]

The Analysis of Mongol Society

The tragedy of Inner Mongolian nationalism led Lattimore to explore several lines of research and speculation which were soon to become central to his scholarly corpus. His explanations were both historical and contemporary, the former finding completed expression in *Inner Asian Frontiers of China*, and concerned the nature of Mongol society and its historical evolution. He wished to determine how a nomadic society with many egalitarian characteristics had come to be dominated by an entrenched nobility and clergy; he also sought to understand why this entrenched élite had so signally failed to provide that leadership which the Mongols required in the crisis of the previous two decades, an enquiry which led to speculation on what future course of action would preserve them as a people. And since the fate of the Mongols was related at every turn to developments in China, Lattimore was led also to contemplate the past and the present of the relationship between these two civilisations, and what failing in Chinese society had prevented that alliance which would have been so advantageous to both peoples.

In an extremely important article published in early 1935 (though not to be found in Lattimore's collected writings) Lattimore considers the relationship between the Mongol past and future and in so doing interprets the Mongol predicament as a particular legacy of history. The history of China and Mongolia may be considered as cyclical, 'a rhythmic recurrence of invasions of China' during which frontier peoples dominated the provinces within the Great Wall, followed by Chinese resurgence during which the frontier peoples were removed to their former habitat, divided and controlled (though at considerable cost) by alliances, subsidies, and trading concessions.[30] Within the Mongol society of the frontier a class of chiefs arose whose role was to

26

impose such leadership upon their followers as would be necessary to extract subsidies from the Chinese during the waxing of the latter's power. From this class of chiefs would emerge, after a cycle of tribal wars, a 'great chief of chiefs' who would lead his people, noble and commoner alike, to the plunder and exploitation which would be the fruits of the next dynasty of conquest in China. The lama church appeared much later on the scene, but the role of the clergy paralleled in some respects the role of the chiefs or nobles. They were used to sanctify and legitimise various claimants to the overlordship of the frontier peoples, but they enjoyed many of the privileges previously the preserve of the noble class. At this point the Manchus stepped in to sidetrack the development of a political-ecclesiastical alliance among the Mongols which would most likely have overwhelmed the declining Ming Empire. As allies of the Manchus the Mongols did, however, share in the exploitation of agricultural China, and by seeking to attach princely families to particular localities and to set nobles and clergy in competition with each other for power and position the Manchus realised their aim of preventing a united Mongol resurgence which would challenge their dominion.

The conditions of the nineteenth century were to impose new and devastating pressures on the society which had thus come into being. To understand these pressures and their consequences especially in Outer Mongolia Lattimore employs Marxian class analysis, an approach he finds 'devastatingly rational' despite the fact that the contending classes were princes and nomadic tribesmen rather than bourgeois and proletarian. The noble and priestly classes Lattimore considers in terms of their function. They evolved as superintendents and chief beneficiaries of the exploitation of China, but since the lesser members of Mongol society derived some benefit from that exploitation they were, on the whole, inclined to accept a subordinate role. All this changed with the advent of frontier railways, the possession by the Chinese of modern armaments, withdrawal or fall in value of Chinese subsidies to the nobility and clergy, and the penetration of Chinese commerce into the nomadic areas which occurred with the shift of attitude of the imperial government towards the frontier. A social structure which was 'organised in such a manner that it would produce united action for aggression'[31] was much less effective in defence. Some princes led their followers in revolts, but many nobles and clergy colluded with traders to exploit their subjects with the result that class became more important than nation:

> Since the existence of special classes depended on exploitation
> and the enjoyment of unearned increment, and since China could
> no longer be exploited, the common Mongol people, who had once
> been simply the lowest rank of a privileged nation, became
> themselves an exploited class, supporting a now useless
> superstructure of upper classes - useless because they were no

longer the spearhead of national expansion, but had become merely the apex of a national pyramid of exploitation.[32]

Lattimore found this situation so far analogous to the opposition of classes described by Marx that he likened the lot of the common Mongols to that of the Western proletariat or the Chinese peasantry, dominated by capitalists and landlords respectively.

With his understanding of the old Mongol society thus clarified Lattimore was in a position to offer a systematic account of events in Outer Mongolia. The Mongol assertion of independence in 1911, bringing a form of national unity after more than two centuries, appeared to offer the Mongols several strategies. Their history might incline them to regard unity as a prelude to renewed aggression against China, but this way was closed by the new circumstances of the time, particularly the presence of western influence in East Asia. There could be no return, thus, to the 'dynamic principles' of the past, instead a 'new phase' must be embarked upon. Here, and with the nature of the Mongol social structure very much in mind, Lattimore poses two alternatives. The Mongols could retain this social structure as it was, and 'become part of a Tsarist Russian advance on China', or they could 'liquidate' that structure 'because it was no longer capable of fulfilling its functions' by the means of social revolution.[33] The fall of the Russian Empire precluding the former, the latter therefore became the only way forward.

In the remainder of this article and at greater length in 1936 Lattimore was also able to account for the failure of Inner Mongolian nationalism by employing the same approach.[34] In Inner Mongolia the features of the new era, particularly railway-fed colonisation, prevented a repetition of the frontier cycle hitherto enacted upon the collapse of a Chinese dynasty. And extensive co-operation by the nobility and clergy in this colonisation had decisively compromised most of them in the eyes of the Mongol commoners. The parlous and decaying condition of the Mongols stimulated the rise of nationalism which, identifying the decline of the Mongols as a people with Chinese interference, sought a remedy in a movement towards self-government. In time 'conservative' and 'radical' groups in this movement became distinguished with respect to the role they wished to accord the old élite in the new political order which they were trying to create.

But the antipathy felt by Mongols towards Chinese disguised the real source of Mongol impoverishment, which was the ruthless exploitation of the frontier peoples. In the manner of one presenting a new and important discovery - and there is no doubt that this theory would influence Lattimore's view of the Mongols henceforth - Lattimore states that the true problem was not the opposition of nationalities but one of 'the relation of social structures to economic systems'.[35] Autonomy under their own princes would have led to little if any improvement among the common people since to equal the power of the provincial Chinese authorities these nobles would have had to place such exactions upon their people (for they were so dispersed and so few) as would lower them to the level of the Chinese peasantry of the frontier; and this despite the fact that the common Mongol herdsman if left to himself enjoys a higher standard of living than his Chinese counterpart. Thus arose a more radical form of nationalism seeking the promotion to power of able commoners, but as most of the nationalists shared a common aristocratic background, treachery and divisions prevented them from choosing any coherent strategy. Some of the disillusioned members of the movement left for Outer Mongolia where they may have contributed to the awareness that developed there of the 'limitations of nationalism'; others looked abroad in the hope of some form of foreign-led liberation. Outer Mongolia eventually took the road of 'economic and social revolution' as a Soviet 'satellite' whereas the élites of Inner Mongolia sought assistance from Japan. Japanese conduct however, showed the 'old nationalism' to be a sham. The Japanese preferred to keep the Mongols under a form of subjection and thus kept alive the power of the old élites in preference to the economic and social renovation which the Mongols so urgently required:

> Intervention [by Japan] has meant only the transfer of control from Chinese overlords to Japanese proconsuls. Without some degree of social revolution, Inner Mongolian nationalism can only be led by the aristocrats. The lower ranks of the aristocracy may be radical in their political beliefs, but they do not hold the decisive power. It is the ruling princes, together with the high lamas, who hold such real power as exists; and they, because of the dichotomy between their class interests and national interests, can never free themselves from subordination to an overlord power. Nor can Inner Mongolia raise itself from being exploited on a colonial level except by an economic revolution interacting with social revolution.[36]

For the Mongols, as a consequence, social revolution was on the agenda: 'the old nationalism is dead'. Accordingly among many Mongols at that time the prestige of Outer Mongolia was on the rise.

By 1935, then, Lattimore had begun to pose certain quite specific questions of Mongol society. He sought to determine whether this social structure could deal with the challenges to and pressures upon it, and he found intelligible an answer which exposed the interests of the various classes found therein. The evidence suggests that Lattimore's thinking took this direction as a result of his own observation and experience which were undoubtedly crystallised by the failure of the Inner Mongolian nationalist movement either to express a unified Mongol point of view or successfully to extract favourable terms from the Nanking government. In his later discussion of the ideas and theories which had affected his work Lattimore notes that 'the most nearly Marxist influence'[37] thereon was Karl Wittfogel who at that time had yet to sever completely his relations with the Communist movement. But whatever influence Wittfogel was to have subsequently he can only have played a small part in this discovery, since it was quite fully enunciated, as has been shown, in an article published at the beginning of 1935 whereas the two men were not to meet until August of that year.[38]

The Prospects for China

Thus possessed of new insights, Lattimore turned his attention to China, the other half, as it were, of the Mongol puzzle. Nanking had failed to adopt an equitable policy towards the Mongols for reasons internal to China and the Kuomintang regime. Sun Yat-sen's ideal of treating the national minorities as 'equal citizens of a federated Republic' had been abandoned with the rise to prominence of colonising and military interests within the regime following 'the abandonment by Nanking of a revolutionary policy for China after 1928'. Writing at the time of the 'Sian Incident' of December 1936, when Chiang Kai-shek was reluctantly forced by a military rebellion into alliance with the Communist Party to resist further Japanese encroachments, Lattimore argues that the root of the Mongol problem lay in China. This problem would not be solved until there was a return to the position of Sun Yat-sen which 'would result in something very much like the "united front" which the Chinese Communists demand and offer'.[39] Lattimore's favourable assessment of the prospects for the Chinese Communists did not depend entirely however on their alleged freedom from special interests. Just as Mao Tse-tung (Mao Zedong) and the other Long Marchers were making their way finally into Shensi (Shaanxi) after their long trek under Kuomintang harassment from the southeast, Lattimore was advancing the view, consistent with his earlier geopolitical observations, that a new and specifically continental chapter was opening in the Asian communist movement. An inland base, such as the communists were soon to construct at Yenan (Yanan), would permit them to make contact with and draw upon the industrialised strength of the Soviet Union in much the same way as had been possible for the People's Revolutionary Party in Mongolia. And in a most prophetic passage, all the more remarkable given the lack of information at that time in Peking about the communists, Lattimore observes that 'those who both evade the government troops and survive the difficulties of the country they traverse will come out with the reputation of supermen'.[40]

The impression that the communists were in China to stay was confirmed when Lattimore travelled to Yenan in June 1937. Acting as a guide and interpreter to two Americans, Philip Jaffe and T A Bisson,[41] Lattimore took part in interviews with Mao Tse-tung and other Chinese leaders and was able to form an estimate of these men and their programme, particularly as it affected the minority peoples. Although he was much later to recall that his interviews at a training school for minorities were abruptly closed when he began to discuss Communist Party policy towards the Mongols in the Mongol language rather than Chinese,[42] at the time he wrote that the communists were neither manipulative nor chauvinistic in their attitude towards Moslems, Mongols and others. In the same articles (written for, though never published by *The Times*) he concludes that irrespective of what course of action Japan adopted the communists would prove to be a force to be reckoned with:

> If Japan does not fight the Communists will emerge as a legal
> party with influence all over China and a sort of provincial status
> in the region they already control. If Japan fights, and the
> Communist theory of the relation between army and population in
> a 'semi-colonial' country is correct, a large part of both army and
> people will go over to the Communists.[43]

In the month following the trip to Yenan the Japanese began their invasion of China proper and Lattimore found the environment for his editorial and research work increasingly adverse. He therefore returned in December 1937 to the United States and under the patronage of University President Isaiah Bowman joined the staff of Johns Hopkins in Baltimore, first as a lecturer and later as Director of the Page School of International Relations, where he remained until 1941. In these years Lattimore began to publish some of the preliminary studies for *Inner Asian Frontiers of China*, he also wrote a number of pieces on the Sino-Japanese War and the part he considered the United States ought to be playing. And he put together a long and reflective account, based on his travelling notebooks, of the various journeys in Inner Mongolia which were the raw material of his observations on Mongol society, history, and politics.[44] The preliminary studies are best considered together with the work to which they gave rise, but Lattimore's writings on the conflict in China deserve some analysis here. They reveal an attempt to combine Lattimore's knowledge of the geopolitics of East Asia with what he had discovered of the dynamics of the societies in question, themes he was to explore at great length in his wartime and postwar writings on the new place of Asia in the world.

As early as May 1936 there are clear indications that Lattimore began to see the problems of East Asia more in global terms. Neither continental conflict between Russia and Japan nor a forward policy towards the Mongols by the Japanese was inevitable: both depended on developments in the West and in the League of Nations. But the pressures within Japan for conquest and expansion were inexorable, and could only be checked by external powers.[45] Writing in 1937, only a month after the Marco Polo Bridge incident which finally precipitated the Sino-Japanese War, Lattimore predicted, correctly as it turned out, that the Japanese would be most likely to capture most if not all of the Chinese coastal areas but would make little headway in the hinterland.[46] Those in the West, Lattimore argued, who preferred such 'limited' war were merely assisting the aggressor, the circumstances calling for resolute assistance to be rendered to China and to the other victims of similar attacks, notably Spain. In a more considered piece Lattimore exposes the geographical basis of the conflict. The failure of the initial Japanese assault on Shansi had prevented them from advancing on China along the traditional avenue of conquest, inland from the north. This failure had in some measure signalled the inability of the Japanese ever to bring their invasion to a successful conclusion. Advancing from the coast and up the river valleys would leave Japan in possession of the greater part of the traditional agricultural heartland but would not offer a decisive advantage. In the hinterland, particularly in the southwest, there existed great potential for development, a potential which only needed 'a new individual mentality and a new social outlook'[47] neither of which was beyond the people or their regime. The insufficiency of Japanese power was underlined by Soviet resolution to defend her Far Eastern borders, and those of Outer Mongolia, particularly as revealed in the outcome of the fighting at Changkufeng (Zhanggufeng) in 1938, when Soviet forces repulsed a Japanese advance in disputed territory where the Manchukuo, Korean, and Soviet borders met.[48] Indeed, the importance of the Soviet Union in any lasting settlement in East Asia could not be understated. In an article devoted to the Central Asian supply route by which Soviet aid reached China Lattimore exposed the likely consequences of British and American vacillation over keeping open alternative routes (notably the Burma Road) to the Chinese hinterland. Chinese development was possible from two new centres - from the northwest, to link up with the USSR and Central Asia, and from the southwest towards the maritime countries. British and American inaction may have decided which of these possibilities was realised.[49]

Notes to Chapter Two

1 'The Gold Tribe, "Fishkin" Tatars of the Lower Sungari', *Studies in Frontier History*, pp 395-402.

2 'Inner Mongolian Nationalism and the Pan-Mongolian Idea: Recollections and Reflections', *Journal of the Anglo-Mongolian Society* VI (1980), no 1, pp 13-15; *Diluv Khutagt*, pp 2-3. At this time Lattimore read an analysis by Merse of the Mongol problem which though critical of present Chinese policy favoured a fair co-operation of the two peoples since they were both the victims of oppression: 'Modern Mongolia', *Pacific Affairs* III (1930), pp 754-62.

3 'Inner Mongolian Nationalism and the Pan-Mongolian Idea:', p 16; *Diluv Khutagt*, p 4.

4 R A Rupen, *How Mongolia Is Really Ruled* (Stanford: Hoover Institute Press, 1979), p 25.

5 The politics of this period are discussed in S Jagchid, 'Mongolian Nationalism in Response to Great Power Rivalry 1900-1950', *Plural Societies* 5 (1974) pp 43-57; 'The Failure of a Self-Determination Movement: The Inner Mongolian Case' in W O McCagg and B D Silver (eds), *Soviet Asian Ethnic Frontiers* (New York: Pergamon Press, 1979), pp 229-45; Joseph Fletcher, 'A Brief History of the Chinese Northwestern Frontier', in M Alonso (ed), *China's Inner Asian Frontier* (Cambridge, Mass: Harvard University Press, 1979), pp 45 ff.

6 H L Boorman and R C Howard, *Biographical Dictionary of Republican China* (New York: Columbia University Press, 1967), I, pp 6 ff. Boorman states that the first Congress of the Inner Mongolian Kuomintang was held in March, and that a further group meeting in October also in Kalgan founded the Inner Mongolian People's Revolutionary Party. Other sources (Jagchid, Rupen, Fletcher) imply there was only a single movement. According to Brown and Onon, the delegates from the Mongolian People's Republic to the 1925 meeting were Dambadorj and Buyannemekh: W A Brown and Urgunge Onon (trans and ed), *History of the Mongolian People's Republic* (Cambridge, Mass: Harvard University Press, 1976), p 806, n 12.

7 James E Sheridan, *Chinese Warlord: The career of Feng Yü-hsiang* (Stanford: Stanford University Press, 1966), pp 197 ff. It was the flight of Feng's former troops into the northwest that delayed the Lattimores for five months in Kuei-hua: *The Desert Road to Turkestan*, pp 18 ff.

8 R A Rupen, *How Mongolia Is Really Ruled*, pp 37 ff.

9 R A Rupen, *How Mongolia Is Really Ruled*, p 36.

10 'On the Wickedness of Being Nomads' [1935], *Studies in Frontier History*, p 418.

11 H L Boorman and R C Howard, *Biographical Dictionary of Republican China*, II, pp 6 ff.

12 Paul Hyer and Sechin Jagchid (eds), *A Mongolian Living Buddha: Biography of the Kanjurwa Khutughtu* (Albany: State University of New York Press, 1982), pp 167 ff.

13 S Jagchid, 'Prince Gungsangnorbu, Forerunner of Inner Mongolian Modernization', *Zentralasiatische Studien* 12 (1979), pp 147-58.

14 Donald G Gillin, *Warlord, Yen Hsi-shan in Shansi Province 1911-1949* (Princeton: Princeton University Press, 1967), pp 213 ff.

15 P Hyer and S Jagchid (eds), *A Mongolian Living Buddha*, pp 170-1: Chinese hostility to Te Wang may be judged by the fact that in 1934 in violation of an agreement made by Nanking the governor of Chahar established a Chinese style administrative district in this area, naming it Huate (Huade: ie pacifying Te Wang). For the events of 1936 see also: James W Morley (ed), *The China Quagmire. Japan's Expansion on the Asian Continent 1933-41* (New York: Columbia University Press, 1983), pp 202-24.

16 Lawrence N Shyu, 'China's "Wartime Parliament": The People's Political Council, 1938-1945', in Paul K T Sih (ed), *Nationalist China During the Sino-Japanese War, 1937-1945* (Hicksville, New York: Exposition Press, 1977), pp 280-1.

17 Chang Mu (Zhang Mu), *Meng-ku Yu-mu Chi* (Menggu Yumu Ji), (Changsha: Basic Sinological Series, 1938).

18 G C Binstead, 'The Tribal and Administrative System of Mongolia' *Far Eastern Review* X (1913-14), no 2, pp 41-8, 70.

19 *Manchuria, cradle of conflict* [additional chapters of 1935], p 318.

20 'Open Door or Great Wall' [1934], *Studies in Frontier History*, pp 76 ff.

21 *Manchuria, cradle of conflict*, pp 326 ff.

22 'Mongolia Enters World Affairs' *Pacific Affairs* VII (1934), pp 21-2. This is also printed as chapter one of *the Mongols of Manchuria*; cf *the Mongols of Manchuria* (New York: Macmillan, 1934), p 136.

23 'The Unknown Frontier of Manchuria' [1933], *Studies in Frontier History*, p 325.

24 'The Unknown Frontier of Manchuria', pp 330 ff.

25 'The Unknown Frontier of Manchuria', p 337; cf 'Mongolia Enters World Affairs', p 25.

26 'Mongolia Enters World Affairs', pp 26-7.

27 'The Phantom of Mengkukuo' [1937], *Studies in Frontier History*, pp 405 ff; 'The Eclipse of Inner Mongolian Nationalism', [1936] *Studies in Frontier History*, pp 430-2; 'Land and Sea in the destiny of Japan', *Pacific Affairs* IX (1936), pp 586-9.

28 'The Eclipse of Inner Mongolian Nationalism', p 435.

29 'The Eclipse of Inner Mongolian Nationalism', p 438; cf 'The Lines of Cleavage in Inner Mongolia', *Pacific Affairs* X (1937), pp 196-201. Here (199) Te Wang is described as having been 'honest throughout'.

30 'Prince, Priest and Herdsman in Mongolia', *Pacific Affairs* VIII (1935), pp 36 ff.
31 'Prince, Priest and Herdsman in Mongolia', pp 39-40.
32 'Prince, Priest and Herdsman in Mongolia', p 40.
33 'Prince, Priest and Herdsman in Mongolia', p 44.
34 'The Historical Setting of Inner Mongolian Nationalism', [1936], *Studies in Frontier History*, pp 440-55; cf 'The Eclipse of Inner Mongolian Nationalism'.
35 'The Historical Setting of Inner Mongolian Nationalism', p 449.
36 'The Historical Setting of Inner Mongolian Nationalism', p 455.
37 'Preface', *Studies in Frontier History*, p 28.
38 G L Ulmen, *The Science of Society. Toward an Understanding of the Life and Work of Karl August Wittfogel* (The Hague: Mouton, 1978), p 189.
39 'Inner Mongolia - Chinese, Japanese or Mongol?', *Pacific Affairs* X (1937), pp 68,71.
40 'The Inland Gates of China', *Pacific Affairs* VIII (1935), p 471.
41 T A Bisson, *Yenan in 1937: Talks with the Communist Leaders*, University of California China Research Monograph (Berkeley: University of California Press, 1973). Lattimore contributes a Foreword, pp 7-9.
42 'Preface', *Studies in Frontier History*; Lattimore was also obliged to discuss this and other incidents on his trip to Yenan in - US Congress: Senate, *Institute of Pacific Relations. Hearings before the Subcommittee ... of the Committee on the Judiciary* (Washington: US Government Printing Office, 1950-1), pp 328 ff.
43 'Unpublished Report from Yenan 1937', J Ch'en and N Tarling (eds), *Studies in the Social History of China and South East Asia* (Cambridge: Cambridge University Press, 1970), p 163. It is Lattimore's opinion that this report was never published because it contradicted the received wisdom of the time that the Chinese did not have the ability or resolve to resist the determined Japanese onslaught which was mounted just as it reached the newspaper.
44 *Mongol Journeys* (London: Jonathan Cape, 1941).
45 'Russo-Japanese Relations', *International Affairs* 15 (1936), pp 525-42.
46 '"Limited" War and World War', *Pacific Affairs* X (1937), pp 450-3.
47 'Japan Hung Up on the Hypotenuse', *Amerasia* 2 (1938), p 480.
48 'Siberia seals Japan's fate' *Amerasia* 2 (1938), pp 380-4.
49 'China's Turkestan - Siberian Supply Road', *Pacific Affairs* XIII (1940), p 412.

CHAPTER THREE

Inner Asian Frontiers

Owen Lattimore returned to the United States at the end of 1937, taking up a position, under the patronage of college President the geographer Isaiah Bowman, initially as Lecturer then as Director of the Page School of International Relations at Johns Hopkins University. *Inner Asian Frontiers of China* was published in 1940 but Lattimore refers to its period of gestation as ten years, and by 1937 his ideas were sufficiently developed for him to write at length on two of the most important themes of the book. The first concerned the dynamics of nomad (especially Mongol) society, the second the abiding characteristics of Chinese civilisation in the era before industrialisation.

The complex of historical issues Lattimore had set himself to investigate had two principal aspects. He had come round to the view (expressed as early as 1932) that the impact of the nomads was a crucial factor in Chinese history. He had also been persuaded of the relative inability of the Chinese to adopt any other way of life than that which permitted the reproduction of a sedentary agrarian pattern. He had therefore to explain both phenomena given that repeated nomad-Chinese interactions had led neither society to alter its fundamentals.

Toynbee on the Nomads

In a lecture delivered in 1936 Lattimore sought to refute Toynbee's interpretation of the major characteristics of nomad civilisation. Toynbee (and Huntington, upon whose work Toynbee relied) had been an important early influence on Lattimore. He had, moreover, quoted Lattimore's writings on Manchuria with approval in the same volume of *A Study of History* in which his views on nomads were expressed. But his argument was the greatest challenge to Lattimore's present views since he maintained that nomadic civilisation though it was an historical '*tour de force*' was a response to external forces and thus was, in essence, a civilisation without an independent history. Nomadism, in Toynbee's view, 'may be conceived as having arisen in response to the searching challenge of desiccation'.[1] Innovation may be allowed to the nomads in that their way of life seems to have evolved subsequent to the discovery of settled agriculture (which permitted the initial domestication of animals, the foundation of nomadism). But thereafter they are the prisoners of their predicament, and the periodic eruptions of these peoples onto the centre-stage of world history are to be understood as the result of the operation of two external forces:

37

The Nomad is occasionally pushed off the Steppe by a fresh turn of the climatic screw which intensifies the pressure to a degree which even the trained and hardened steppe-dweller cannot endure; and again he is occasionally pushed out of the Steppe by the suction of a social vacuum which has arisen in the domain of some adjacent sedentary society through the operation of historic processes, such as the breakdown and disintegration of a sedentary civilization ...[2]

That is to say, whenever the nomad appears on the stage of world history he is either forced from his accustomed habitat by adverse changes in weather conditions or drawn towards settled societies by the superfluity of goods therein. In a lengthy annexe to this volume of his book Toynbee attempted to prove that nomadic history could be explained in its entirety by the operation of these 'two mechanical causes', though he had the foresight also to append a note by G F Hudson which pointed out some of the difficulties of the Huntington view of desiccation, the more important of the two causes. Hudson argued that desiccation need not necessarily lead to a reduction in the amount of pasture available to nomadic peoples, and that such empirical evidence as was available did not support in several instances the chronology of nomadic history drawn up by Toynbee himself.[3]

Although he accepted Toynbee's view that nomadism was a relatively late human development, Lattimore took issue with the assertion that the nomads had no history, treating this as a serious hypothesis rather than as an echo of Hegel. He accepted that, in the initial stages, the environment was likely to be a powerful determinant upon a primitive society, but he also argued that the very marginality of the nomad habitat could lead to the exercise of choice and initiative. Mongol society, for example, was replete with instances both of cultural survivals and adaptations. And a study of Mongol history revealed not so much a cycle as a spiral form of development: the empire of the Hsiung-nu (Xiongnu) (209 BC - AD 155) could not be compared with that of Chinggis (AD 1206-1227). Moreover, relations with sedentary societies often led the nomad to modify his way of life through commerce or even by way of adopting the practice of oasis agriculture. As these relations were important throughout most of Mongol history, 'it is the poor nomad who is the pure nomad'.[4]

The Dynamics of Chinese Society

In tackling the problem of the dynamics of Chinese society Lattimore turns Toynbee on his head.[5] He does not go so far as to suggest that the Chinese have no history, but he does observe that reliance over many dynasties upon a relatively fixed frontier zone, the Great Wall, suggests that some constant factors have been at work in that history. Following Carl Whiting Bishop,

Karl Wittfogel, and a number of geographical authorities from von Richthofen to Thorp[6], Lattimore develops the view that geography was of vital importance in determining the extent to which Chinese civilisation could expand. Arising in the readily cultivated loess regions of the north, and extending with the development of more extensive irrigation systems under state tutelage into the river regions of central and south China, this civilisation could only incorporate those new territories in which such a pattern of life could be reproduced. Chinese society was 'cellular' in character, each agricultural region being dominated by a walled city in which was conducted such market exchange of artisan and agricultural produce as was necessary. Long range transport was generally restricted to the carrying of tribute grain to the capital by way of a canal system operated by state stipendaries. Political unification had not destroyed this cellular structure, and as there were no insuperable obstacles to its reproduction in the southern margins, China expanded indefinitely in that direction. Particular historical circumstances did give rise to the control of the oasis regions of Sinkiang, Ninghsia, and Kansu, but these areas never assumed major importance.

In the north, however, the Chinese were confronted by 'the factor of range', the very term Toynbee employs to account for the geographical delimitations of nomad societies.[7] Although attempts were made by successive Chinese dynasties to expand in the north beyond those territories suitable for intensive, sedentary agriculture, notably in the Ordos (Mu Us) region, these attempts were in the long run unsuccessful. In considering the impact of this frontier upon Chinese civilisation once the Ch'in (Qin) and former Han dynasties had endeavoured to give it a hard and fast definition, Lattimore finds that these marginal territories exercise a 'pull' on their inhabitants every bit as important as the 'pressure' brought to bear by tribal barbarians upon China. Here Toynbee's argument is recast, with the inhabitants of the sedentary empire being pulled towards the steppe as much as the steppe nomads are being pulled by a temporary power vacuum towards the fleshpots of a settled civilisation. In seeking to act beyond the natural 'range' of the political and social forms that were the enduring foundation of Chinese civilisation successive Chinese empires created a population of frontiersmen upon whom their new environment exercised a sometimes fatal attraction:

> The Ch'in unification of the Great Wall Frontier, by acquiescing
> in the development of a special frontier population, not wholly
> Chinese in its characteristics, compromised the idea of rigidity that
> was essential to the Great Wall theory of frontier delimitation. It
> exceeded the effective range of action of the newly established
> imperial state ... making it possible for disruption to begin under
> the feet of the successful conquerors.[8]

Although the imperatives of the fixed pattern of Chinese society required the existence of a definite frontier, the geography of the region was transitional, permitting to the borderers more than one way of life. From the Ch'in dynasty to the eighteenth century, then, attempts to delimit the frontiers of China in the north and northwest presented a problem insoluble in the long run.

Thus were the origins of the policy of the frontier 'reservoir' described in Lattimore's earlier writings. To hold the frontier the co-operation of the 'partly sinicized nomads and semibarbarized Chinese' of the marginal zones was necessary. Their role was therefore crucial not merely for the maintenance of a particular dynasty but for the larger pattern of Chinese history:

> In passive phases they represented the balance, at any given time, between China and the Frontier; but in active phases they were agents of ferment in frontier relations, causing new adjustments of the balance and preventing it from ever becoming static and permanent. Because of this, it is not always necessary to search the core of China for the causes of the great periods of Chinese expansion. Nor are the origins of great nomadic conquests to be found only in the widest regions of the true steppe.9

The Argument of 'Inner Asian Frontiers of China'

Inner Asian Frontiers of China is largely the depiction, on a far broader historical and geographical canvas, of the themes dealt with in Lattimore's essays of 1936-38. The study falls into two parts, an enquiry into the historical geography of Chinese frontiers (with particular emphasis on the Great Wall), and an historical exemplification of that enquiry over the three periods of Chinese history - the earliest period, the era of Chinese states, and the Imperial age.

The work is a comprehensive and wide-ranging synthesis of much scholarship that was then current - archaeological, historical, and sociological - and as might be anticipated in many respects it has now been overtaken by subsequent research. Lattimore's account of the spread of early bronze working into China, for example, itself based on Bishop, Creel and others, would now be rejected by historians.10 Similarly, Lattimore's treatment of the Imperial (post-Ch'in) age as a single historical entity would now be regarded as an over-simplification. In its time, however, the book was extremely influential and deservedly so. Chinese history writing in English at that time tended to exhibit a bias towards philosophical and political developments to the exclusion of other factors. And the influence of traditional historiographical materials often focussed historical accounts upon the metropolis and the bureaucracy. Lattimore's writing was timely in that the findings of archaeology and economic history had begun to force the revision of many conceptions derived from these sources. Moreover contemporary events - the activities of Soviet Russia and Japan in frontier regions, and the forced withdrawal of the Kuomintang government to Chungking (Chongqing) after 1937 - demanded a new geographical and geopolitical view of China's past.

In order to consider the development of Lattimore's ideas, as well as to assess the extent of his permanent contribution to scholarship, the following discussion will be restricted to a review of the principal themes of *Inner Asian Frontiers of China*. These themes, stated simply, are how the Chinese and the frontier nomads came to be distinguished, and how their civilisations and ways of life have interacted. More generally they include the role that Lattimore accords to geographical factors in his analysis. This will be followed by a consideration of the response his ideas have generated among specialist scholars.

The Origins of Pastoral Nomadism

It is Lattimore's contention that for millennia mixed patterns of ways of living including hunting, agriculture, and shepherding could be found over much of East and Inner Asia.[11] From this mixed pattern more specialised hunting and agricultural societies are likely to have evolved. Hunting peoples especially in the margins between forest and steppe in northern Asia could have turned to herding as a supplement to or a modification of their way of life, but nomadism as a distinctive form of society and economy could only have developed with the domestication of appropriate animals. This in turn could only have been possible in a pre-existing agricultural society able to provide food for relatively closely confined animals from cultivated crops. It is Lattimore's further contention that the factor responsible for setting the seal on pastoral nomadism as a distinct civilisation in Inner Asia was man's mastery of the horse. Horse riding imparted the mobility and skills which permitted an abandonment of permanent relations with marginal peoples and habitats in favour of the extensive grazing of mobile herds entirely on the steppe. The skills learned at herding could also be employed in warfare, and the pastoral nomads in time produced a 'natural cavalry' only to be contained militarily by neighbouring sedentary societies at ruinous cost.[12]

Lattimore postulates that marginal societies, forced towards the steppe by more vigorous agricultural communities, turned to animal control as a primary rather than ancillary activity. These societies may have combined with some populations from the Siberian forest or Central Asian oasis zones to form a people thoroughly adapted to the steppe environment.[13] With the acquisition of the horse their transformation into a separate people was complete. Lattimore goes on to argue that Chinese historical sources are now to be viewed in a different light. The Jung (Rong) and Ti (Di) barbarians of the Spring and Autumn period of Chinese history (c722-481 BC) were not thus to be equated with the northern barbarians of later times, still less were the original Chou (Zhou) conquerors who supplanted the Shang dynasty (c1027 BC). The Jung, Ti, and other tribes are to be considered rather as merely less developed and organised peoples excluded or absorbed by the expanding Chinese statelets of the time. True 'barbarians' can only be said to have come into existence when these statelets ceased their expansion into the territory more or less suited to agriculture which was open to them, and began to war with each other, creating as a by-product a 'new steppe society [which] was both independent of the society of China and alternative to it'.[14] This is confirmed by the appearance of *mounted* nomads in Chinese historical sources at the end of the fourth century BC. Thereafter the cycles of nomadic history, beginning with the states organised by T'u-man (Tuman) and Mao-tun (Maodun, Modun) of the Hsiung-nu, were inextricably bound up with the history of China.

The Origins of Chinese Civilisation

The emergence of Chinese civilisation may be attributed to the presence of extensive deposits of readily cultivated loess soil in the middle reaches of the Yellow River (Huang He), these geographical conditions making possible the formation of the earliest communities of sedentary intensive agriculturalists. From a very early time the uncertain climate encouraged the development of irrigation, and in the original cradle of the civilisation in valley after valley there evolved forms of co-operative and collective enterprise, the granaries of which were safeguarded against less developed neighbours by a warrior class. In an account which shows an indebtedness to Bishop, as well as to Wittfogel and his Chinese colleagues Chi Ch'ao-ting (Ji Chaoding) and Wang Yü-ch'üan (Wang Yuquan)[15], Lattimore offers an interpretation of the formation of the centralised Chinese empire.

With the extension of techniques evolved in the loess region to the Chinese plains large scale co-operation particularly in the management of canal systems for irrigation and transport required an authority larger in scope than petty feudal lords. First statelets and then kingdoms came into existence, and 'feudalism was burst asunder by this growth'. From the old nobility there emerged a 'scholar-gentry' class whose function was to administer schemes of water control and conservancy of ever greater complexity which demanded ever larger inputs of corvée labour for their execution.[16] Ultimately the centre of gravity of the civilisation moved towards the south, a region of potential grain surplus from which was drawn through canal borne transportation[17] the revenues for the administrative capital, and into which the civilisation could expand without requiring a change in its habitual pattern.

But in this expansion lateral integration of the state remained weak. Lattimore returns to the description offered earlier of the 'cellular' character of Chinese society, the formation of which comprised:

the adding together of innumerable units, which in spite of local differences were essentially homogeneous, each consisting of a rural landscape watched over by a walled city - never, in the more fertile parts of the country, more distant than a day's walk from the next city.[18]

Apart from a limited variety of commodities, typically salt, iron, tea, and silk, which were traded at longer range, the village was the unit of agricultural production and the walled city provided such artisan craft goods as were necessary to supply local demand. High population densities and early reliance upon large scale mobilisation of labour for state administered water conservancy and transportation projects hindered the development of labour saving devices and machines. And the bureaucratic ethos of the administrative class recruited in the main from the landed gentry who held the empire together dominated the towns, holding the development of commerce in check by monopolies and other controls and frustrating other innovations such as mining.[19]

The Pattern of Chinese History

If Bishop and the geographers were the principal inspiration for those portions of *Inner Asian Frontiers of China* which dealt with the geographical basis and pre-history of Chinese civilisation - as Lattimore records, Bishop's 'patient criticism helped me to find my way step by step into the Stone Age, and at least part way out of it'[20] - the ultimate source of Lattimore's characterisation of the later pattern of the Chinese political and economic systems is clearly the Marxian conception of the Asiatic mode of production. Now it was this conception and its elaboration which had already been Wittfogel's preoccupation for a decade, a preoccupation which had led to the severing of his connections with the official communist movement.[21] And Lattimore acknowledges that after his father, David, and Bishop, Wittfogel was the most significant source of stimulus and support in the writing of his book. Indeed, the intellectual biography by Wittfogel's amanuensis claims that Wittfogel wrote a 'long memorandum' to Lattimore after reading the original draft, which resulted in many changes to the published version.[22] A review, therefore, of Lattimore's treatment of the dynamics of Chinese and Inner Asian history will reveal the extent both of his originality and of his indebtedness to others.

In Marx's conception of the Asiatic mode of production the social and political structures which dominated the numerous agricultural village communities were constituted such that no progress or historical development (from indigenous sources) was possible. The state machine, in providing crucial aspects of the material conditions of production (especially waterworks, made possible by the geography of large river systems) controlled the ownership of landed property and continuously appropriated most of the production surplus, thereby preventing the formation of other classes who might usurp those functions.[23] Commerce and a merchant class could be found, and populous cities came into being, but all were subordinated to the autocratic and bureaucratic ethos of the ruler and the state machine. The parade of dynasties in oriental history was of no greater significance than the passing of clouds in the sky since the fundamental reality remained constant.

Wittfogel evidently accepted much of this sketch but sought to give it a more historical dimension. In particular, from his earliest scientific writing on China he endeavoured to explain the fact that though dynasties rose and fell, and the civilisation endured periodic crises, the mode of production remained unchanged. The best exposition of his answer is to be found in an article written in 1935, 'The Foundations and Stages of Chinese Economic History'[24], a source to which Lattimore is clearly indebted. There Wittfogel maintains that with the commuting of labour rent to rent in kind and then money rent, and with the completion of the Grand Canal and the shifting of the economic centre of gravity to the lower Yangtze (Chang Jiang) basin, a mature political and social order emerged. Though this order was destined to have a prolonged life, it could never escape a periodic cycle of crisis. The efficiency of the political system depended upon as large a tax revenue as possible, the agents for the collection of which were ultimately the officials. But these same officials, or the 'gentry' or landlord class from whom they were recruited, were in their private capacity intent upon securing for themselves the largest landed estates possible and the largest practicable surplus from those estates. There was thus a tendency for the gentry to shift more and more of the tax burden onto the peasantry and away from their own holdings. This had the effect of impoverishing elements of the rural population and reducing them to tenant status, thereby diminishing further the tax base of the regime. At the same time the government's need for liquid assets encouraged the use of money, the introduction of which facilitated the emergence of a merchant class. As the merchants were not, in general, superintending any new form of production, their activities served essentially to absorb a growing proportion of the surplus. Under these conditions either increasing rural impoverishment led to peasant rebellions which unseated the ruling dynasty, or the enfeebled state was no match for invaders from without. This understanding of the cycle of Chinese history was the basis for a long article on the Ch'ing dynasty by one of Wittfogel's Chinese colleagues which Lattimore also cites with approval.[25]

It is Lattimore's contention that once the feudal stage of Chinese history had been surpassed, and with it a clear delineation had emerged between the Chinese and nomadic pastoral ways of life, the internal dynamics of Chinese civilisation produced a cycle of the kind described by Wittfogel. At one point the decline of dynasties is specifically attributed to 'the overdevelopment of the "scholar-gentry"' in the provinces and the corresponding evisceration of imperial revenues, though elsewhere Lattimore observes that overpopulation and the dwindling marginal returns of human labour in agriculture may also have provoked political and social crisis.[26] But this is only part of the story since, for Lattimore, one of the sources of Chinese history is to be found on the frontiers where quite a distinct cycle could be discerned. It is necessary therefore to consider Lattimore's view of the forces at work in nomadic society, and the impact of these forces on Chinese civilisation, before his analysis of the pattern of Chinese history can be properly appraised.

Cycles of Nomadic History and the Appearance of Marginal States

Within the societies of the steppe Lattimore identified the following characteristic phases of evolution. The need for mobility on the part of the steppe dwelling nomads imparted considerable powers to the tribal chiefs who regulated the allotment of pastures and migration routes. A chief with a superfluity of stock and followers might be tempted to employ his mobile followers on new endeavours, either 'to raid China if China were then weak, or to patronize trade if China were strong, or even to experiment with agriculture'.[27] These 'departures from the steppe norm' produced in time a 'mixed society' of steppe, marginal, and sometimes agricultural territory which, despite various expedients tried by the rulers of such states, in time broke asunder into its incompatible constituents. The nomadic norm was reasserted in the steppe, and the cycle began afresh.

In this cycle the role of 'marginal' territories and 'marginal' men was crucial. T'u-man who rose to prominence among the Hsiungnu was a man from the Ordos, forced to migrate through Chinese pressure.[28] His son, Mao-tun, 'the first great khan of the Hsiungnu', was the master of a new kind of society which exercised the power of attraction on some at the margins of the new Chinese empire and which had to be dealt with through a combined policy of trade, tribute, and warfare.[29] A similar pattern may be seen in the later history of the Toba Wei, the Hsien-pi (Xianbi), the Juan-juan (Ruanruan), the Liao and Chin (Jin) dynasties, the Mongols under Chinggis and his successors and the Manchus.[30] And the original leaders of most of these federations of peoples were 'marginal men', individuals from the periphery in a social as well as in a geographical sense. They were 'men of the border, who knew the structure of power both in the steppe and in China'.[31]

Lattimore gives some consideration also to the expedients that were employed to bridge the gap between steppe and sown in this succession of mixed states. Here the concept of the 'tribal reservoir' first discussed in Lattimore's work on Manchuria enters as the device whereby a conquering dynasty of nomadic origins kept more distant tribesmen at bay while providing a ready source of levies for its rule of agricultural China.[32] Inner Asian conquerors and rulers of marginal states also employed specialised administrators of non-Chinese origin, sometimes in conjunction with religion in an attempt to give longevity to their domains. Thus Chinggis used central Asian, Persian, and other servants to avoid becoming the captive of a Chinese bureaucracy.[33] Khobilai (Kublai, Qubilai) also patronised the Buddhist church, Tibetan monks being among his closest advisers, and he was venerated by them as an incarnation of Maitreya, though Lattimore does not point out the irony of the fact that it was at this time that Sung (Song) neo-Confucianism was brought under Mongol patronage to north China ultimately to become the philosophical orthodoxy.[34]

Lama Buddhism did not put down lasting roots in the period of the Mongol dynasty but it was revived in the sixteenth century by Altan Khan of the Tumet (Tümed) whose relations with the Tibetan bSod-nams rgya-mtsho recalled those that had existed between Khobilai and his preceptor 'Phags-pa. Lattimore's interpretation of these events places emphasis upon the mixed character of Altan's state, rather than the ideological convenience this relationship had for both participants. Altan was 'a city-building prince' seeking to rule a state inhabited by both pastoral and agricultural subjects, who pursued an active and successful policy of enriching his domains through trade with China. In such a state a 'unifying agency' was required, and Altan's patronage and employment of Lama Buddhism supplied this without ensnaring him in the net of Chinese culture. The church provided for the state a body of literate administrators, moreover:

> a celibate church with monastic property made possible a better management of the most important working problem of all such border states of mixed economy and society. The church's co-operative, impersonal title to property achieved a higher degree of integration between mobile pastoral property and fixed landed property than the society of the time could manage in any other way. It both stood between and linked together the families that were attached to the tribal structure of power and those whose power was based on landed estates, tenantry, and city activities.[35]

Though the ultimate source of Manchu power was quite different, Manchu patronage in the following century of the Buddhist hierarchy among the Mongols provided them with a useful device to reduce the Mongols to vassalage. The Ch'ing rulers were thus:

> able to perpetuate a Mongol church that was independent of the princes, thus creating a permanent dyarchy in Mongol affairs, with a church that looked toward Tibet (whose pontiffs were granted Manchu patronage) and princes that looked directly to the Manchu court in Peking.[36]

In considering the character of mixed states Lattimore revises his previous remarks on the role and character of the tribal 'reservoir' of frontier dynasties. His emphasis had formerly been on the function of the reservoir as a source of troops and administrators for use within China, and as a military screen against peoples further out in the steppe. Now his work on nomads and their contacts with sedentary civilisations, not to mention his personal experiences of nomads and their environment, led him to a more complex view. All mixed states were bound to experience, to some degree, a tension between the peoples of their two habitats. These peoples followed different patterns of life, but some frontier Chinese sought integration with the steppe, and some nomads desired greater contact with the trade and commodities of China. In this way the varying form of mixed states was to be explained, and the reservoir could be seen to have the additional function of muting or mediating these internal tensions.[37] But a consideration of the conflicts within mixed states raises the fundamental issue of the historical pattern of interactions between nomads and Chinese, the second major theme of the work.

Nomad - Chinese Interactions

At several points in the book Lattimore pauses to review the relationship between nomads and Chinese. Having offered a characterisation of pastoral nomadism, Lattimore considers the evidence, given the relative self-sufficiency of the nomadic way of life, of climatic changes causing cycles of concentration and dispersal among the peoples of the steppe. Such cycles would impinge upon the neighbouring sedentary societies, resulting in competition for land, or warfare. But, quite apart from those reasons already considered for rejecting the desiccation hypothesis, Lattimore finds that the historical record shows that nomadism was never a 'closed world'. Irrespective of climatic fluctuations the nomads had always engaged in a complex variety of contacts with adjacent societies involving trade, political domination, and warfare. The continuity of these contacts, and the need to consider them in any account of the evolution of nomadic societies, was sufficient for Lattimore to describe nomad-Chinese interactions as a 'symbiosis'.[38]

Lattimore then turns his attention to the formation in China of national states, and the differentiation in the period from about the sixth to the third centuries BC of the two distinct ways of life, nomadic and sedentary. As Chinese civilisation expanded to occupy those areas suited to intensive cultivation and warfare between the states became endemic, a 'frontier style' appeared in Chinese history. This is exemplified, according to Lattimore, in the contrasting approach of those states at the outer limits of the civilisation, Chao (Zhao), Yen (Yan) and Ch'in:

> In Chao the Frontier dragged away from China; the Chao borderers were centrifugal. In Ch'in the Frontier was part of a co-ordinated centripetal process; it contributed to the pressure of Ch'in on the rest of China.[39]

In Chao, and also to an extent in Yen, the marginal character of the territory and the use of 'barbarian' tactics in warfare led the borderers of those states to adopt a mixed way of life. The resulting tensions in Chao pulled the state apart. By contrast Ch'in expanded to the northwest into territory in which Chinese style agriculture, sometimes in oasis form, was still possible. The Chinese way of life prevailed, and the borderers recruited into the Ch'in cavalry became the military instrument for the unification of China. Thereafter Lattimore finds this pattern repeated in the history of the control of the frontier regions:

> a distinct 'Frontier style' in Chinese history became recognisable:
> either a dynasty was founded beyond the Frontier or on the
> Frontier, and moved inward to establish its control over China, or
> it was founded within China and moved outward to establish
> control over the Frontier and sometimes beyond the Frontier.[40]

At the end of *Inner Asian Frontiers of China*, having by then reviewed the imperial age of Chinese history, Lattimore brings his argument together, taking into consideration also previous attempts to explain the larger pattern of that history. The era of the Western Han (206 BC - AD 8) saw the coming to maturity of the 'Great Wall' character of China's relations with Inner Asia, a character that persisted until its disruption by the Europeans in the nineteenth century. Now most writers on Chinese history from the first great Chinese historian Ssu-ma Ch'ien (Sima Qian, 145-90 BC) onwards have agreed that that history is periodic or cyclic, and Lattimore devotes some attention to those contemporary scholars who have influenced him the most. It was Ch'ao-ting Chi's view that the most important cycle was the regular fluctuation from political unity to political division, a fluctuation to be explained in terms of the pre-eminence of 'key economic areas'. Building on Chi and Wittfogel, Wang Yü-ch'üan sought to explain the regular fall of dynasties by the operation of a bureaucratic cycle, the scholar-gentry gradually permitting the class from which they sprang, the landlords, to escape an increasing proportion of their taxation, thus enfeebling and ultimately strangling the state.[41] It is Lattimore's contention that in the periods of disorder which followed, a cycle of dynastic formation was repeated because the conditions were conducive to the rise of 'marginal men' able to lead the rebellious peasantry but sufficiently familiar with the old order to be able to work with or manipulate the great wealthy clans and to restore the apparatus of the state when the time was appropriate. Although it is a topic of only passing interest to the traditional Chinese historians upon whom he had to rely for evidence, Lattimore finds a related phenomenon in the foundation of the dynasties of the steppe similarly by marginal men.

But how is that interaction of steppe and sedentary orders which resulted in dynasties from beyond the Great Wall ruling China to be explained? Wittfogel traces successful nomadic irruptions to the taxation cycle already mentioned. He also points out that the nomadic capacity for and interest in invasion was bound to be greater than corresponding Chinese interest in conquering the steppe.[42] Lattimore refines this analysis by pointing out that these nomadic dynasties actually emerged from peoples not of the deep steppe but marginal to Chinese civilisation, possessed of leaderships with the military and political acumen to rule territory of more than one type. It is they who evolved the policy of the tribal 'reservoir' to control their diverse domains.

Why then is there no integration between China and the steppe despite this long history of interaction? The explanation is ultimately to be sought in the environment. Agricultural China and the true steppe regions are hosts to ways of life so disparate that there could be no unity of them in historical times. Industrialism might have provided a bridge, but in China the surfeit of labour, and in the steppe excessive mobility, prevented its appearance. The history of East and Inner Asia is thus the history of two separate civilisations each with its own cycles: the Chinese cycle helped to define and form the nomadic cycle, but thereafter the nomadic cycle brought to bear on the Chinese an independent force:

> Inasmuch as the evolution of the Chinese agriculture and society, by the pressure it put on the people of the steppe margin, helped to create the true steppe society, the nomad cycle was at least in part a product of the Chinese cycle. Once established ... the nomad cycle acquired a vigor that enabled it to interact on the cyclical history of China with independent force.[43]

The Geographical Factor and the Social Structure

Considering the intellectual influences on Lattimore to this point, it is significant that many accorded greatest weight to the role of geographical factors in the explanation of history. Thus Huntington attributed the migrations of the peoples of the steppe to climatic fluctuations, and Toynbee, though in general committed to quite a different view of human civilisation, held that the nomadic form of life having evolved the nomads were thereafter trapped by the exigencies of their environment. Although there are statements in *Inner Asian Frontiers of China* that suggest a form of geographical determinism, this is not Lattimore's position.

In Manchuria, argues Lattimore, the three types of terrain (agricultural land, steppe, forest) have led to the evolution there of three types of history. For primitive peoples geography strongly conditions the way of life they adopt, and the distinctive social and economic pattern of early Chinese civilisation could only have appeared in the loess lands of the middle Yellow River basin. Although the Chinese sought military control of the west as a means to turn the flanks of the nomads, they held this region for extended periods of time because the Taklamakan, without a zone of continuous pasture to provide a base for nomad activity, favoured a Chinese type of agriculture practised in oases scattered around the central desert basin.[44] But as has been shown the evolution of pastoral nomadism is no simple response to the problem of survival posed by a particular environment, requiring the application of techniques (especially the domestication of animals) that could only have appeared first in sedentary societies. And the actual history of nomads is inextricably bound up with the civilisations of other environments. How then can Lattimore's evaluation of the geographical factor be characterised?

Geography clearly establishes parameters: the environment accounts for the fundamental and incompatible differences between nomadic and Chinese civilisation. However, the human species possesses an immense capacity for invention and adaptation, a belief which inclines Lattimore to view with some scepticism those interpretations of early Chinese history which explain the appearance of new techniques (bronze working, for example) solely in terms of the diffusion of ideas from outside the civilisation. Moreover, once a pattern of life has become well established the society acquires a momentum of its own. Here, and especially in his propounding of cyclic interpretations of nomadic and Chinese history, Lattimore reveals an abiding indebtedness to Toynbee and Spengler. Lattimore's account of the Chinese attitude towards marginal environments is an excellent illustration of this social momentum, and of the particular unwillingness of the Chinese to modify long-standing habits and practices. Here a reliance upon extensive agriculture without irrigation supplemented by livestock grazing would have supported a significant population of Chinese, but:

> This was not possible for the new society of China, which, being committed to irrigation, could not flourish unless the population was concentrated - in order to furnish the maximum supply for the necessary key enterprises, the canals ...[45]

This tendency led in the mixed states to attempts to stabilise the dominant 'social order' in the geographical area the state occupied. Thus the Orkhon Turks patronised agriculture in river valleys in the far north of the steppe. But the parameters imposed by the environment are evident in the eventual Sinification of dynasties of steppe origin, and in the use by the Chinese élites in marginal territories of barbarian practices. Lattimore's work on the contemporary period must be considered before a definitive view of his approach to the geographical factor and to the ability of civilisations to accept or generate change can be offered.

Lattimore and Modern Scholarship

The impact of *Inner Asian Frontiers of China* may be assessed in a variety of ways. At the general level Lattimore's influence, and in particular his 'cellular' description of traditional Chinese society, is manifest in the standard university textbooks of John Fairbank and his collaborators[46], as well as in subsequent work on spatial relationships in the Chinese economy and society. In work on the political geography of boundaries and frontiers it is also clear that Lattimore's ideas have been of seminal importance.[47] Concerning the question of Lattimore's originality, however, his impact on the study of nomadism and the relationship between nomadic and sedentary societies has been of lasting value.

In historical work Lattimore's hypothesis that the appearance and evolution of nomadic societies and states could partly be understood as a response to developments within neighbouring sedentary civilisations has been taken up by scholars working on particular problems. Barfield, with the inspiration of Lattimore very much in evidence, has explained the apparent paradox of the emergence from a small population and an extensive but undifferentiated economy of a relatively sophisticated Hsiung-nu state in terms of its relationship with China. State forms were required to manage the trade and plunder made possible by geographical propinquity.[48] Similarly Sechin Jagchid has underlined the essential antagonism between the two ways of life in East and Inner Asia, nomadic and agricultural.[49]

One measure of the worth of a piece of scholarship is whether or not its influence transcends disciplinary boundaries. Here it is significant that anthropologists of Africa have embraced Lattimore's nomadic hypothesis with enthusiasm. Weissleder has found that the relationship in Ethiopia between the Amharic central government and the Adal nomads bears a close resemblance to that linking the two societies of China's Inner Asian frontiers.[50] And in an important survey article Dyson-Hudson has lamented the fact that Lattimore's influence was not felt earlier:

> In 1940 ... Lattimore's *Inner Asian Frontiers of China* had appeared, with the clear suggestion that nomadism could be a controlled political response and not merely an environmentally induced reflex. But the implications of that powerful suggestion were not systematically taken up ...

Dyson-Hudson observes that 'nomadism' as a concept is vague and inadequate, since it links two phenomena not necessarily related, livestock rearing and spatial mobility.

Yoking the two sets of phenomena together is what has facilitated the erroneous assumption that nomadic movement is caused simply by environmental factors. Separating them out allows us to see that such movement may have social and (as Lattimore tried to tell us thirty years ago) political causes as well.[51]

Finally, in the definitive and encyclopaedic work of Khazanov, Lattimore's contribution to the study of nomads is highly appraised. Khazanov's own view is that there may have been more than one path of development leading to the evolution of that distinct form of society. He finds Lattimore too much inclined to regard nomadic societies as potentially autarchic, and he also holds the view that Lattimore's rejection of the possibility that desiccation or climatic change may have been a factor in the formation of particular nomadic societies is arbitrary.[52] But in the difficult but necessary task of bridging anthropological and historical research in order to provide an adequate characterisation of nomadism, 'in every respect Lattimore's brilliant book stands out on its own'.[53]

Notes to Chapter Three

1   Arnold Toynbee, *A Study of History*, III, 2nd edition (Oxford: Oxford University Press, 1935), pp 7, 8.
2   *A Study of History*, III, p 15.
3   *A Study of History*, III, pp 395-452; 453-4.
4   'The Geographical Factor in Mongol History' (1936), *Studies in Frontier History*, p 257.
5   'Origins of the Great Wall of China: a Frontier Concept in Theory and Practice' (1937), *Studies in Frontier History*, pp 97-118.
6   C W Bishop, 'The Rise of Civilization in China with reference to its Geographical Aspects', *The Geographical Review* 22(1932), pp 617-31; Karl Wittfogel, 'The Foundations and Stages of Chinese Economic History', *Zeitschrift Für Sozialforschung* IV(1935), pp 26-60; James Thorp, *Geography of the Soils of China* (Nanking: National Geological Survey of China, 1936); G B Barbour, 'Recent Observations on the Loess of North China', *The Geographical Journal*, LXXXVI(1935), pp 52-64.
7   'Origins of the Great Wall of China', pp 98, 105-6; cf *A Study of History*, III, p 395.
8   'Origins of the Great Wall of China', p 111.
9   'Origins of the Great Wall of China', p 116.
10   *Inner Asian Frontiers of China* (London: Oxford University Press, 1940), pp 262-74; C W Bishop, 'The Beginnings of North and South in China', *Pacific Affairs* VII(1934), pp 297-325; H G Creel, *Studies in Early Chinese Culture* (Baltimore: Waverly Press, 1937), pp 218-34.
11   *Inner Asian Frontiers of China*, p 327.
12   *Inner Asian Frontiers of China*, p 64.
13   *Inner Asian Frontiers of China*, pp 328, 354-5.
14   *Inner Asian Frontiers of China*, p 382.
15   Chi Ch'ao-ting, *Key Economic Areas in Chinese History. As revealed in the development of public works for water-control* (London: Allen and Unwin, 1936); Wang Yü-ch'üan, 'The Rise of Land Tax and the Fall of Dynasties in Chinese History', *Pacific Affairs* IX(1936), pp 201-20.
16   *Inner Asian Frontiers of China*, pp 373, 393.
17   Quoting Wittfogel: 'The Foundations and Stages of Chinese Economic History', p 52, Lattimore refers to the Grand Canal as an 'artificial Nile': *Inner Asian Frontiers of China*, p 42.
18   *Inner Asian Frontiers of China*, p 41.
19   *Inner Asian Frontiers of China*, pp 393-4, 42-4.
20   *Inner Asian Frontiers of China*, p xx.
21   G L Ulmen, *The Science of Society. Toward an Understanding of the Life and Work of Karl August Wittfogel*, pp 59 ff; U Vogel, 'K A Wittfogel's

Marxist Studies on China, 1926-1939', *Bulletin of Concerned Asian Scholars* 11(1979) no 4, pp 30-7.

22 G L Ulmen, *The Science of Society*, p 199. Ulmen, however, did not sight this memorandum but based his account solely on Wittfogel's conversations (personal letter, 13 July 1981).

23 M Sawer, *Marxism and the Question of the Asiatic Mode of Production* (The Hague: Martinus Nijhoff, 1977), pp 40 ff; G Lichtheim, 'Oriental Despotism', *The Concept of Ideology and Other Essays* (New York: Vintage Books, 1967), pp 62-93; S Avineri (ed), *Karl Marx on Colonialism and Modernization* (New York: Anchor Books, 1969).

24 On the circumstances leading to the writing of this article, see: G L Ulmen, *The Science of Society*, pp 179 ff.

25 Wang Yü-ch'üan, 'The Rise of Land Tax'.

26 *Inner Asian Frontiers of China*, p 45.

27 *Inner Asian Frontiers of China*, p 71, see also pp 519 ff.

28 *Inner Asian Frontiers of China*, pp 45-9.

29 *Inner Asian Frontiers of China*, p 461.

30 *Inner Asian Frontiers of China*, pp 526 ff, 544 ff.

31 *Inner Asian Frontiers of China*, p 543. On the character of Chinggis as a 'marginal man', see: Paul D Buell, 'The Role of the Sino-Mongolian Frontier Zone in the Rise of Cinggis-Qan', in Henry G Schwarz (ed), *Studies on Mongolia. Proceedings of the First North American Conference on Mongolian Studies* (Bellingham: Western Washington University, 1979), pp 63-76.

32 *Inner Asian Frontiers of China*, pp 247 ff.

33 *Inner Asian Frontiers of China*, pp 81 ff.

34 On the rise of neo-Confucianism, see W T deBary, *Neo-Confucian Orthodoxy and the Learning of the Mind-and-Heart* (New York: Columbia University Press, 1981), pp 1-66; Hok-lam Chan and W T deBary (eds), *Yüan Thought. Chinese Thought and Religion Under the Mongols* (New York: Columbia University Press, 1982).

35 *Inner Asian Frontiers of China*, p 85; cf L W Moses, *The Political Role of Mongol Buddhism* (Bloomington: Indiana University Asian Research Institute, Uralic Altaic Series no 133, 1977); H Serruys, *Sino-Mongol Relations During the Ming, II. The Tribute System and Diplomatic Missions (1400-1600), Mélanges Chinois et Boudhiques*, XIV (Brussels: Institut Belge Des Hautes Etudes Chinoises, 1967). Moses and Serruys note the political role played by Buddhism in the frontier states of the time. Serruys observes (pp 89 ff) that the potential of such a role was not lost on the Chinese, who tried to send their own monks to Altan as a means of influencing him.

36 *Inner Asian Frontiers of China*, p 89.

37 *Inner Asian Frontiers of China*, pp 247-50; cf *Manchuria, cradle of conflict*, pp 36-42.

38 *Inner Asian Frontiers of China*, pp 331, 334.

39 *Inner Asian Frontiers of China*, p 422.

40 *Inner Asian Frontiers of China*, p 409.

41 *Inner Asian Frontiers of China*, pp 531 ff; Chi Ch'ao-ting, *Key Economic Areas in Chinese History*; Wang Yü-ch'üan, 'The Rise of Land Tax'.

42 K A Wittfogel, 'Die Theorie der orientalischen Gesellschaft', *Zeitschrift Für Sozialforschung*, VII(1938), pp 109-14.

43 *Inner Asian Frontiers of China*, pp 550-1.

44 *Inner Asian Frontiers of China*, pp 103 ff, 261, 27 ff, 170.

45 *Inner Asian Frontiers of China*, p 325.

46 J K Fairbank, *The United States and China*, third edition - first published 1948 (Cambridge, Mass: Harvard University Press, 1971), chs 1-4; J K Fairbank et al, *East Asia. Tradition and Transformation* (Boston: Houghton Mifflin, 1973).

47 Ladis K D Kristof, 'The Nature of Frontiers and Boundaries', *Annals of the Association of American Geographers* 49(1959), pp 269-82.

48 Thomas J Barfield, 'The Hsiung-nu Imperial Confederacy: Organization and Foreign Policy', *Journal of Asian Studies* XLI(1981-2), pp 45-61.

49 Sechin Jagchid, 'Patterns of Trade and Conflict Between China and the Nomads of Mongolia', *Zentralasiatische Studien* 11(1977), pp 177-204; Sechin Jagchid, 'Kitan Struggle Against Jurchen Oppression - Nomadism versus Sinicization', *Zentralasiatische Studien* 16(1982), pp 165-85.

50 W Weissleder, 'The Promotion of Suzerainty Between Sedentary and Nomadic Populations in Eastern Ethiopia' in: W Weissleder (ed), *The Nomadic Alternative. Modes and Models of Interaction in the African-Asian Deserts and Steppes* (The Hague: Mouton, 1978), pp 275-88.

51 N Dyson-Hudson, 'The Study of Nomads', *Journal of Asian and African Studies* VII(1972), pp 5, 23-4.

52 A M Khazanov, *Nomads and the Outside World* (Cambridge: Cambridge University Press, 1984), pp 117, 172; 70; 95.

53 A M Khazanov, *Nomads and the Outside World*, p 11.

CHAPTER FOUR

Geopolitics and Foreign Policy

Between 1941 and 1950 Owen Lattimore's reputation in the scholarly community and in public life rose to considerable heights. In June 1941 he was chosen by President Roosevelt as his personal adviser to Chiang Kai-shek, a position he held until the end of 1942 when he returned to the United States to become Director of Pacific Operations of the Office of War Information. In the latter capacity he accompanied a party led by Vice-President Henry Wallace which, between 20 May and 5 July, visited the Soviet Far East, China and Mongolia. At the end of the war, having by this time resumed his academic career, he acted as an economic consultant to the American Reparations Mission to Japan led by Edwin W Pauley. At Johns Hopkins University he organised an Inner Asia Seminar devoted to the study of the Chinese border regions. To assist these researches, he brought to the United States a number of Mongol émigrés who were later to make important contributions to the study of their language and society. During and after the war he was an important participant in conferences of the Institute of Pacific Relations, and in 1949 he attended as a State Department nominee the American-Indian conference convened in New Delhi. In 1950 he went to Afghanistan as a member of a United Nations Technical Assistance Mission. But in March of that year he was forced to return to the United States to face the controversy which effectively ruined his career.[1] In these years the scope of his work broadened and as a result of the exigencies of wartime and his connections with members of the United States government and administration he became almost exclusively concerned with contemporary issues. The intellectual foundations of his position can be traced however to his writings and experiences of the 1930s.

America and the Sino-Japanese War

Until the outbreak of the Pacific War Lattimore was concerned to cajole his countrymen into an awareness of what was at stake in the conflict between China and Japan. By opening the Burma Road the Chinese had shown that they had the will to defend themselves, but the war would surely result in such poverty and dislocation that the country would be in danger of succumbing to Bolshevism. If this happened, the Chinese example would set a powerful precedent for the remainder of Asia.[2] Indeed, Lattimore found American policy made a poor comparison with that of the Soviet Union, a reflection of the fact that up until the German invasion of July 1941 with only a fraction of the resources at its disposal Russia's military and economic aid equalled that of the United States.[3] Lattimore pleaded for the United States to exercise more fully the undoubted economic leverage she possessed to curb Japan's military adventures. His own appointment was an indicator of the personal interest taken in China by Roosevelt: while in Chungking Lattimore had a direct line to the President by way of Lauchlin Currie in the White House.[4] However, despite having abrogated the commercial treaty with Tokyo in July 1939 and banned steel exports to Japan in 1940, the United States remained a major purchaser of Japanese goods and a source of some materials with war potential until 1941.

In Chungking Lattimore found Chiang Kai-shek disappointed and demoralised due to the fact that, despite shouldering the burden of the war against Japan, China was still without a formal alliance and excluded from the diplomatic and military deliberations of the non-Axis powers. In a cable to the President in August he conveyed two proposals, the adopting of either of which Chiang believed would show that China was taken seriously in the counsels of the 'anti-aggression peoples'. On the initiative of Roosevelt, China should either be drawn into a pact with Russia and Britain which would provide for joint military action in the event of an attack on one of the latter powers by Japan, or China should be involved in joint defence planning with the British, Dutch and Americans in the Pacific.[5] Nothing came of this advice, and as fighting continued between China and Japan through 1941 Chinese apprehension of possible isolation was heightened when it became apparent that Washington and Tokyo were negotiating with the objective of arranging a *modus vivendi* in the Pacific. Lattimore reported that Chiang was 'really agitated' at the prospect that Japan might as a result be able to resume purchasing oil and other commodities from the United States. Just as the closure of the Burma Road for three months in 1940 as a result of Japanese pressure destroyed British credibility in China so these negotiations fatally undermined American prestige and may have tipped the hand of those Chinese who wished to abandon the struggle with Japan in the interests of 'oriental solidarity'.[6] Now it is clear that this resumption of limited trade with Japan was the price American policy makers were prepared to pay for securing a partial Japanese withdrawal from Indochina, a move they evidently felt would not only improve the security of the Philippines but would reduce the likelihood of an eventual Japanese attack on the Burma Road supply line to China. Indeed, in early drafts of a document outlining this *modus vivendi* the Americans had proposed a withdrawal of Japanese forces from China and Sino-Japanese talks on the status of Manchuria, but by the time the Chinese government received official notification of these diplomatic manoeuvres American policy makers had become convinced that they would have to begin with much more limited objectives.[7] In the event nothing came of these proposals, with the consequence that Japanese forces remained in southern Indochina, the United States maintained the embargo on oil exports to Japan imposed in July, and Japan's leaders decided to launch the war in the Pacific.

Unusual in commentators of that early stage of the war, Lattimore devoted some attention to internal events in China and to the effect on those events of external pressures. There were good geographical reasons, he maintained in mid-1941, for holding the view that the Japanese had so far failed to gain a strategic advantage in China. While they did not hold the traditional invasion routes through Shansi, the Yellow river crossing at T'ung-kuan (Tongguan), and the Han river basin they could not hope to dominate the country, despite the fact that they had occupied many of the most populous areas. 'Strategic and economic geography lead to political geography', and the authorities in power in unoccupied China ought to be able to turn the labour and resources of the inland to advantage. Both the Kuomintang and the Communist Party must strive to generate as much support as possible from the population and avoid morale sapping conflict since it 'would be extremely dangerous for China as a whole if Free China were in fact sharply divided between a major area controlled by Generalissimo Chiang Kai-shek and a minor area dominated by the Communists'.[8] External powers would contribute to the efforts of the Chinese population to the extent that they supported the 'United Front' as opposed to one or other of the two forces in the country. With hindsight it can be seen that Lattimore, though he was then optimistic of Chiang Kai-shek's leadership capacity, had identified in 1941 the two most important issues that were to bedevil American policy makers in the years to come. In 1944 the attempt by General Joseph Stilwell to involve communist forces in operations he hoped to mount against the Japanese in the southeast was one of the issues which forced his recall. By that time Yenan was blockaded by large contingents of Kuomintang troops despite the fact that the CCP-Kuomintang alliance agreed at Sian in 1936 was still formally in effect. And it was a continuous refrain of those aware of the true state of affairs in the country (including Stilwell, and John S Service and other US Foreign Service officers) that too little of the supplies provided at great cost by the Americans for Chungking found their way to those armies fighting the Japanese, the greater bulk which escaped misappropriation being earmarked instead for the forthcoming duel with the communists.[9]

In a singluarly prescient piece, written in April of that year, Lattimore addressed himself to the question of why it was that the Chinese had been able to sustain their resistance to Japan through four terrible years. He found that they had been motivated by a revolution defined in terms of two objectives, internal reform and genuine national independence. Lattimore was inclined to think that the Chungking government was capable of leading the country to the attaining of those goals, but his concluding remarks struck a cautionary note:

> ... two things have already been proved in these four years. The first is that in a war of aggression the people can be cheated, but in a war of defense a government must make concessions to the needs of the people if it demands the loyalty and sacrifices of the

people. The second is that in China a right wing government can stand if it has a certain amount of foreign support and approval; but if foreign attack overweighs foreign support, it must get on with the revolution or it will find that the revolution can get on without it.[10]

American War Aims in the Pacific

With the entry by the United States into the war, Lattimore's position became superfluous, though he stayed in Chiang's service until the end of 1942. Much of his time was spent in Washington endeavouring to put the case for the greatest support for Chungking and for giving priority to the war in the China theatre.[11] In his writings he turned his attention almost immediately to the post-war settlement. Writing for an American audience he argued that a return to the status quo was both undesirable and impossible. The war was a fight for democracy; it was no accident that in Asia those nations that had mounted the strongest resistance to Japan, China and the Philippines, were fighting with the promise of democratic self-government in mind. According to Lattimore the Chinese were fighting for a new democracy, and their struggle would have an impact throughout Asia. Lattimore also took the position that for the United States events in the Far East were of greater moment than events in Europe: 'this is a war about Asia'. And if democracy was to triumph in Asia after the war it could not co-exist with imperialism. Americans should recognise their complicity in the old imperialist world order and resolve to bring it to an end. This would be consistent with their own principles, it would also ensure that the solidarity of the countries of the United Nations would be maintained. Here Lattimore appeared to believe that the Soviet Union would regard an end to the colonial order in Asia as congruent with its own 'nationality principle' which 'makes no distinction whatever between the citizenship of Asiatics and the citizenship of Europeans'. But although Lattimore revised his earlier opinions about the practicality of self-government for the Chinese, he admitted that not all of the peoples of Asia were as prepared for self-government as the Philippines.[12]

Thus began a phase of Lattimore's writing in which he returned repeatedly to the problem of the possible shape of the post-war world particularly in Asia, a problem which will be reviewed later in this chapter. Personal experiences in these years provided the background and impetus for themes which recur in his writing. Lattimore developed an interest in new geographical areas; he also acquired new insights into the problems of colonial and post-colonial Asia. Residence in Chungking made him aware of the economic and political potential of southwest China. No longer tied to the coast and to the old economic regions, the development of Yunnan was likely to be an indicator of the shape of the new China. The opening of the Burma Road which was achieved by the Chinese themselves pushing outwards marked the beginning of a new era as surely as the renunciation of the old Treaty Port privileges in 1942 by Great Britain and the United States. The impact of this example on Southeast Asia would be considerable, and China could well become an ally of the nations in the region should the Western countries attempt to restore the old colonial order after the war is over.[13]

Lattimore's extended trip to the Soviet Far East also led to writings on the character and potential of the region. Travelling the great circle air route from the continental United States by way of Alaska made him aware that the road to Asia lay north rather than west.[14] This gave him additional reasons for holding a view he had already expressed, that events in the heartlands of the continent would be of greater consequence for the future than events that affected the rim. Thus Japan could never be held as a base against the Soviet Union. And after the war the struggle for the loyalties of the various minority peoples of Inner Asia would be crucial. Here the Soviets held an immense advantage over China in their mutual frontier zone in that their policy towards these peoples had so far been an 'outstanding success'. The Chinese had hitherto been hampered by the need to compete with foreign imperialists, and by the assumption of cultural superiority bequeathed to them by the Confucian tradition. Unless a revolutionary China was able to mobilise these peoples by offering them 'an opportunity to go forward rapidly in conjunction with a Chinese economy, society, and political structure which is changing as rapidly as their own', the power of attraction exercised by the Soviet example would prove too strong. In stating this view Lattimore develops a point which became a major preoccupation in his later writings. For the peoples of Inner Asia, despite the vague appeal of such notions as democracy, their practical political choices could only be informed by what was familiar to them. At present they were confronted with the fact that the superiority of Soviet as opposed to Chinese minority policy meant that the Soviets were '*the* standard of progress from the Ussuri and Amur rivers to the Pamirs'.[15]

Lattimore devoted several popular writings to Soviet minority policy. He argued that the close and apparently voluntary identification of the minorities with the central government could be explained by the fact that the rights of the former had been granted by the Bolsheviks.[16] This opinion was no doubt partly a product of the superficial and carefully managed nature of the visit of the Wallace mission, but it is also in accordance with statements already published in *Inner Asian Frontiers of China*. There Lattimore, basing himself on the testimony of refugees and on the contents of government statements, expressed the view that as a result of Soviet policy:

> the Khalkha Mongols now have, under the Mongol People's Republic, the most popular and representative government they have ever had and a rising standard of living shared equally throughout the country.

61

Russian intervention in Sinkiang, by contrast with the previous policy of the Chinese, was similarly altruistic. It sought to:

> eliminate as far as possible the subjection by force of one people, religion, culture, or economic activity to another, and to set up at least the beginnings of an equal and proportional representation of the different interests within the province.[17]

It may be conjectured that Lattimore's approach to the Soviet nationalities was conditioned by his Mongol experiences. He imagined that their societies were also forced to choose between the stark and mutually exclusive alternatives - internal revolution or extinction - faced by the Mongols. The Mongols as a distinct people had been saved by Soviet intervention, therefore the same must be true of the rest of Inner Asia's minorities. Certainly none of Lattimore's observations in 1944 in Ulan Bator or Tihwa (Urümqi), restricted though they were, caused him to revise his opinions. But the superficiality of the Wallace mission as a sound foundation for the analysis of any aspect whatever of Soviet policy in the Far East is revealed by the fact that one of the localities visited was Kolyma, the site of the Arctic death camps controlled by Dalstroi (Far Northern Construction Company). Even at that time, as Robert Conquest points out,[18] accounts of these camps by former inmates were becoming available, but Lattimore, oblivious to Dalstroi's true function, enthused about the atmosphere in the gold mines, finding it a far cry from the disorder of the American frontier:

> It was interesting to find, instead of the sin, gin, and brawling of an old-time gold rush, extensive greenhouses growing tomatoes, cucumbers, and even melons, to make sure that the hardy miners got enough vitamins.[19]

Lattimore much later defended his conduct, arguing that he could not then have known of the character of these Siberian settlements, but he was never led to revise his assessment of Soviet nationalities policy.[20]

American Policy in Postwar Asia

Back in the United States Lattimore, in addition to his work with the Office of War Information, became a popular and influential speaker at universities and colleges. In two lectures at Claremont College he developed at greater length his views on the war and the direction United States policy should take at its conclusion. So important did he regard the conflict in China that he even expressed the view that the major battle with Japan should be fought there, rather than in the Pacific theatre. America should ensure that the postwar world order was democratic, which implied a demolition of the old colonial system. As to the prospects for China, Lattimore was confident that civil war would be averted under the leadership of Chiang Kai-shek who he regarded as 'a world statesman of real genius'. However, he also developed the general argument that as revolutionary upheavals are the product of bad government rather than subversion, American policy should aim to support governments prepared to provide property, security, and hope for their populations. America must not 'make the mistake of assuming that strong government is more important than good government'.[21] Here it is clear which side Lattimore inclined towards in the dilemma which has confounded United States policy makers from that time to the present: whether to back as allies those states with similar foreign policy interests irrespective of the nature of their internal political systems, or to embrace only those states similarly dedicated to the same democratic ideals.

Lattimore elaborated on these themes in lectures delivered in 1944 and published the following year as *Solution in Asia*. There Lattimore argues that America, in imposing a punitive peace on Japan should allow some industry to be rebuilt but should not protect the institution of emperor which could never be the focus of a democratic political order without an internal revolution. In any case, it was Lattimore's belief that events in Japan would be subordinate to events in China, the shaping of which should have been the United States' chief preoccupation.

In considering China Lattimore develops a much more detailed analysis than he had attempted before, and one which he was able to describe thirty years later as 'pretty sound'.[22] China, in his view, was in the grip of an upsurge of nationalism stimulated by the external pressure of imperialism and the revolutionary example of Soviet Russia. In the pursuit of national unity the wide coalition of forces led by Sun Yat-sen gave way in 1927 to a narrower grouping of 'bankers, industrialists, employers, landlords, and military leaders'. Chiang Kai-shek became the focus of this grouping but he never became a dictator since his true character was to be a 'coalition statesman of genius'.[23] The struggle between the communists and the Kuomintang that then occurred resulted in a 'Red Terror' and a 'White Terror' both born of desperation. As to their respective merits:

> The White Terror, it should be pointed out, was as bad as the Red Terror in the things done. For every landlord or 'bourgeois' killed, scores of peasants were slaughtered, tortured or burned in their villages; untold numbers of peasant girls were sold into brothels and boys into bondage. In China, as in Pilsudski's Poland ... the White Terror was worse than the Red because in a peasant country revolution attempts to break the grip of a minority, while counterrevolution attempts to break the will of a majority.[24]

The nature of this struggle was transformed, however, by the growth of the Japanese menace which made co-operation between communists and Kuomintang possible. The Communist Party widened its base of support and modified its position, according to Lattimore, to become a 'coalition party' with a policy no longer antagonistic but now merely alternative to that of the government. At the same time the move to the interior weakened the hold of the bankers and industrialists over the Kuomintang. The party became bureaucratised, and came to rely increasingly for its support in this predominantly rural area on the landlord class. By contrast the Communist Party in Yenan was forced to address itself to the needs of the peasantry and pursuing a moderate policy on the land question came to embody the broad peasant interest. In the circumstances of their base area at Yenan, being dependent upon the support of the local population the communists had created a sizeable enclave where basic economic conditions were better than in the regions controlled by the Kuomintang, and where taxation and conscription were more equitably managed. Political conditions in Yenan also compared favourably with those in Chungking:

> The political structure under the Communists is more nearly democratic than it is under the Kuomintang. It is a fact that governing committees and representative committees are elected, and that the Communists limit themselves to one third of the representation; whereas in Kuomintang-controlled territory it is increasingly difficult to hold a public position without joining the Kuomintang and accepting its discipline.[25]

On the basis of this assessment of the two parties' characters and records, Lattimore advocated as the best way forward, the creation of a coalition government before a unified military structure was formed. Only Chiang was strong enough to head such a government but the creation of political freedoms prior to the merging of military forces would ensure that parties other than the Kuomintang would be able to play a role. What were the alternatives if this course of action were rejected? There was a danger of China becoming 'a Poland in Asia', with the United States drawn into the role of 'the not too enthusiastic backer of a "legitimist" group with too many Chinese "Polish colonels" and not enough popular support'. This in turn would have brought the United States into collision with the Soviet Union which would be bound to support 'a group which is legally "dissident", but has growing support among moderate groups as well as the peasants'.[26]

For, returning to an argument we have encountered before, in postwar Asia the Soviet Union would exercise a 'power of attraction' by virtue of the example of its minorities policy and the progress, evident to Asiatics, of Soviet border regions. The United States could only hope to match this power of attraction by adopting the role of patron and cautious promoter of Asian independence. But the two nations should not be in competition. Lattimore was a firm believer in the need to promote a multilateral policy involving the Soviet Union, aimed at producing peace and stability in Asia. The Soviets had already shown their good faith by the material support they gave to Chungking in the knowledge that some of these supplies were destined for the forces attempting to blockade Yenan. Such a multilateral policy, in his view, was in the interests of all of the United Nations.

Kohlberg's Campaign Against Lattimore

Lattimore's opinions, though not uncommon among commentators on Chinese affairs at that time, had not been expressed without attracting some adverse comment at least on his views concerning China policy. Although the full effect of the criticism was not felt until some years later, Lattimore's role in the Institute of Pacific Relations and his ideas on postwar co-operation between the United States and the Soviet Union were the subject of a critique authored by Alfred Kohlberg and published in October 1945.

Kohlberg was a businessman who had made his fortune importing lace from China. He was a man of singular and strongly held opinions, as is shown by the fact that, having concluded in 1940 that the Japanese were bent upon merciless aggression in China, he volunteered his services to the Royal Canadian Air Force as a kamikaze pilot. He later conducted an on-the-spot personal investigation into charges that there was extensive graft among the recipients of American aid to China. Finding no evidence for these allegations but ignored by officials Kohlberg turned his attention to those who he regarded as responsible for the false image held in the United States of Kuomintang China. By late 1944 he had become convinced that the source could be traced to the machinations of the communist conspiracy working through the Institute of Pacific Relations and its publications. For some years Kohlberg had been a member of the Institute, which had existed since 1925 to promote the study in the United States and internationally of Asia and the Pacific region. After a lengthy campaign Kohlberg's charges became the subject of a ballot in 1947 of members of the Institute who rejected them out of hand.[27] Kohlberg then shifted his attention to other matters,[28] but he had made up his mind on the question of who was to blame for the communist takeover in China. He finally adopted the role of Lattimore's *nemesis* when he met Senator Joe McCarthy in March 1950. Kohlberg subsequently advised McCarthy on the communist infiltration of Washington, and his charges were to become the basis, such as it was, of the Senate inquiry into the functioning of the Institute in 1951.[29]

Kohlberg found much to criticise in Lattimore's stewardship of the Institute's principal publication, *Pacific Affairs*, which he alleged exhibited the editor's pro-Soviet bias. Concerning *Solution in Asia* Kohlberg alleges that the baleful likely outcome of the impartiality between the contending forces in China which Lattimore advises, would be 'to lock China into the Communist World System'.[30] In his reply Lattimore argued that the spread of communism in Asia was neither desirable nor inevitable but as the Soviet Union as a power on the continent was there to stay some form of agreement with the Soviets was preferable to conflict. His overall intention, he maintained, in his scholarly as in his public career, had been always to work for the spread of democracy rather than of communism.[31]

Although Kohlberg's charges were wild and inaccurate, Lattimore had held a high and optimistic estimate of the Soviet Union since the major focus of his work had shifted to the Mongols. He had become sufficiently interested in Russia to spend three months in the winter of 1936 learning the language, though it is clear that this was largely to permit him access to Russian materials on Inner Asia. As has been shown the most that could be said for Lattimore's enthusiasm for Soviet nationalities policy was that it was tenuously based on inadequate information. Nor had Lattimore confined himself to comments on those aspects of the Soviet Union closest to his area of expertise. Writing in an editorial in *Pacific Affairs* in 1938, as Kohlberg was able to point out, Lattimore had referred to the Moscow trials as fully credible and likely to improve the prospects for 'democracy' in the Soviet Union.[32] Here he was in good company, but no sound assessment of a man's views can properly be based on his *obiter dicta*. However, as one who regarded a victory in China for the communists as the worst of all possible worlds, Kohlberg was correct in identifying Lattimore as an antagonist. Lattimore had never been the proponent of a single party in the Chinese conflict. Moreover, a careful reading of his statements on China shows a shift in his opinion as he came to revise his estimate of the Kuomintang and its leadership.

Postwar Political Solution in China

In 1944 Lattimore published with his wife a short popular history of China, entitled *The Making of Modern China*. Insofar as the views expressed therein are original, they are mostly drawn from *Inner Asian Frontiers of China*. The concluding section speculates on the future political settlement likely to occur in the country, and here Lattimore was optimistic on the role of the Kuomintang. Although China was not a democracy by any procedural definition, it 'is a democratic country in the sense that the Party and the Government represent what the vast majority of the people want'.[33] The Kuomintang monopolised political power, but it was committed to an abolition of its tutelary role in conformity with the original programme of Sun Yat-sen. The functioning of the People's Political Council (reconstituted by the Kuomitang authorities as an advisory body including other parties in 1942) may be taken as a sign that freedom of association was on the way, just as the growing freedom of the press showed that the party was more prepared to permit open criticism of at least the details of government measures. The communists even more than the Kuomintang must have been prepared to compromise to avert the possibility of a civil war which would be in no party's interest.

In the second edition which appeared in 1947 it is noteworthy that the prognosis was less optimistic. Lattimore repeated the argument found in

Solution in Asia that under wartime conditions the Kuomintang and the Communist Party had both undergone an inner transformation. The Kuomintang had come to stand also for a centralising and authoritarian approach to government, and its appeal to the people had been damaged in that 'in its efforts to impose control over them it appeals not to them but to foreign arms and foreign support'.[34] American policy had become unbalanced, with the channelling of aid to one side in the domestic conflict at the end of the war. The mission to China of General Marshall in December 1945 in an attempt to encourage a political and military agreement between Chiang and the Communist Party was a proper attempt to correct this imbalance, but some in the United States were still of the opinion that full scale intervention would have been appropriate. This would have been a mistake:

> In the long run ... stability and progress in China must be judged by the ability both of the country as a whole and of the major political parties to rise above the level of asking for subsidies for hand-to-mouth maintenance. China, and China's political parties, must produce their own proofs of their ability, politically, to stand on their own feet, and their ability, economically, to absorb loans for productive purposes. Stability and progress ... are within the reach of a people which elects its government, but not within the reach of a people which is subject to its government - especially if the government can keep up a 'strong' rule over the people only at the price of being so weak that it has to ask continually for outside support.[35]

Nothing short of the assumption by America of a colonial role in China would have given American power the leverage to influence developments in that country, and such a role would be quite inappropriate if the United States was to be an opponent of imperialism elsewhere. In other words, by 1947 Lattimore was prepared to countenence a communist victory in China if, as looked to him increasingly likely, the Kuomintang conclusively demonstrated its political and economic incompetence to maintain effective government and complete China's unfinished revolution.

Although Lattimore referred to the development of a third political force in wartime China, if an agreement or coalition between the Communist Party and the Kuomintang proved impossible, the alternative to Kuomintang rule was a communist victory. What expectations did Lattimore have in the years immediately after the war, of the character and programme of a communist dominated regime? As we have seen Lattimore believed that Chinese communism had largely been transformed by the exigencies of the wartime struggle. Its growth had been almost entirely dependent upon its nationalist stance, and its careful attempts to mobilise as wide a spectrum of peasant opinion as possible. Doctrinaire opinions had been abandoned and as the party owed little to Soviet support a communist regime in Peking would not be greatly beholden to Moscow. The party could only expect to form a successful government by following the practices evolved in Yenan:

> Chinese Communist practice differs in many ways from Russian Communist practice. It is significant that the Chinese Communists, as a minority movement fighting for survival, have perforce drawn on non-Communist allies. A large part of their rank and file is non-Communist. The countryside which supports them is peopled with peasants who are fighting primarily for the private ownership of land and the right to be represented in government. These peasants have arms in their hands. They can be led by the Communists, if the Communists go in the direction in which they want to be led. They cannot be dictated to either by the Communists, whom they are now following, or by the Government, which they are now resisting.[36]

It is evident that Lattimore believed that the social and economic structure in the Chinese countryside was ripe for radical reform. In an essay of 1947 he delineated the features of the 'Asiatic paradox' which produced 'perennial malnutrition' in those districts where grain productivity per acre was highest. This was the result, in conditions of labour superabundance, of landlords setting tenant against tenant in a competition to produce the highest rental. A corollary of the paradox was that the growth of industry was obstructed since this would have attracted labour and reduced the landlord's control over his tenants.[37] The failure of the Kuomintang to address these problems, a failure made more certain by the growth of the landlord interest in the party during the years in Chungking, undoubtedly inclined Lattimore to the view that a communist regime would be no bad thing for the rural areas. Indeed, communist mobilisations of the peasantry in Yenan had demonstrated that this party could tailor its programme to the perceived needs of the rural population.

Changes in world politics also led Lattimore to the belief that a reforming regime with a significant communist presence largely independent of Soviet control was possible in China. Writing in 1947 during a trip to Central Europe Lattimore discerned significant portents in developments in Czechoslovakia. There a communist movement with a solid electoral base was co-operating with non-communist parties in a moderate programme of reconstruction aided by an economic treaty with the Soviet Union. This suggested to Lattimore that the Czechoslovak Communist Party was experimenting with a new road to communism 'with prosperity all along the way and without massacre or coercion'. This showed that it was incorrect to describe the world as divided between two all-embracing camps:

> There already exist in the world several different kinds of socialism or communism, and several different kinds of capitalist enterprise. In Czechoslovakia they exist side by side.[38]

Lattimore also held sanguine expectations of Soviet policy in Eastern Europe, finding there a fear not of Soviet but of German power which the United

States was fuelling by underwriting the industrial reconstruction of West Germany. In the event these expectations were to be disappointed. Indeed, prior to Lattimore's visit to Prague the Czechoslovakian government had been forced, under Soviet pressure, to withdraw its earlier acceptance of Marshall Plan aid for reconstruction from the United States; within six months of Lattimore's optimistic words a communist coup had replaced the Czechoslovak coalition government with one subservient to Moscow.

In early 1948 Lattimore returned to the argument that there was room for a third bloc or 'Third World' between the contending major powers. Though the lines were being drawn in Europe the possibility nevertheless that such a bloc might exist had been shown by events in Asia. Guerrilla warfare in Indonesia and Indochina had demonstrated that there were limitations to the extent to which the United States and the Soviet Union could influence events in other countries. The independence of Burma had created a nation which would be dependent upon outside assistance in its development for some time, but would never return to any form of colonial status. Lattimore still believed that the failure of either side in the civil war in China to achieve a military victory would result eventually in a compromise.[39] But it can be seen that he would anticipate that a defeat for the Kuomintang might lead to the formation of a regime led by the communists but with participation by other groups, committed to sensible reforms and reconstruction and ready to place China in the emerging Third World of nations.

The Failure of American Policy

In *The Situation in Asia* published in April 1949 Lattimore brings these ideas together in a sustained review of events in postwar Asia and the issues confronting American policy makers as a result. Asia was 'out of control', engulfed by a wave of nationalist sentiment which no outside power could check. Most of the nations of Asia were destined to belong to the 'third force' or 'third quotient of power' which was making its appearance in world politics and which the United States could only hope to influence from without.

Lattimore repeated his analysis of the origins of the Chinese revolution, though he now emphasised the role the western powers played in the original formation of the Nanking regime. By putting together a coalition of landlords, bankers and industrialists under the leadership of Chiang Kai-shek, an instrument was forged which in 'smashing the political organisations of the peasants and the industrial workers' permitted those powers to retain many of their privileges. But even now Lattimore defended Chiang against charges of dictatorship and personal failure, seeing in his decline the last phase of the 'old diplomacy' in China.[40] He revised, however, his assessment of the Kuomintang. In 1940 he expected the party, identified as it was with industrial and mercantile interests, 'to raise China from mediaeval agrarianism to modern industrial capitalism' following the precedents of state led modernisation established by Germany, Japan and then Turkey. By this time he had come to believe that the experience of the war years had so transformed the party that its policies after 1945 amounted to nothing less than 'an attempt to bring modern economic activities under feudal control'.[41] It was American inability to recognise that the Kuomintang did not stand for capitalism in China that drove many exasperated business people and managers into the arms of the communists.

As to the Chinese Communist Party, they would continue to embody the peasant interest until industrialisation and mechanisation could make a decisive impact on rural life. The course of the Chinese revolution had thus been utterly unlike the revolution in Russia. Communist land redistribution had engendered in the peasants the political will and the military power to protect and conserve the fruits of the revolution:

> By 1949, many millions of peasants had come to feel thoroughly
> comfortable in a triple combination of ownership of land,
> experience in the use of arms to defend their ownership, and rough
> but workable town meeting democracy for the definition of rights,
> the assignment of duties, and the election of representatives.[42]

Communist prestige was therefore high, but the party could not 'indulge in experiments which the peasants do not accept' because the peasants had the power to resist them. The co-operatives were a realistic alternative to collectivisation which would never be introduced 'merely for the sake of Marxist orthodoxy' since it would be irrational without mechanisation. Given the nature of the Chinese revolution and the nationalist roots of communist power it would be reasonable to conclude that any future Soviet attempt to override Chinese interests could bring into being 'a Chinese Titoism'.[43]

In retrospect, although Lattimore's remarks on the weaknesses of the Kuomintang appear accurate enough, his expectations of the CCP were very much wide of the mark. Contemporary observers of wartime Yenan also found there much to praise in the organisation and dedication of the inhabitants of the region by comparison with the corrupt and hopeless atmosphere of Chungking. But it is now clear that it was at that very time that the foundations were being laid for the personal and ideological dominance of Mao Tse-tung. By 1951 a start had been made on the introduction of wider forms of co-operative organisation in agriculture, a movement which was to have its culmination in 1958 in the introduction of large scale Rural People's Communes. In these Communes, not only were peasants initially forbidden much against their will to cultivate even small plots on the now collectively owned land, but peasant enthusiasm was to take the place of mechanisation. It should be pointed out that Lattimore was not alone at this time in the conviction that for the leadership of the CCP nationalist goals were likely to be given high and perhaps exclusive priority. But the initiative taken by Richard Nixon in 1971-72 to open American relations with China following the Sino-Soviet split in 1960 shows that there may well have been some room even in the late 1940s for an astute American policy to attempt to detach China from the socialist camp. The irony of this observation is that Nixon's original rise from obscurity was founded upon the relentless urging in an atmosphere of national crisis of the view that, not only was there no such room but that those who argued that there was (including Lattimore himself) were witting or unwitting tools of the communist conspiracy.

Looking beyond China, Lattimore developed a critical comparison of the European role in Asia with the methods of rule employed by Russia and the Soviet Union. For Asians Russia is a land power and a neighbour whose relations with the peoples of Asia had been distinctive. In the days of the Russian Empire the Russians extended their control into East and Inner Asia by assimilating the upper classes of the peoples with whom they came into contact. More recently Soviet Asia had been for many bordering peoples an example of the advantages that industrialisation and education could bring. By contrast the Europeans in Asia had been maritime colonialists whose traditional policy was to assume that leadership of the landlord class which was hitherto exercised by Asian despots. So closely were the interests of colonialists and 'feudal' landlords identified that the landlord class 'remained loyal to imperialist rule long after other groups in colonial societies had turned nationalist' as a result of nationalists taking land reform as their chief cause.[44] Despite the events of the war Europe retained important colonial possessions and the European countries were bound therefore to seek to resist the nationalist tide in Asia. This continuing entanglement which Lattimore described as 'a direct negation of democracy' distorted even the internal politics of these countries: 'The survival of empire is what explains the strength of right-wing socialism and trade-unionism in Britain, France, Holland, and Belgium'.[45] It is also the principal reason why American and European goals in Asia do not necessarily coincide.

The mistakes of American policy in the postwar period had been the result of a confusion of aims and a lack of preparedness to react to the new circumstances of the time. Lattimore castigated the Truman doctrine of March 1947 in which the President announced his readiness to help any nation prepared to resist the onslaught of the militant communism camp, as having 'originated more in out-of-date British thinking than up-to-date American thinking'. And he blamed the fiasco of what he saw as the 'attempt to imitate ... Japanese policy in China' on 'the fire breathers in the 80th Congress and the tom-tom beating in the jingoistic sections of the press'.[46] On this view when Secretary of State Marshall, in January 1947, abandoned his attempt to mediate between the parties in the conflict raging in China, he was quite correct to see that events there were beyond the limitations of American power to control.

Lattimore reaffirmed the view that between the Soviet sphere and American power in Asia a gulf populated by 'third force' nations was likely to emerge. United States policy should have been independent, seeking to exercise influence rather than mastery and aimed at matching the power of attraction exercised by the Soviet Union while channelling the nationalist tide in Asia in a way that would keep the continent open to American business and trade. The 'beachheads of empire' around the Pacific rim of Asia should have been abandoned following the general rule that no government should be maintained if it cannot stand alone. America had become associated in Asia with 'bad government' and this trend had to be reversed. Interference in the internal politics of Japan should have been abandoned, and in Korea the 'weak and unreliable police state' character of the regime should have been recognised.[47] In the case of the latter country, far from learning from their mistakes American policy makers in using former collaborators and émigrés had 'manufactured' their 'own Kuomintang'. In Asia as elsewhere a 'cold truce' was to be preferred to a 'cold war', and this would best be achieved through a competition attuned to the political and social realities rather than conflict:

> Nationalism is the only bedrock on which a political structure can be built in China - or anywhere in Asia - today. If we are as quick as the Russians and the Communists of Asia are to build on that bedrock, then the new political structures that are being built in China and all over Asia will incorporate many features of capitalism, private enterprise, and political democracy in their 'third country' architectural design. If the Russians and the Communists continue to keep ahead of us in accepting Asia on its own terms, there will be more socialism in the superstructure.[48]

Lattimore and his Critics

In March 1950 the members of the Inner Asian Seminar at Johns Hopkins under Lattimore's leadership published the first in what it was hoped would be a series of volumes devoted to the history, politics and economics of that region.[49] But at that very time Lattimore was dragged into the maelstrom generated by Senator McCarthy's allegations. As he was to recall later this put an end to the Seminar and blighted the careers of the participants.[50]

In the coming years Lattimore was to have little time for academic or popular writing, but neither events in Asia nor the reception of his ideas in America caused him to change the fundamentals of the views he expressed in 1949. Thus, despite the outbreak of the Korean war, Lattimore was insistent at the end of 1950 that there was very little sign yet of the abandonment of the old colonial approach to Asia in American foreign policy, the direction of which was increasingly in the hands of 'fanatics and cranks'. A multilateral policy involving America's allies and the free nations of Asia was overdue.[51] In two opinion pieces devoted to Korea, though Lattimore expressed approval of Truman's decision to intervene and the principle of collective security which lay behind it, he was fearful of the consequences of allowing 'the same incompetent, tired old reactionaries' to resume control of the state. If America acted as their patron 'our future in Asia is black indeed'.[52] On the question of the outcome of a treaty with Japan, Lattimore argued that in the longer term it would probably be advantageous for the Japanese, given their geographical position, to seek a middle course between the Soviet Union and the United States. American public opinion had to be prepared for the fact that the Japanese, irrespective of the conditions of any treaty (and here Lattimore evidently had in mind the US-Japan Security Treaty of 1951), would not wish to act as makeweight against China and the Soviet Union in the Pacific.[53] And in a piece devoted to the construction of new transportation and industrial corridors along the land border between the Soviet Union and China, Lattimore returned to his old preoccupation with the geopolitics of Inner Asia. The Soviets were building a base of support in this region because they were transforming the material conditions of life of the population, and drawing at least the younger generation into developing an interest in this transformation. American policy makers, bemused by the ideological contest, were not addressing themselves sufficiently to the struggle of interests going on in Asia. Nor was enough attention paid to the side effects of offering military alliances and aid to Asian countries deemed friendly.[54] It is evident that in the early 1950s Lattimore believed that American policy had yet to take account of the true situation in Asia.

Notes to Chapter Four

1   Because Lattimore's career became a subject of controversy there are many sources devoted to the discussion thereof. Among the recollections of those who were associated with him, the following are of particular value: J M Blum (ed), *The Price of Vision: The Diary of Henry A Wallace 1942-1946* (Boston: Houghton Mifflin, 1973). This diary was the basis for a book published by Wallace on the 1944 trip to the Far East (*Soviet Asia Mission*); J K Fairbank, *Chinabound: A Fifty-Year Memoir* (New York: Harper & Row, 1982); T H White, *In Search of History* (London: Jonathan Cape, 1979). Lattimore is himself writing an account of his experiences as adviser to Chiang Kai-shek.

2   'American Responsibilities in the Far East', *Virginia Quarterly Review* 16(1940), pp 161-74; 'Not China's Lifeline, But America's', *The China Monthly* (November 1940), p 8.

3   'As China Goes, so Goes Asia', *Amerasia* 4(1940), 253-7; I C Y Hsu, *The Rise of Modern China*, third edition (New York: Oxford University Press, 1983), pp 599-601.

4   'America and the Future of China', *Amerasia* 5(1941), pp 296-7. This is the text of Lattimore's first public address in Chungking in 1941. On Lattimore's contacts with Roosevelt, see Christopher Thorne, *Allies of a Kind. The United States, Britain, and the War Against Japan, 1941-45* (Oxford: Oxford University Press, 1978), p 81.

5   US Department of State, *Foreign Relations of the United States, 1941* IV, The Far East (Washington: US Government Printing Office, 1956), p 362.

6   *Foreign Relations of the United States. 1941* IV, The Far East, p 652.

7   *Foreign Relations of the United States. 1941* IV, The Far East, pp 623 f.

8   'Stalemate in China', *Foreign Affairs* 19(1941), pp 627, 9.

9   Joseph W Stilwell, *The Stilwell Papers*, (ed) T H White (London: MacDonald, 1949); Joseph W Esherick (ed), *Lost Chance in China. The World War II Despatches of John S Service* (New York: Random House, 1974).

10   'After Four Years', *Pacific Affairs* XIV(1941), pp 151-2.

11   US Department of State, *Foreign Relations of the United States. 1942*, China (Washington: US Government Printing Office, 1956), pp 46, 175 f, 185 f.

12   'The Fight for Democracy in Asia', *Foreign Affairs* 20(1942), pp 694-704.

13   'Yunnan, Pivot of Southeast Asia', *Foreign Affairs* 21(1943), pp 476-93.

14   'The Inland Crossroads of Asia' [1944], *Studies in Frontier History*, pp 119-33.

15   'The Inland Crossroads of Asia', p 131.

16 'Minorities in the Soviet Far East', *Far Eastern Survey* XIII(1944), pp 156-8. See also 'Yakutia and the Future of the North' [1949], *Studies in Frontier History*, pp 455-66.

17 *Inner Asian Frontiers of China*, pp 199, 200.

18 R Conquest, *Kolyma. The Arctic Death Camps* (New York: Viking Press, 1978), pp 200-13.

19 'New Road to Asia', *The National Geographic Magazine* LXXXVI(1944), p 657.

20 'Left-Wing Consciences', *New Statesman* 76(1968), 11 October, p 461. See also the letters by Gross and Conquest, 18 October. Lattimore's piece was occasioned by a review by Gross of R Conquest, *The Great Terror. Stalin's Purge of the Thirties* (London: Macmillan, 1968).

21 *America and Asia. Problems of Today's War and the Peace of Tomorrow* (Claremont: Claremont Colleges, 1943), p 45.

22 *Solution in Asia* (New York: AMS reprint of Little, Brown edition of 1945, 1975), p iv.

23 *Solution in Asia*, pp 77, 84.

24 *Solution in Asia*, pp 93-4.

25 *Solution in Asia*, p 121.

26 *Solution in Asia*, pp 193-4.

27 J N Thomas, *The Institute of Pacific Relations. Asian Scholars and American Politics* (Seattle: University of Washington Press, 1974), pp 38 ff.

28 Alfred Kohlberg, 'Stupidity and/or Treason', *China Monthly* 9(June 1948), pp 151-2.

29 Stanley D Bachrack, *The Committee of One Million: 'China Lobby' Politics 1953-1971* (New York: Columbia University Press, 1976).

30 Alfred Kohlberg, 'Owen Lattimore: "Expert's Expert"', *China Monthly* 6(October 1945), p 26.

31 'Reply to Mr Kohlberg', *China Monthly* 6(December 1945), pp 15-17.

32 'The Moscow Trials: Comment', *Pacific Affairs* XI(1938), pp 370-2.

33 *The Making of Modern China. A Short History* [1944] (London: Allen and Unwin, 1945), pp 182-3.

34 *The Making of Modern China. A Short History* revised edition (New York: AMS reprint of Norton edition of 1947, 1975), p 203.

35 *The Making of Modern China. A Short History* revised edition, pp 212-3.

36 'The Chessboard of Power and Politics', *Virginia Quarterly Review* 24(1948), p 182.

37 'Inner Asian Frontiers: Chinese and Russian Margins of Expansion' [1947], *Studies in Frontier History*, p 140.

38 'The Czech Exception Disproves the Rules', *The New Republic* 117(1947), 22 September, p 6.

39 'The Chessboard of Power and Politics', pp 184-5.

40 *The Situation in Asia* (Boston: Little, Brown, 1949), pp 71, 174-6.

41 'American Responsibilities in the Far East', p 166; *The Situation in Asia*, p 73.
42 *The Situation in Asia*, p 159.
43 *The Situation in Asia*, pp 160, 163.
44 *The Situation in Asia*, p 68.
45 *The Situation in Asia*, p 64.
46 *The Situation in Asia*, pp 218, 165. See also, 'Our Failure in China', *Nation* 169(1949), 3 September, pp 223-6.
47 *The Situation in Asia*, pp 181 ff, 120, 97.
48 *The Situation in Asia*, p 180.
49 *Pivot of Asia. Sinkiang and the Inner Asian Frontiers of China and Russia* (Boston: Little, Brown, 1950; New York: AMS reprint, 1975). An earlier draft of parts of this text appeared as 'Sinkiang Survey', *Far Eastern Survey* XVII(1948), no 5, pp 56-63.
50 'Introduction' to AMS reprint.
51 'We Need Asia', *Nation* 171(1950), 16 December, pp 556-9.
52 'Safeguard Democracy!', *Nation* 174(1952), 9 February, p 134; see also 'Korea: We Win a Round', *Nation*, 173(1951), p 44.
53 'When Japan Has a Treaty', *Nation*, 173(1951), 4 August, pp 88-9.
54 'Battle of the Corridors', *Nation*, 178(1954), 23 January, pp 69-71.

CHAPTER FIVE

Opinions on Trial

Between 1950 and 1955 Lattimore, from being a figure not widely known outside the community of Asia scholars, was propelled into the public consciousness to the extent that his name was emblazoned on hostile propaganda produced for the 1952 American elections. Senator Joseph McCarthy was principally responsible for Lattimore's rise to notoriety, though in the long run the activities of McCarthy's colleague, Pat McCarran, were to result in far greater damage to his reputation. Generations of Americans have puzzled over the meaning of these extraordinary events with the consequence that Lattimore's ordeal and the background to it are illuminated in a glare of light, and his writings and scholarly contributions are often interpreted solely with them in mind.[1] As new evidence of those years becomes available the record is reassessed. Thus the release from 1977 of the files on Lattimore held by the Federal Bureau of Investigation and other US government departments has resulted in a more complete account of his case than has been available hitherto.[2] Given that this ground has been well traversed by historians of America I wish here principally to consider what these episodes reveal about the evolution of Lattimore's ideas and his understanding of them in the light of the fact that he was repeatedly required to recapitulate his arguments and views and explain the precise chronology of their development. But the context must first be established with a sketch of the episodes of the ordeal.

The Tydings Loyalty Hearings

On 9 February 1950, at an obscure venue in Wheeling, West Virginia, Senator Joseph McCarthy announced that he had 'here in my hand' a list of 205 names of 'active members of the Communist Party and members of a spy ring' who, despite this information being passed to the State Department, were still government employees shaping the nation's foreign policy.[3] These sensational charges quickly became the subject of a hearing on the loyalty of State Department officers before a specially constituted Subcommittee of the Senate Committee on Foreign Relations. The Chairman was Senator Millard E Tydings, and between March and June 1950, his Subcommittee heard the testimony of 35 individuals including John S Service whose name had been given prominence by McCarthy at Wheeling. But as a result of further statements by McCarthy, and evidence given by other witnesses (most notably, ex-communist Louis Budenz), Lattimore became the most important subject for the Subcommittee's scrutiny despite the fact that he had never served in the Department.

In his evidence at the hearings McCarthy first described Lattimore as one of the 'principal architects' of American Far Eastern policy with a 'procommunist' record going back many years. In a later executive session McCarthy went further, charging Lattimore with being within the government service 'the top of the whole [spy] ring of which Hiss was a part'.[4] By this time Alger Hiss, a former assistant to the Assistant Secretary of State, had been convicted on perjury charges which implied that he had been a communist agent while in US government service. After Lattimore's initial appearance at which he strongly defended his record and opinions, the Subcommittee heard from other witnesses, notably Freda Utley and Louis Budenz, who attempted respectively to give some substance to the allegations of Lattimore's sympathies and connections.[5] Lattimore was given a second chance to appear to rebut their testimony, though its basis was patently insubstantial. In any event Budenz's charges that Lattimore was known to the communist underground were undermined by information from the FBI that despite a thorough investigation (including many sessions with Budenz) there was nothing to indicate that Lattimore was a communist or a subversive; they were also refuted by the statements of other ex-communists. As Lattimore's connections with senior policy makers in the State Department were sporadic at best, there was no substance to anything McCarthy had said. The Subcommittee in its final Report found accordingly, concluding that 'we have seen a distortion of the facts on such a magnitude as to be truly alarming'.[6]

McCarthy, however, was only the proximate cause of Lattimore's arraignment before the Senate Subcommittee. Such facts as he had in his infamous 'file' had been provided largely by Alfred Kohlberg who was the ultimate source also of earlier statements attacking Lattimore's allegedly communist sympathies in an influential article by Max Eastman and J B Powell. There the authors had argued that American policy makers were offered the choice of backing in China a democratic Chiang Kai-shek or a totalitarian Communist Party. This choice was being obfuscated by means of a deliberate communist plot to introduce false notions of Chinese and Soviet communism into the American consciousness. Lattimore was singled out for his assertion that the Soviets practised a 'form of democracy' in Asia which was bound to be attractive to neighbouring peoples.[7]

In addition it may be conjectured that Lattimore was suffering for his acquaintance with John S Service and the fact that between 1937 and 1941 he had been nominally on the editorial board of *Amerasia*. Service, a career officer with the United States Foreign Service, had met Lattimore in China in 1933 and again during the war years in Chungking. He had been at the centre of the '*Amerasia* affair' in 1945, when with four others he was arrested by the FBI for passing confidential government documents to Philip Jaffe, the editor of that decidedly left-wing journal. It will be recalled that Jaffe had been one of the two Americans for whom Lattimore had acted as translator in Yenan in 1937. The outcome for Service was that later in the year he was cleared of any improper conduct in passing to Jaffe his personal copies of some of the factual memoranda he had prepared on conditions as he had seen them in the communist controlled areas of China.[8] Though exonerated, in the increasingly tense atmosphere of Washington as the Cold War developed and the beginnings of the Hiss case gave new impetus to fears of national betrayal, Service was subjected to further loyalty and security reviews in 1946, 1947, 1949, 1950 and 1951. Despite his clear record he was finally discharged from the State Department, though he was eventually declared to have been wrongfully dismissed in a decision by the US Supreme Court in 1957. From evidence now available it can be confirmed that Service was under FBI surveillance in 1945.[9] On the Sunday prior to his arrest regarding the *Amerasia* affair Service had attended a barbecue at Lattimore's house with other guests among whom were Andrew Roth and Professor George F Carter of Johns Hopkins. During the Tydings hearings the barbecue was discussed as a result of some of McCarthy's remarks. Roth, Service, and Lattimore had allegedly spent some of the afternoon 'declassifying' some documents, although the version of events given by most of those present was that they were examining the proofs of Roth's forthcoming book on Japan. University intrigue played a part in the prominence given to this episode as it is now apparent that despite being a guest in his house Professor Carter had developed a strong animosity to Lattimore and had consequently passed this story to McCarthy.[10]

Following the publication of the Report of the findings of the Tydings hearings Lattimore, his reputation apparently vindicated, resumed his work at Johns Hopkins. But though McCarthy moved on to other targets, his activities had drawn extensive public interest and had had a significant effect on the elections of 1950. Among those who had lost seats was the Senator from Maryland, Millard E Tydings, and a more conservative Congress, stirred by the 'loss' of China and the impasse of the Korean War, cast about for sacrificial victims. As a result Lattimore once again became the centre of controversy, this time of a far more serious nature.

The McCarran Investigation into the Institute of Pacific Relations

In 1951 the Internal Security Subcommittee of the Senate Judiciary Committee of the Senate chaired by Senator Pat McCarran of Nevada formed a special Subcommittee to investigate the organisation and the influence of the Institute of Pacific Relations (IPR). The character, conduct, and outcome of these hearings, which were conducted under the chairmanship of Senator James O Eastland of Mississippi, were in every sense a contrast to the Tydings hearings. Although the Institute as a whole was under scrutiny Lattimore, as editor of the Institute's principal journal from 1934 to 1941, became the central figure of the investigation partly no doubt because McCarthy's earlier charges had shown the way.

To understand why the IPR became a target of the Subcommittee it is necessary to say something of its history.[11] Originally founded in 1925 it soon came to be dominated by Edward C Carter who became its secretary-general in 1930. From an organisation originally conceived to facilitate cultural exchange it became under Carter one concerned as much if not more with economic and political issues in the Asian-Pacific area. Although its American section, composed of academics and opinion leaders as well as some figures from commerce, was by far the most important, the Institute had an international dimension. National affiliates or 'councils' (in Britain the Royal Institute of International Affairs) contributed to the workings of the Institute including its publications and periodic conferences. In the circumstances of the 1930s the various aims of the Institute often came into conflict. At the international conferences of the Institute national sensibilities could easily be offended when such contentious issues as Sino-Japanese relations or colonialism were discussed. This situation was sometimes exacerbated by Lattimore's penchant for controversy. As editor of the Institute's major journal he sought to publish along with academic contributions opinion pieces on the problems of the time even though the latter sometimes occasioned complaints from one or other of the national councils. Although the Soviet council of the Institute contributed little to its activities Lattimore was very keen to draw the Soviets into a greater collaboration, this being the principal reason for his trip with Carter to Moscow in 1936. He therefore sometimes edited articles critical of the Soviets, or sought to 'balance' such materials with other more complimentary contributions. This, it may be suspected, was also a factor in his favourable personal treatment in the pages of *Pacific Affairs* of Soviet books under review.

In the wartime period the activities of the Institute took on a more influential character. The Institute conferences of that time (at Mont Tremblant, Canada, in December 1942 and Hot Springs, Virginia, in January 1945) became forums for semi-official exchanges of opinion between delegations which included a number of senior government officials.[12] In the United States particularly the expertise of many individuals associated with the Institute was employed for the war effort, including that of Owen Lattimore who entered the Office of War Information.

For the purposes of the Subcommittee the Institute was a convenient target. Though membership did not denote belief in any particular views, criticising those many academics and others who had any relationship with the Institute (though this sometimes amounted to nothing more than receiving IPR journals) by way of that relationship gave those opinions the Subcommittee found reprehensible and potentially treasonable an apparent coherence and influence. Moreover the Subcommittee had in its possession the files of the Institute. These permitted members to call witnesses to account for any connections they had with the IPR going back two decades. The Subcommittee had heard allegations that various individuals who had published in IPR books or journals were covert communists. Finally the Subcommittee had the testimony of Louis Budenz, amplified further from his statements before the Tydings hearings, to the effect that Frederick V Field had organised a communist cell within the IPR in order to mount favourable propaganda for the communist cause. Here at least there seemed to be some link with communism. Field was a noted leftist - in his later autobiography he admitted his unofficial though close links with the American Communist Party[13] - as well as secretary of the American Council of the Institute (1934-1940) and a member of its Board of Trustees. He had also on occasions given the Institute donations from his substantial personal fortune.

Although much of the ground covered in the Tydings hearings was traversed again - Budenz embroidered his already fanciful tales - many more witnesses were heard over a period of eleven months.[14] They included a number of former Soviet citizens, the burden of whose testimony was that Lattimore and others had co-operated in the use by the Soviet Communist Party of the Institute as a propaganda and intelligence gathering organ. Hostile academic witnesses including Karl Wittfogel and Kenneth Colegrove also made appearances. Wittfogel damned Lattimore's writings and maintained that he had known (despite his denials before the Senators) of the communist connections and sympathies of various contributors to *Pacific Affairs* and other IPR publications. Some former members of the State Department testified regarding the allegedly pernicious influence of Lattimore on foreign policy and policy makers. And the atmosphere of the hearings was totally different from those of 1950. Tydings had permitted Lattimore to read a prepared statement at the outset, and the proceedings for the most part were conducted in a fair and orderly fashion with some consideration shown for those who had drawn McCarthy's charges. Lattimore had already attended an executive meeting of the Subcommittee but at his first public appearance on 26 February 1952 he was able to read only a paragraph of a lengthy opening statement before he was subjected to a relentless series of cross-examinations from counsel to the Subcommittee which continued through the three days it took simply to complete this statement. Eastland and his assistants held the inestimable advantage that they had scrutinised the files of the Institute which had earlier been seized at the orders of the Subcommittee. From the first it was evident that their tactics would be to ensnare Lattimore in inconsistencies and contradictions, a tactic which was bound to succeed since he did not share their access to his letters and files some of them almost twenty years old.

The findings of the Subcommittee, published in July 1952, could hardly have been more damaging for Lattimore. The Institute, and particularly *Pacific Affairs*, under the direction of members who were 'either Communist or pro-Communist', was found to have been used as a means to influence decision makers and public opinion in favour of the communist cause.

Lattimore and John Carter Vincent (another of McCarthy's original targets who had been counsellor at the US Embassy in Chungking, and later Director of Far Eastern Affairs in the State Department) were charged with bringing about 'a change in United States policy in 1945 favorable to the Chinese Communists'. And in a sweeping judgment unique in the document Lattimore was described as being 'from some time beginning in the 1930's, a conscious articulate instrument of the Soviet conspiracy'.[15] The Report further recommended that 'the Department of Justice submit to a grand jury the question of whether perjury has been committed before the subcommittee by Owen Lattimore'.[16] This had been the strategy that had finally captured Alger Hiss when direct charges of espionage could not be sustained.

Lattimore's career was in ruins. The hearings were a travesty, weight being given to the uncorroborated statements of witnesses it is clear now were totally untrustworthy, and Lattimore being subjected to questioning, according to the opinion of his eminent counsel, '*not* asked in order to obtain information, but for the purpose of entrapment'.[17] Although colleagues at Johns Hopkins had gathered an impressive body of scholars to give testimony to his contribution to oriental studies,[18] in the public mind such sentiments were far outweighed by the depiction of Lattimore in a number of inaccurate and tendentious studies as one of those chiefly responsible for delivering much of East Asia to the communists.[19] In a dishonourable chapter in the history of American academic affairs, though he was accepted back at Johns Hopkins ultimately to find a home in the History department, Lattimore's School was disbanded and the scholars he had collected for his project on Inner Asia were scattered, some not to resume an academic career in the United States. Nor did the affair end there because the McCarran Subcommittee's suggestion that Lattimore be charged with perjury was followed, though only as a result of McCarran's personal intervention with the Justice Department.

Aftermath: the Perjury Charges

In a sorry episode in American justice McCarran ensured that a perjury charge concerning Lattimore be put to a Grand Jury even though, as is now abundantly evident from the records available, neither the Justice Department nor the FBI were of the opinion that such a charge could be sustained, and when President Truman himself did not wish to see Lattimore subjected to further injustice.[20] In confirmation hearings before the Senate Committee on the Judiciary McCarran extracted a promise from James P McGranery, nominated by Truman as Attorney-General, that he would support the presenting of a case against Lattimore to a Grand Jury. To ensure further that the Justice Department did not flag in its efforts McCarran pressured McGranery into appointing Roy Cohn as a special assistant. Cohn, who later gained notoriety working with McCarthy, drafted an indictment against

Lattimore on seven counts of perjury which was accepted as a basis for prosecution by a Grand Jury in December 1952. In retrospect the charges that Lattimore had lied at the McCarran hearings appear either absurd or trivial. The government sought to maintain that Lattimore had been a 'follower of the communist line', though only later was a definition offered of this totally nebulous notion. It was also alleged that though Lattimore had insisted that *Pacific Affairs* under his stewardship had not published any contributions from communists (apart from Soviet authors), he had known that two of his authors were members of the communist movement. Although in May 1952 Federal Judge Luther Youngdahl destroyed the prosecution's case by dismissing the specific charges, and finding the more general ones so vague as to prohibit a fair hearing, Lattimore was not finally cleared until June 1955 after a series of prosecution appeals one of which went so far as to impugn Youngdahl's neutrality. Lattimore was undoubtedly fortunate, given the nature of the times, in finding in charge of his case a judge concerned to see that justice was done without fear or favour. It is an irony in retrospect that the political affiliations in the 1930s of Chen Han-seng and Chi Chao-ting, both of whom had contributed articles on China to Institute publications, so much discussed on the basis of so little evidence during the McCarran hearings, were as the Senators had hypothesised. Both had been Comintern agents and members of the CCP since the 1920s.[21]

Lattimore at the Tydings Hearings

Before the Tydings Subcommittee Lattimore offered a cogent defence of his role and opinions. As to the statement that he had been unusually influential in foreign policy making he was able to show that there were many occasions where his appeals had been ignored, as for example in 1940 when he urged the adopting of a much tougher line towards Japan by the United States.

The Senators were much preoccupied with policy towards China and Lattimore answered questions both on his past record and on his recommendations for the future. He identified himself as a supporter of Chiang Kai-shek, hopeful until 1946 that he would 'stop the advance of communism by instituting a few, necessary reforms'. Thereafter he regarded the Marshall mission as the only way of retrieving something of Chiang's position, finally coming round in 1947 to the view that 'the Kuomintang was beyond salvage'. On the record of his statements regarding the Chinese communists, Lattimore defended the views he had expressed in 1945. The communists in Yenan had shown themselves capable of working with other political groups, and their regime clearly enjoyed a good measure of popular support. On the alternatives open to America in 1950, with a CCP regime firmly ensconced in Peking, Lattimore forthrightly expounded a view later and with some irony to be associated with Richard Nixon. Accepting that a close identification of China with the Soviet Union would be the least preferred likely eventuality, Lattimore favoured the use of American influence to foster in China any development likely to lead to the creation there of 'Titoism'. Formosa, which had become the final refuge of the Kuomintang and was then threatened by imminent communist invasion, would accordingly have to be abandoned. Not only was a reconquest of the mainland by the Kuomintang an impossibility, but whatever support was given to Chiang Kai-shek would only serve to drive Peking into the arms of Moscow.[22]

Concerning United States policy towards Asia, Lattimore offered recommendations based on the premises expounded in *Situation in Asia*. Making public a memorandum written in October 1949 at the request of Philip Jessup of the State Department, Lattimore rejected any further attempts to pursue 'the type of policy represented by support for Chiang Kai-shek'. Neither in Japan nor elsewhere should attempts be made to create or sustain through economic or political interference allied or client regimes which do not rest on popular support. If there was to be conflict with Russia it would not be won, in Lattimore's view, by defeating northern Korea, Vietnam or China, thus America should avoid 'premature or excessive strategic deployment in the Far East'. A positive policy towards the emerging nationalist regimes of Asia represented the greatest hope for the strengthening of democracy in that region and world-wide.[23] It followed that the regime in Korea could not be supported:

> we are there in a position which is, I think, untenable for a democracy ... [in] backing an inefficient police state against the ruthless and efficient police state of the Russians in North Korea.
> I am afraid that if that situation goes on, it will only mean a cumulative loss of prestige for us, and a very dangerous advertisement for us in the rest of Asia.[24]

As an indicator of how little regard was held in the State Department for Lattimore's point of view, he noted that since his memorandum was sent to Jessup not only was the United States 'still supporting a little Chiang Kai-shek in South Korea' but 'we have ... taken on another one in Indochina'.[25] It was Lattimore's fear that the United States was becoming involved in positions in Asia without a careful review of the options. Commitment to Formosa and Korea was not merely commitment for the wrong reasons, but it would also absorb energies and resources which would be much better directed elsewhere:

> At the present time anything put into Formosa is being frittered away. Anything put into India, Pakistan, Indonesia, has a chance of developing into a big going concern, and I think it is a grave defect of our policy ... that so much attention is concentrated on these holding-point positions which cannot ... be anything but temporary situations, and the main field of action is being neglected.[26]

Finally, given Lattimore's preoccupation with the Mongols, he was granted the opportunity of defending his views on the Mongolian People's Republic. In the 1949 memorandum he had stated that he was in favour of diplomatic recognition of this 'increasingly important potential listening-post country' strategically situated between Russia and China, and this was still his opinion. Taxed on the exact status of the country Lattimore at one point described it as a 'satellite' in which 'high policy' was only decided with Russian participation. At a later point he discussed internal developments in the country, although he did not have the evidence to say whether these events were as a result of Russian promptings or were in imitation of events in the Soviet Union. And he revealed that he had tendered advice to Chiang Kai-shek on the Mongol question during his time as Chiang's adviser when the Kuomintang still maintained that China retained a legal title to all of Mongolia. He had then stated that in the event of China regaining a role in Outer Mongolia Chiang should offer a positive role to the Mongols in order to be able to counter the influence of the communists whose strength in the neighbouring areas exceeded that of the national government.[27]

Lattimore at the McCarran Hearings

Before the McCarran Subcommittee Lattimore was called to account in a punishing series of verbal duels for opinions he had held over two decades. Much of the same ground was covered but the aggression of the Subcommittee and particularly of its counsellors, and their access to a great body of Lattimore's correspondence dating back to 1934, revealed new details.

In a letter written in November 1936 which was made an exhibit Lattimore offers a perceptive exposition of Japanese tactics which were aimed at so weakening the Nanking regime that it would be forsaken by western friends and would eventually capitulate. Even before his trip to Yenan in 1937, Lattimore could see that the communist presence in China was a new factor likely to have profound consequences. If Nanking resisted Japan, military defeat was certain, but then the Japanese would be faced by 'a genuine national resistance', a war 'with mud huts and impoverished farms' in which the employment of modern armaments may not make a great difference. In this conflict the communists would have the considerable advantage of 'veteran military and political organizers and a nucleus of hardbitten partisan armies already inured to that kind of war'.[28]

In an exchange on the status of the Mongolian People's Republic Lattimore defended the view that though it was now an independent state, from 1921 the influence of the Russians has been 'very strong' though they had exercised this influence 'primarily at the request of the Mongols themselves'. Bearing in mind the reliance of the hearings on the rememberings by diverse witnesses of snatches of conversation which occurred ten or fifteen years before it is noteworthy that Lattimore in accepting that Mongolia was now a Soviet 'satellite' could not suppose that he used the term before 1945 since this 'is a post-war expression'. In fact Mongolia is thus described in an essay of Lattimore's of 1936, this perhaps being the first instance of the modern political use of this term.[29] Following this up the Subcommittee questioned William C Bullitt, former American ambassador in Moscow, whom Lattimore had met during his visit to the Soviet Union in 1936. Bullitt reported a conversation he had had with him in which Lattimore had urged him to telegraph President Roosevelt to extend diplomatic recognition to the Mongolian People's Republic which was now fully independent. Bullitt made the point to the Subcommittee that this was even in advance of the official Soviet position on Mongolia. Though a 'protocol of mutual assistance' between Russia and Mongolia had been signed earlier in 1936, in an exchange of diplomatic notes with Nanking the Soviet Union had affirmed Chinese sovereignty over that region. Bullitt, from his conversations with Soviet officials convinced of Moscow's almost complete control of Mongolia, drew the inference that either Lattimore was not as well informed as he ought to be on his area of specialty or he was purposely advancing the communist cause.[30]

From Lattimore's recollection in 1982 of these events it is clear that his intentions then, though 'politically quite unsophisticated', were to seek to involve the United States in the struggle for Mongol loyalties lest they go by default to Japan. Indeed, Lattimore still maintains, as he did at the hearings though this was not mentioned by Bullitt, that following his exposition to Bullitt of the situation in Inner Mongolia, the Ambassador was sufficiently impressed as to arrange an interview for him with Stomonyakov of the Soviet Foreign Office in order to have Lattimore refute the Soviet interpretation of the Inner Mongolian nationalists as pro-Japanese traitors. Lattimore subsequently explained 'to a somewhat impassive audience' that Nanking had little control over the regional warlords who were driving the Mongols from their lands and thus by their actions fomenting nationalist feeling which, if it went unrecognised, might force the Mongols into the arms of the Japanese.[31]

Allegations of Lattimore's influence over American foreign policy elicited a memorandum he had written for Truman shortly before the President's departure for the Potsdam conference. It may be supposed from other testimony at the time that here Lattimore was unwittingly the victim of rivalries between China and Japan specialists within the State Department. Grew, then Acting Secretary of State (and a former Ambassador to Japan), had quashed a proposal by Vincent that Lattimore be appointed as an occasional consultant to the Department - it transpired later from Vincent's testimony for his special knowledge of Inner Asia. The Japan hands Ballantine and Dooman had then been replaced in 1945, and Vincent (a China hand, and Lattimore's friend) had been put in charge of the Far Eastern Division. Dooman testified that in his view Vincent and then Under Secretary of State Dean Acheson were under Lattimore's baleful influence particularly in the views they held regarding American policy towards Japan. Dooman quoted the disparaging remarks in *Solution in Asia* on Washington's supposed Japan experts (including Grew), and the views therein expressed on the need to dissolve the *zaibatsu* and turn the emperor over to the Chinese for internment if the Japanese people did not themselves disestablish the monarchy. He found Acheson and others espousing similar views which became American policy shortly after his retirement. And he charged that the Pauley report following the visit of the reparations mission to Japan which called for the 'pastoralisation' of that country was drafted by Lattimore. Here the Subcommittee could confirm that in executive session Lattimore had stated that he had 'co-ordinated' the drafting of this report.[32] It is certainly the case that Lattimore was forthright in 1945 in stating the case for the destruction of the business interests that had supported Japan's expansionist policy. In a broadcast discussion in July 1945 he had also advocated the internment of the imperial family whose return would have to be ratified by plebiscite. America should be concerned to point out that it did not wish to punish the Japanese people as a whole, but without these measures a recrudescence of militarism would be possible. Nor did Lattimore spare the Japan hands of the Department of State. For without these measures the 'decent people' of Japan 'will not be able to get in touch with the people in the State Department who stand for a Japanese equivalent of a Darlan policy, a Badoglio policy'[33], that is compromising with former supporters of the old regime in exchange for their present support.

But the memorandum to Truman, though it mentions Japan, is concerned largely with China. Here Lattimore argued that America must use her influence lest China become divided into two irreconcilable camps which would in turn lead to a confrontation with the Soviet Union. An agreement between the Kuomintang and the Communist Party backed by an agreement between the big powers was necessary if this division was to be avoided. The former would entail the creation of a coalition government in which the communists would have 'minority standing' but 'proportionate to their real strength, not just token representation'. In the absence of a clear American policy made credible to Chiang by Soviet concurrence he would assume that America, which he was advised was 'heading for a long-term conservative trend', would come down on the Kuomintang side 'if he hits the right timing in a civil war'. In view of Lattimore's earlier statement that he had backed a reformed Kuomintang until 1946, it is noteworthy that here he is optimistic in assessing Chiang's capacity to accept advice: 'Chiang is tenacious but has shown in the past that he knows when to give in and try a new policy'.[34]

Lattimore defended, against hostile interrogation, the positions he had come to hold by 1949 including his conviction that no useful purpose would be served by further American involvement in Korea and Formosa. These positions were exemplified in the transcript of a round table discussion on

China policy held in the State Department in early October of 1949 which was reviewed by the Subcommittee. Quite contrary to the assertion at the McCarran hearings by one of the other participants, University of Pennsylvania President Harold Stassen, Lattimore did not dominate the proceedings nor was he part of a 'leading group', but he does express a variety of forthright views on American policy. The Chinese communist regime should be recognised as part of a package concerning admissions to the United Nations (inevitably including the Mongolian People's Republic). There is a potential for nationalist sentiment even in the communist leaders of Asia - Lattimore mentions Ho Chi Minh - which could be exploited by an adroit American policy. Lattimore also recognises that the approach taken by the United States regarding aid to and trade with Asia in the years ahead will be of the greatest moment. All aid monies will have a political impact which must be recognised. America must give preference to those countries, and here he has India particularly in mind, in which the 'modernization of their political forms' has 'created the political condition under which economic improvement can be carried forward'. It would be a mistake to close to American commerce any country in Asia including China. This would effectively destroy any leverage the United States might have in the countries of the region against the Soviet Union.[35]

Lattimore's Academic Critics

Much of the proceedings before the McCarran Subcommittee were taken up with the question of whether the publications and activities of the IPR exhibited any systematic bias. Contending analyses of the articles appearing in *Pacific Affairs* and in other Institute publications - a practice which probably had its origins with Alfred Kohlberg - were presented to demonstrate or refute charges of bias or selectivity. In an age which values freedom of opinion and expression this now seems an extraordinary exercise, but it was at least made possible by the structure of the Institute which sought to reconcile objectives which came into conflict in the 1930s. As has been shown the Institute's publications were expected to make contributions to science but the federal nature of the Institute, which was based on a number of national councils, did lead in time to attempts by the Soviet and Japanese constituent bodies to influence publication policy. In addition the editor of the principal journal, *Pacific Affairs*, had the task of ensuring that it was a topical publication which did not avoid controversy. Lattimore was a man of strong and sometimes careless opinion, and this as much as his need to keep the national councils content with the publication was reflected in his conduct as editor. He made strenuous efforts to extract contributions from his Soviet affiliates (who wrote very little for the journal), and was conciliatory in responding to their complaints against particular articles. He had little time for the Japanese, however, nor was he afraid to encourage criticism of European colonialism. Of course such an approach is a long way from the communist conspiracy, but the McCarran hearings were able by taking a small sample of the Institute's work to exhibit some notable favourite causes. Lattimore's lack of a university degree and the journalistic nature of some of his writings were also used in an attempt to discredit his professional standing.

To the credit of the American academic community, many scholars were prepared to attest to his scholarship. In March 1950 John K Fairbank sent a circular letter to some forty China specialists urging them to write to Senator Tydings with their views on McCarthy's charges. All but one did so. When Fairbank himself was drawn into the McCarran hearings George Boas, professor of the history of philosophy at Johns Hopkins, assembled the testimonials of thirty-seven scholars, most of them orientalists, in support of Lattimore's integrity and contributions to learning.[36] But at the McCarran hearings the predominant academic voice was given to six university teachers who, for one reason or another, were prepared to criticise Lattimore's scholarship or politics.

Rowe, McGovern and Colegrove on Lattimore

Professor David Rowe, a political scientist from Yale (who from his evidence may perhaps have been a disappointed suitor for the hand of Eleanor Holgate, later to be Lattimore's wife), was an outspoken critic. Lattimore was 'probably the principal agent of Stalinism' in the United States. The mildest of cross-examination revealed, however, that Rowe had no reason to suppose that Lattimore was 'a formal Communist affiliate', which left him with the mere supposition that Lattimore was no more than 'a fellow traveler'. Notwithstanding, Rowe was given the opportunity to introduce an analysis of the publications of the Institute prepared by Richard L Walker, then of Yale (and most recently US Ambassador in Seoul), which purported to show a systematic bias.[37] William McGovern, professor of political science at Northwestern University, who had first met Lattimore in the late 1920s, spent some time charting the various changes he had observed in his political views since 1937 when they had seen a great deal of each other in Peking. From exhibiting a 'warm admiration' for the communists in 1937-38 ('they represented the real people'), Lattimore had shifted towards enthusiasm for Chiang Kai-shek in the winter of 1941. When their paths crossed again towards the end of the war Lattimore was a proponent of a punitive peace for Japan; he also advocated giving the Chinese communists a favourable mention in Office of War Information propaganda. Indeed, he had gone so far as to say in 1945, regarding American policy, that 'we have to build on the forward-looking elements in China', that is 'the people in Yenan'. Now whether or not this was an accurate recollection it reflected sentiments which were bound to be differently interpreted at a time when the United States was locked in a sanguinary and apparently prolonged conflict with the Chinese communists in Korea. McGovern also commented on Lattimore's post-war views of Japan and Korea, and expressed the opinion that Lattimore's influence could be seen in the 'Kunming telegram' sent by Wallace to Roosevelt in late June 1944. Now the telegram did advocate putting American support behind a 'new coalition' only to be led by Chiang if he was sufficiently astute to see the need for reform; Wallace's visit also cleared the way for an American military observer mission to be sent to Yenan.[38] But according to the testimony of Vincent and Alsop who were there, and former Vice-President Wallace himself Lattimore had no hand at all in any of this.[39] Nevertheless, McGovern is adamant that Lattimore had always followed the 'Stalinist' line.[40]

Another professor from Northwestern, the political scientist Kenneth Colegrove, was prepared to offer an even more damning indictment of Lattimore's ideas and influence. From his evidence it is clear that the two men had disagreed violently in late 1943 when Colegrove had been offered a position in the Office of War Information with Lattimore. At that time he had taken strong exception to Lattimore's condemnation of colonialism in India and Indonesia, and to his belief that at the end of the war the Japanese imperial family should be interned in China. His analysis of Lattimore's view at that time that the Chinese communists were mere 'agrarian reformers' not under the control of Moscow is worth a more lengthy consideration as it conveys in a striking fashion the manner in which the Subcommittee interpreted academic comment:

Senator FERGUSON. ... that was the Communist line?

Mr COLEGROVE. Yes. I do not charge him --

Sen FERGUSON. With being a Communist?

Mr COLEGROVE. No. I did not charge him with following the Communist line. I simply told him I was sure he knew better, that Mao Tse-tung was not a democrat and a mere agrarian reformer ... Also I discussed with Lattimore the policy of the United States toward the Emperor ...

Sen EASTLAND. Why did you decline a job in San Francisco [with OWI]?

Mr COLEGROVE. Largely personal. I did not trust Owen Lattimore. I did not care to be associated with him.

Sen EASTLAND. You thought they were following the Communist line out there?

Mr COLEGROVE. I can't say I was that alert, Senator. Some of us professors are not as alert as we should be. I could not say that Owen Lattimore was following the Communist line. I didn't like his attitude on Asiatic problems.

Sen EASTLAND. You say it was a Communist line?

Mr COLEGROVE. Yes. I say it was the Communist line.

....

Sen FERGUSON. You have no doubt about it now?

Mr COLEGROVE. That was the Communist line. As you look back over the situation and compare it with the editorials in the Daily Worker, you can see definitely that was the Communist line.[41]

Colegrove also detected in Lattimore's 1949 memorandum on foreign policy views which, if put into practice, would have furthered the communist cause in Asia. He also commented on other issues but his most outspoken remarks were reserved for the State Department round table of October 1949. According to Colegrove, there Lattimore had led a 'pro-Kremlin' group which dominated the discussion, one of the consequences of which was the severing of aid to Formosa in late October. But as an academic witness with a duty to pass judgment on complex matters of fact Colegrove rather undermined his own credibility, if only to posterity, by assenting to the proposition that 'there was a conspiracy by people in the State Department to throw China to the Communists'.[42]

Nicholas Poppe on Lattimore

A wholly serious witness, and probably the only academic called to the hearings with a sound knowledge of Lattimore's specialty, was Professor Nicholas Poppe. Poppe, perhaps the world's leading Mongolist, had not been in the United States for very long and, being a former Soviet citizen, was anxious to co-operate with the members of the Subcommittee. At the same time, from his testimony, and from his later autobiography, it is clear that he wished to give a fair interpretation of the facts. On the scholarly standing of the Institute's Soviet affiliates, Poppe recounted his experience of the evidence of Communist Party control of all academic matters, including Voitinsky's purge of the Oriental Institute in Leningrad. On the relationship between the Soviet Union and Mongolia Poppe pointed out that Mongolia's independence was only nominal - all visits to the country, even by Soviet scholars, had to have political approval from Moscow and Lattimore must have known something of this in his attempts to arrange permission for such a visit through his Soviet contacts. Indeed, this latter point may be inferred from Lattimore's correspondence with Moscow, though this also bears another construction. As Mongolia's southern borders were closed a Soviet visa would have been required to traverse territory not normally open to foreigners, and only Soviet good offices, Mongolia not being recognised by any other country, would have gained Lattimore entry. On Lattimore's works, Poppe praised his writings on Manchuria and *Inner Asian Frontiers of China*, but found some of his other books superficial and uncritical. But though the Senators were evidently anxious to hear Poppe label Lattimore a communist, he carefully resisted their attempts to do so even though he regarded as nonsense all talk of Russia exercising a power of 'attraction' over Mongolia in view of the commitment of Soviet troops to suppress an extensive rebellion there against the communist regime.[43]

Karl Wittfogel and George Taylor

The most damaging academic critic of Lattimore to appear before the Subcommittee was Karl August Wittfogel, by this time a professor at the Far Eastern and Russian Institute of the University of Washington in Seattle as well as Director of the Chinese History Project at Columbia. George Taylor, also from Seattle, supported some of Wittfogel's remarks concerning particular incidents, but Wittfogel's contribution was of far greater importance. A great deal of credence was placed in his testimony because of his unique qualifications, as an academic and an undoubted influence on Lattimore's scholarship, as one closely acquainted with Lattimore for a considerable period, and as a former communist. In retrospect it is clear that the members of the Subcommittee were not possessed of the acumen or the inclination to consider critically the bearing of these diverse (and perhaps inconsistent) qualifications on some of Wittfogel's more remarkable statements. On the latter point, it is specifically stated in the record of the hearings that the Subcommittee (like the Spanish Inquisition in this if not in other respects), far from fearing the danger of recidivism or distrusting the character or motives of those who could become communists in the first place, accorded particular weight *a priori* to the evidence of ex-communists.

Wittfogel was given the widest brief to discuss Lattimore and the Institute, and the reader of the proceedings repeatedly feels the lack of interventions by counsel to the Subcommittee, Robert Morris, who in peremptory fashion normally required witnesses to keep to the point and answer the question at hand. Indeed, at the end of his contribution Morris unashamedly contrived to allow Wittfogel a grand peroration with the rather broad inquiry, 'Now, Dr. Wittfogel, what have you done in the last 10 years to express your opposition to the Communist movement ...?'[44]

Many of Wittfogel's remarks concerned his relationship with Lattimore and their estimation of mutual acquaintances. Wittfogel was adamant that Lattimore knew of his communist affiliations, and of the communist connections of several contributors to *Pacific Affairs*, though curiously enough on the former question no words actually passed between them. An example of this unspoken understanding - Lattimore was supposed to have given Wittfogel a knowing smile during a conversation - was to provoke a sardonic response:

> The truth is that I have not the faintest recollection of this whole
> conversation, but if I smiled at all, it was certainly a non-

Communist smile. Now I would be willing to believe that
Communists have an arsenal of secret signals, but I would never
suppose that it included anything as good-natured as a smile. In
fact, I thought that these grim conspirators regarded a smile as a
bourgeois gesture - practically as an enemy of the state. If I am
wrong, and if a smile is a secret Red signal, I confess that I used to
smile a great deal. In the pre-McCarthy days I used to think that
life was lots of fun.[45]

Wittfogel also freely testified on the leftist or communist sympathies of a
number of individuals connected with the Institute. But he was sufficiently
scrupulous not to name Lattimore directly as an organised communist - he
preferred to profess ignorance on this question, though he found his political
position in retrospect to be consistently 'pro-Soviet'. And he denied that
Lattimore's lack of formal academic qualifications should have any bearing on
his scholarly standing, though he was of the opinion that Lattimore's
considerable authority in a limited academic field did not justify a claim to
'global' expertise.

According to Wittfogel's account, at a point in 1947 he had come round to
the view that he detected in Lattimore's past statements, particularly on the
post-war fate of Korea and American treatment of the Japanese imperial
family, a careless and irresponsible lack of integration. Lattimore had been
due to contribute a preface to the volume prepared by Wittfogel on the Liao
dynasty as the first fruits of his connection with the Chinese History Project at
Columbia. However, with their relationship soured by political disputes
Wittfogel was no longer prepared to incorporate such a preface in the book.
The precise dating of this break in their relations is important since Wittfogel
criticised Lattimore at the McCarran hearings *inter alia* for views which he
had expressed in 1944 and 1945. Lattimore declared himself puzzled during
the hearings that although Wittfogel had definitely broken with communism in
1939, he was still able to write to Lattimore describing him as 'an expert to
end all experts' in March 1945.[46]

It may be conjectured that Wittfogel's relations with Lattimore were
constituted of a tangle of scholarly and political as well as personal
considerations. When Wittfogel arrived in China he was virtually unknown in
the American China field. His friendship with Lattimore had opened doors, at
the same time as his ideas had contributed to the structure of *Inner Asian
Frontiers of China*. From his later writings and behaviour it is evident that he
found it difficult to be beholden to any other person apart from figures such as
Marx and Weber who were safely dead. It is noteworthy, therefore, that
Wittfogel's 1949 work on the Liao dynasty, in its incorporation of a new
approach to the history of 'barbarian' conquest dynasties in China, built on the
major theoretical preoccupation of *Inner Asian Frontiers of China* which was
the relationship between frontier and heartland in Chinese history.[47] At the
McCarran hearings Wittfogel went so far as to refer to the 'historical and

institutional analysis' of Lattimore's 1940 book as having 'so faithfully followed my ideas', but Lattimore's greatest theoretical debt to Wittfogel lay, as has been shown, in his analysis of the social and political pattern of the Chinese agricultural heartland.

In the early 1940s Wittfogel's political views began to harden. From letters of 1943 and 1944 it is apparent that Lattimore had found Wittfogel's increasing 'vehemence' more and more difficult to accommodate. As he says in the latter:

> About confining myself to conventional phrases during your brief visit here, the fact is that I was completely dazed. I thought we were meeting as old friends for the first time in a long period and was at a loss as to what to say when you opened with a violent personal attack on another old friend for whom I have as much respect as I do for you. You followed that up by a very forceful presentation of political opinions on which I, myself, have either no opinion or only an unformed or half-formed opinion. In such cases I find it very difficult to be expected to endorse somebody else's strongly held opinions, even if I know that his opinion is based on experience and knowledge. I still cling to the privilege of what I believe is known legally as the 'Scotch verdict' - that is, the right to say that I don't know.[48]

From his peroration at the McCarran hearings it can be seen that Wittfogel had come to see by this time all issues, personal relations as well as scholarly questions, in terms of 'the Soviet issue':

> I may have been one of the first persons who raised the question among the Orientalists that we have to adjust ourselves to a world which is not one world. We held the first convention of American Orientalists in the spring of 1946, and the president of our professional organization discussed the lessons of the war. In my own paper I took the line that the Orientalists have to become realists and to be aware that we are not going to live in one world ... Year by year I have tried to show we cannot work in the modern field of oriental history and study what is going on in modern times without understanding communism ...[49]

For Lattimore, as has been shown, the Soviet issue was never pre-eminent. Lattimore had little interest in ideological issues (as a number of his rather bemused references in the 1930s and early 1940s to Wittfogel's views demonstrate), and his recommendations for post-war foreign policy were never based on a need to contain or defeat world communism as a first priority. Indeed, he believed that there were limits within which the United States and the Soviet Union could co-operate, and that in some circumstances a heedless opposition to communism would not be to America's advantage. It is not surprising, therefore, that by 1952 Wittfogel was prepared to swear under oath that 'Lattimore's special and unusual talents were increasingly furthering the aims of total power' thereby doing 'great harm to the free world'.[50]

But how was this harm manifest? Here, as has been shown, Wittfogel felt that too many of Lattimore's ideas on foreign policy ran parallel to those of the world communist movement. Wittfogel, however, appeared before the Subcommittee principally as a scientist and so he offered also an example of a deliberate scientific distortion which had appeared in Lattimore's work because of his increasing sympathies for the Soviet Union. He showed, first of all, that Lattimore earlier was aware of the importance for the communists of obscuring the bureaucratic nature of traditional East Asian society (lest their own plans to create a similar bureaucratic system of total power become apparent) by insisting that such society was 'feudal'. He showed that Lattimore's own past writings rejected the application of the 'feudal' denotation to imperial China. But in one of the preparatory studies for *Pivot of Asia* published in 1948 Lattimore and his collaborators referred to the presence of 'semifeudal agrarian relations' in Sinkiang. *Ergo*, Lattimore's science had been vitiated by the influence of Marxism.[51] The response of the normally assiduous Morris was 'I think that is enough of that'. Lattimore's later reaction was to comment that he did not know that the communists had a 'patent' on the term 'feudal', but perhaps this is an instance of a sin against science on Wittfogel's part for political reasons. Sinkiang is hardly agricultural China, and the application of the term feudal to some aspects of Sinkiang society does not amount to any comment on the nature of traditional or modern China.

Lattimore and the Debate on Postwar Policy

It was almost inevitable that in the atmosphere of the early 1950s, Lattimore's writings and opinions would be interpreted in the light of the debate on the 'loss' of China. Seen in that context his views were neither extreme nor particularly original. The creation of a coalition government in China incorporating the Communist Party as a measure to avoid civil conflict was one of the objectives of Ambassador Hurley's five point agreement of November 1944 which he unsuccessfully endeavoured to have the CCP and the Kuomintang accept. Hurley, who later blamed the State Department China specialists including Service and Davies for undermining Chiang's regime with their misleading reports on the communists, believed at the time and went on saying until 1951 that the Chinese communists were not 'real communists'.[52] What is perhaps most noteworthy is that Lattimore was one of the earliest commentators to see the potential for a communist led guerrilla resistance dedicated to the destruction of the Japanese invaders. But, despite his overall assessment of the Kuomintang, he remained hopeful of Chiang

Kai-shek's powers of leadership long after others familiar with conditions in China had come to see his cause as hopeless.

On the shape of the post-war settlement in Asia Lattimore was more outspoken. But it should be recalled that in connection with proposals for a hard peace with Japan, in 1943 and 1944 a similar proposition for the 'pastoralisation' of Germany (the Morgenthau plan) had been accepted for a time by the allies. Even on the issue of Korea the United States Congress had delayed the aid package assembled in 1949 on the grounds that Korea was a lost cause, and Eisenhower was later to rue the day that he was forced to have dealings with the administration of Syngman Rhee. In Indochina American policy makers in a Republican administration were to decide, in 1954, against a direct military role in Vietnam though of course this decision was later reversed with tragic consequences. And the unequivocal American commitment to defend the Kuomintang on Taiwan, a commitment which Secretary of State Acheson had not wished to make, only came about with the outbreak of the Korean War. Indeed, it has now been established that in 1949 Acheson was already willing to countenance diplomatic recognition of Peking.[53] It must be concluded that Lattimore suffered less for his opinions than for the times in which he had held them.

Lattimore also suffered for his associations. The leftish sympathies of some of the individuals who had been his colleagues in the Institute were clearly a liability in the United States of the early 1950s. But important also, though a factor which is not so evident from the McCarran hearings, was Lattimore's membership of the New Deal generation who were now held to account for America's failure to win the peace, in Asia and elsewhere. Lattimore owed his position as Roosevelt's emissary to Chiang to Lauchlin Currie, Roosevelt's administrative assistant who in superintending lend-lease aid to China was an important influence on China policy at that time.[54] And Roosevelt himself had reacted with enthusiasm when Wallace had informed him that on Currie's suggestion he was taking Lattimore, as an expert on Inner Asia, on his 1944 mission.[55] Roosevelt's idealistic desire to admit China to the ranks of the post-war powers is well documented, as is the distaste with which he viewed the colonial status of much of Asia. These two views were at the bottom of Roosevelt's approach to post-war policy in the region, as shown in the last letter written by Lattimore to Chiang Kai-shek in his capacity as Chiang's adviser. This informs Chiang of a conversation with the President in which he put forward the view that in Southeast Asia a new form of trusteeship would need to be evolved as a restoration of the old colonial order in Asia would not be desirable. It also reports the President's conviction that after the war China would be one of the 'four "big policemen" of the world' along with Britain, the United States and Russia.[56] Insofar as these beliefs were to provide a faulty foundation for subsequent American China policy, Lattimore was bound to be seen as one who shared the blame.

Lattimore's Assumptions and the Evolution of American Foreign Policy

It should be observed by way of conclusion that certain of Lattimore's fundamental beliefs contravened the assumptions which came to be most prominent in the thinking of American foreign policy makers as the Cold War developed. In the later 1940s Lattimore formed the strong conviction that Asia would be dominated by an upsurge of nationalist sentiment and by popular yearnings for (an inevitably ill-defined) democracy. He also remained convinced of the veracity of an idea that he had come to accept in the 1930s, that the coming age was one in which land based power rather than sea power would be dominant. A successful United States policy in Asia would need to take all these factors into account. The drift of American policy, however, was in quite the opposite direction. In the period from George F Kennan's 'long telegram' of February 1946 on the fundamentals of Soviet policy to the declaration of the Truman Doctrine in the following year, Washington moved towards a policy of confronting a Soviet bloc whose conduct was regarded as aggressive and inimical to American interests. This doctrine of 'containment' was expounded in the National Security Council's NSC-68, drafted at the beginning of 1950 and formally accepted as American policy by Truman later in that year when the outbreak of the Korean War seemed to validate its postulates. Though John Foster Dulles at the beginning of the Eisenhower administration sought to distance himself publicly from State Department policy hitherto, it is well established that 'containment' of the Soviet bloc remained the principal American objective well into the 1960s.[57]

As a response to the Korean War and events in Europe, the United States participated in or prompted the formation of a series of agreements and pacts to replicate in Asia the security system created in Europe by the North Atlantic Treaty. Thus between 1951 and 1955 the United States entered into security treaties with Japan, the Republic of Korea, and the Republic of China on Taiwan, and prompted the creation of ANZUS, SEATO, and CENTO. As a concomitant of this security system, restrictions were placed on economic contacts with the communist world, including a boycott on all trade with the People's Republic of China. American strategy aimed at holding the existing line in Asia through the maintenance of a ring of military bases from which air and maritime power could be projected. Neutrality by the third countries in the region was to be positively discouraged, and American business was to be induced to concentrate its efforts on developing links with those countries who were active participants in this strategy.

The fundamentals of this strategy clearly ran contrary to Lattimore's views of the situation in Asia. The United States appeared to be seeking to dominate Asia in the old way. From offshore military bases America could well be thought by Asians to be imposing an external and unsought hegemony on peoples whose national and material aspirations were being subordinated to the global contest against America's principal enemy. Such a strategy denied the existence (and would thus delay or prevent the emergence) of nationalist diversity within the expanded communist bloc and it would be likely also to drive the third countries into the embrace of the very enemy from whom they should be shielded. And the essentially maritime approach to the region denied the new reality of continentally based land power as the key to the control of the new Asia, a power America could not match by clinging to the Asian fringes.

As more becomes known of the detailed thinking at this time of American policy makers it is becoming clear that Lattimore's views were less at variance with those of leading figures in the government than his critics made out in the early 1950s. The most influential individual in the making of policy in these years was Kennan. Though he was the principal architect of the containment doctrine, on policy towards Asia he was both more cautious and less preoccupied with the single factor of communist expansion than later practitioners of that doctrine. The best approach to Asia, he believed, was not to fight communism where and when the communists chose but to hold strong points (Okinawa, the Philippines, Japan) from which an appropriate response could be mounted. He proposed exploiting the differences that were bound to develop within the communist camp and to this end did not favour any entanglement in China where 'Titoism' could well appear. He held a low opinion of Chiang Kai-shek and even suggested at one point in 1949 that the Kuomintang be expelled from Taiwan and the island held possibly as an American strong point.[58] There is good evidence that Dulles, though in his public pronouncements a proponent of the view that communism was monolithic, was aware as early as 1953 that Sino-Soviet disagreements could be exploited. Indeed, United States pressure on China in 1954 (following the Mutual Defence Treaty with Taipei) and again in 1958 was exerted partly to induce a reassessment in Moscow of the costs of underwriting Chinese foreign policy.[59] The real difference between the Truman-Acheson approach to world politics and that of Dulles was that whereas for the former containment was a means to the end of influencing Soviet conduct and inducing the Soviets to negotiate on their differences with the United States, for the latter containment became almost an end in itself. This was largely a result of the changes wrought by McCarthy and his allies in domestic politics as a result of which anything less than implacable opposition to world communism could be construed as treasonable.[60] In the new era of the 1950s Lattimore's dogged adherence to those positions he had espoused in the previous decade was a personal strategy very much against the current of official opinion.

Notes to Chapter Five

1   See the accounts in: Richard H Rovere, *Senator Joe McCarthy* (New York: Harcourt, Brace, Jovanovich, 1959), pp 119 ff; Richard M Fried, *Men Against McCarthy* (New York: Columbia University Press, 1976), pp 58 ff; David M Oshinsky, *A Conspiracy So Immense. The World of Joe McCarthy* (New York: The Free Press, 1983), pp 139 ff.

2   Robert P Newman, 'Lattimore and His Enemies', *Antipode* 15(1983), no 3, pp 12-26, Newman, 'Bureaucrats As Heroes. The FBI In The Age Of McCarthy', *Pitt - Supplement*, February 1982, pp 14-19, Newman, 'Clandestine Chinese Nationalist Efforts To Punish Their American Detractors', *Diplomatic History* 7(1983), no 3, pp 205-22, Newman, 'The Self-Inflicted Wound: The China White Paper of 1949', *Prologue* 14(1982), pp 141-56; Stanley I Kutler, *The American Inquisition. Justice and Injustice in the Cold War* (New York: Hill and Wang, 1982), ch 7.

3   US Congress: Senate, *Hearings on State Department Loyalty. Hearings before a subcommittee of the Committee on Foreign Relations* (Washington: US Government Printing Office, 1950), p 1761.

4   *Hearings on State Department Loyalty*, pp 92, 281.

5   *Hearings on State Department Loyalty*, pp 417-86 (Lattimore's first appearance), pp 487 ff (Budenz), pp 737 ff (Utley).

6   US Congress: Senate, *Hearings on State Department Loyalty: Report* (Washington: US Government Printing Office, report no 2108, 1950), p 74. Lattimore published a spirited account of his experiences before the Tydings committee: *Ordeal by Slander* (New York: Greenwood reprint of Little, Brown 1950 edition, 1971).

7   Max Eastman and J B Powell, 'The Fate of the World is at Stake in China', *Readers' Digest* 46(1945), June, p 15. In 1949 the House Committee on Un-American Activities, probably prompted by Kohlberg, was also keeping a file on Lattimore: Robert K Carr, *The House Committee on Un-American Activities 1945-1950* (Ithaca: Cornell University Press, 1952), p 254, 402 n.

8   On this affair see: US Congress: Senate, Committee on the Judiciary, Subcommittee to Investigate ... Internal Security ..., *The Amerasia Papers: A Clue to the Catastrophe of China* (Washington: US Government Printing Office, 1970); Anthony Kubek, *How the Far East was Lost: American Policy and the Creation of Communist China, 1941-1949* (Chicago: Regnery, 1963); John S Service, *The Amerasia Papers: Some Problems in the History of US-China Relations* (Berkeley: University of California China Research Monograph no 7, 1971). Service demolishes Kubek's tendentious editing of the *Papers*. According to Jaffe's later account, from 1930 to 1945 he was 'a close fellow-traveler of the American Communist Party': Philip J Jaffe, *The*

Rise and Fall of American Communism (New York: Horizon Press, 1975), p 12.

9   Newman, 'Lattimore and His Enemies', p 15.

10   David Harvey, 'Owen Lattimore. A Memoire', *Antipode* 15(1983), no 3, p 6. Andrew Roth's book, *Dilemma in Japan* (London: Gollancz, 1945) favoured the same punitive treatment of the Japanese Emperor advocated by Lattimore.

11   John N Thomas, *The Institute of Pacific Relations. Asian Scholars and American Politics* (Seattle: University of Washington Press, 1974); William L Holland, 'Source Materials on the Institute of Pacific Relations', *Pacific Affairs* 58 (1985-86), pp 91-7.

12   Christopher Thorne, *Allies of a Kind. The United States, Britain, and the War Against Japan, 1941-1945* (Oxford: Oxford University Press, 1978), pp 212 f, 540 f.

13   Frederick V Field, *From Right to Left. An Autobiography* (Westport, Conn: Lawrence Hill, 1983).

14   US Congress: Senate, *Institute of Pacific Relations. Hearings before the Subcommittee ... of the Committee on the Judiciary* (Washington: US Government Printing Office, 1951-2). The text occupies almost 6,000 pages. Kutler, *The American Inquisition*, pp 198-203, provides an excellent account of the hearings.

15   US Congress: Senate, *Report of the Committee on the Judiciary. Hearings held ... by the Internal Security Subcommittee* (Washington: US Government Printing Office, report no 2050, 1952), pp 223-4. The standard account of Vincent's experiences in these years is: Gary May, *China Scapegoat. The Diplomatic Ordeal of John Carter Vincent* (Washington: New Republic Books, 1979).

16   *Report of the Committee on the Judiciary*, p 226.

17   On the veracity of Budenz, see: Herbert L Packer, *Ex-Communist Witnesses* (Stanford: Stanford University Press, 1962), pp 121-77. This judgment of the proceedings is from the account by one of the counsel acting for Lattimore (though he was rarely permitted to speak): Thurman Arnold, *Fair Fights and Foul* (New York: Harcourt, Brace and Co, 1961), pp 214-27.

18   George Boas and Harvey Wheeler, *Lattimore the Scholar* (Baltimore: Boas and Wheeler, 1953).

19   Freda Utley, *The China Story* (Chicago: Regnery, 1951); John T Flynn, *The Lattimore Story* [1953], revised edition (New York: Devin-Adair, 1962). For an account of the contemporary press reaction to the McCarran hearings, see: Earl Latham, *The Communist Controversy in Washington. From the New Deal to McCarthy* (Cambridge, Mass: Harvard University Press, 1966), pp 270-84.

20   Brian Gilbert [pseud], 'New Light on the Lattimore Case', *The New Republic* 131(1954), 27 December, pp 7-12; Kutler, *The American*

Inquisition, pp 203-11; Newman, 'Lattimore and His Enemies'; Newman, 'Bureaucrats as Heroes'.

21 Harold R Isaacs, *Re-encounters in China. Notes of a Journey in a Time Capsule* (Armonk, New York: M E Sharpe, 1985), p 122; Philip J Jaffe, *The Rise and Fall of American Communism*, p 12.

22 *Hearings on State Department Loyalty*, pp 820, 853-4, 438-9.

23 *Hearings on State Department Loyalty*, pp 459-62.

24 *Hearings on State Department Loyalty*, p 459.

25 *Hearings on State Department Loyalty*, p 440.

26 *Hearings on State Department Loyalty*, p 859.

27 *Hearings on State Department Loyalty*, pp 462, 860, 842-3.

28 *Institute of Pacific Relations. Hearings before the Subcommittee ... of the Committee on the Judiciary*, p 3584.

29 *Institute of Pacific Relations. Hearings before the Subcommittee ... of the Committee on the Judiciary*, pp 3634-5; 'The Historical Setting of Inner Mongolian Nationalism' [1936], *Studies in Frontier History*, p 454.

30 *Institute of Pacific Relations. Hearings before the Subcommittee ... of the Committee on the Judiciary*, pp 4522-7. On the Soviet view of the status of the Mongolian People's Republic at that time, see: G M Friters, *Outer Mongolia and Its International Position* (London: Allen & Unwin, 1951), pp 142-50.

31 Personal interview with Owen Lattimore, Cambridge, 19 March 1982; *Institute of Pacific Relations. Hearings before the Subcommittee ... of the Committee on the Judiciary*, p 3328.

32 *Institute of Pacific Relations. Hearings before the Subcommittee ... of the Committee on the Judiciary*, pp 722 ff; *Solution in Asia*, pp 27, 187-9.

33 *Institute of Pacific Relations. Hearings before the Subcommittee ... of the Committee on the Judiciary*, p 5667.

34 *Institute of Pacific Relations. Hearings before the Subcommittee ... of the Committee on the Judiciary*, pp 3387-8.

35 *Institute of Pacific Relations. Hearings before the Subcommittee ... of the Committee on the Judiciary*, pp 1663, 1613, 1591.

36 Fairbank, *Chinabound*, p 338; Boas and Wheeler, *Lattimore the Scholar*.

37 *Institute of Pacific Relations. Hearings before the Subcommittee ... of the Committee on the Judiciary*, pp 3984-5, 4014 ff.

38 *Institute of Pacific Relations. Hearings before the Subcommittee ... of the Committee on the Judiciary*, 1384; Tang Tsou, *America's Failure in China 1941-50* (Chicago: University of Chicago Press, 1963), pp 162-8.

39 *Institute of Pacific Relations. Hearings before the Subcommittee ... of the Committee on the Judiciary*, pp 1812-13, 1447-8, 1365-71.

40 *Institute of Pacific Relations. Hearings before the Subcommittee ... of the Committee on the Judiciary*, p 1012.

41 *Institute of Pacific Relations. Hearings before the Subcommittee ... of the Committee on the Judiciary*, pp 914-15.

42 *Institute of Pacific Relations. Hearings before the Subcommittee ... of the Committee on the Judiciary*, p 933.

43 *Institute of Pacific Relations. Hearings before the Subcommittee ... of the Committee on the Judiciary*, pp 2691 ff, Nicholas Poppe, *Reminiscences* (Bellingham: W Washington University, 1983), pp 214-16.

44 *Institute of Pacific Relations. Hearings before the Subcommittee ... of the Committee on the Judiciary*, p 338.

45 *Institute of Pacific Relations. Hearings before the Subcommittee ... of the Committee on the Judiciary*, p 3103.

46 *Institute of Pacific Relations. Hearings before the Subcommittee ... of the Committee on the Judiciary*, pp 329-30 (letter of 18 February 1947), p 3611 (letter of 4 March 1945).

47 K A Wittfogel and Feng Chia-sheng, *History of Chinese Society. Liao. Transactions of the American Philosophical Society* n s 36(1946) (Philadelphia: American Philosophical Society, 1949), pp 4-25. Wittfogel here acknowledges (34) Lattimore's 'unique knowledge of Chinese frontier society and history'.

48 *Institute of Pacific Relations. Hearings before the Subcommittee ... of the Committee on the Judiciary*, p 5311, cf p 5307.

49 *Institute of Pacific Relations. Hearings before the Subcommittee ... of the Committee on the Judiciary*, p 340.

50 *Institute of Pacific Relations. Hearings before the Subcommittee ... of the Committee on the Judiciary*, p 5310.

51 *Institute of Pacific Relations. Hearings before the Subcommittee ... of the Committee on the Judiciary*, pp 334-6. Wittfogel develops this point in a later work: *Oriental Despotism. A Comparative Study of Total Power* (New Haven: Yale University Press, 1957), p 410 n.

52 Tang Tsou, *America's Failure in China 1941-50*, pp 288 ff, 183 ff.

53 Warren I Cohen, 'Acheson, His Advisers, and China, 1949-1950', Dorothy Borg and Waldo Heinrichs (eds), *Uncertain Years. Chinese-American Relations, 1949-1950* (New York: Columbia University Press, 1980), pp 13-52.

54 Michael Schaller, *The US Crusade in China, 1938-1945* (New York: Columbia University Press, 1979), p 53; Barbara W Tuchman, *Sand Against the Wind: Stilwell and the American Experience in China 1911-45* (New York: Macmillan, 1970), pp 226-7.

55 J M Blum (ed), *The Price of Vision: The Diary of Henry A Wallace*, pp 311, 321.

56 US Department of State, *Foreign Relations of the United States. 1942. China*, pp 185-7.

57 John Lewis Gaddis, *Strategies of Containment. A Critical Appraisal of Postwar American National Security Policy* (New York: Oxford University Press, 1982), chapters 1-6.

58   Gaddis, *Strategies of Containment*, pp 39 f; J L Gaddis, 'The Strategic Perspective: The Rise and Fall of the "Defensive Perimeter" Concept, 1947-1951', Borg and Heinrichs (eds), *Uncertain Years*, pp 61-118.
59   Gaddis, *Strategies of Containment*, pp 142 f.
60   Gaddis, *Strategies of Containment*, p 79.

CHAPTER SIX

Chinese and World Frontiers

Lattimore was never again to exert influence in political circles in the United States, but the experiences of 1950-1954, though they exacted an immense physical and psychological toll, did not bring his work to an end. He continued to be a prolific writer, often returning to and elaborating on ideas first considered in the 1930s. He remained at Johns Hopkins until 1963, finding a home in the department of History when the Page School was liquidated, and moving to Leeds University in 1963 to become foundation professor of Chinese Studies. Following his retirement in 1970 and the death of his wife and co-worker, Eleanor, he lived first in Paris (working with his Japanese collaborator in research, Fujiko Isono) and then in Cambridge (where he became attached to King's College), before ill health forced his return to the United States to live with his son in 1985.

Three major themes have dominated his more recent writings. The history and contemporary condition of the Mongols which has been his major preoccupation will be considered in the following chapter. The present chapter will review his more speculative work on the wider historical and political impact of the frontier on civilisations and empires, and his essays on contemporary China (in which the consideration of frontier problems is prominent) many of which were occasioned or stimulated by his assumption of the Leeds chair. But first the background to both of these themes will be sketched in through a consideration of those aspects of his work of the 1940s.

Frontiers and Foreign Policy in Asia

In those books and articles published towards the end of the war Lattimore repeatedly emphasised that the old colonial era in Asia was drawing to a close, and that policy makers in the United States would need to abandon the old maritime view of Asia which was an inheritance from that era if they were successfully to take the measure of the new Asia.[1] The postwar era was destined to be one dominated by land rather than sea powers, and consequently developments in the Asian hinterland would be of much greater moment than events on the Pacific rim.[2] The 'success' of the Soviet policy towards the national minorities in that portion of the Asian hinterland which lay within the USSR was thus of much greater than local significance.[3] In 1945, as has been shown, Lattimore expressed the view that Soviet Russia exercised a potent 'power of attraction' for the peoples of Inner Asia by virtue of the material progress and 'democracy' to be found in the Central Asian Soviet republics. The fundamental orientation of Soviet policy, Lattimore asserted, was the principal cause of this power of attraction, though the continuous geographical relationship between Russia and Asia gave even the empire of Tsarist times much greater integration than was seen in the other European empires. The strength of the Soviet power of attraction is particularly manifest in relations with Mongolia. These establish a 'standard' deserving of 'careful and respectful study' if Soviet influence is to be matched or emulated by others (here Lattimore has China particularly in mind).[4]

Having returned to Johns Hopkins late in 1944, Lattimore embarked on a number of studies of Inner Asian frontier regions which were to have their fruits in collaborative publications particularly on Sinkiang, the most important of which was *Pivot of Asia*.[5] Of the greatest importance for his own intellectual development was a comparative study Lattimore made using a diversity of Russian sources of the expansion of the Chinese and Russian empires. Published in 1947 this was to provide a new basis for all his subsequent discussion of the history of and contemporary developments in Inner Asia.[6] The lack of a clear geographical division on the Russian frontier between land suited for agriculture and steppe led from the beginning of Russian history to an interpenetration of economic, political, and social forms. The mode of life and the economic role of the principal agents of Russian expansion in the early modern period, the Cossacks, were emblematic of this interpenetration. When the spread of railways and the growth of industrialisation in Russia enabled the Tsarist empire to expand administratively it could readily incorporate a variety of peoples within its territories, often extending its power in Asia by absorbing the old ruling classes into the imperial social and political order. A greater contrast with the Chinese frontier could not be imagined. If China could not absorb and assimilate frontier peoples and habitats to the Chinese way of life these were rejected, and any political and social order which attempted to straddle the frontier was inherently unstable. The construction of railways and the extension of industrially based power by the Chinese into the frontier regions exacerbated these incompatibilities.

The Russian method of imperial expansion by 'incorporation' thus produced, by comparison with the Ch'ing empire, a far more integrated political entity. The Russian revolution, so Lattimore's argument went, reinforced this integration by introducing the additional bonds of class solidarity. In the civil war in Asiatic Russia the old ruling élite, to preserve their privileges, threw in their lot with the White forces. The Bolshevik victory was attained with the help of a good part of the 'common people' who were then able to improve their economic and social conditions by drawing upon Russian industrial power:

> As a result of the Russian Revolution a new standard has been
> established, which may be called the standard of utilization.
> Within the Russian theater of activity, under a system of
> socialization and collectivization, it is no longer adequate to speak

of 'the frontier-conquering civilization'. What we appear to have is a merging of 'the frontier' with 'civilization', and a common utilization of the total resources of the total area. This common utilization is characterized by rapid industrialization of both Russian and non-Russian societies within the Soviet political structure and by the integration of both pastoral and agricultural economics with the industrial economy.[7]

Again, but for an additional reason, the Russian association with Mongolia is of singular importance. In a manner which 'appears to resemble the Rooseveltian Good Neighbour policy' the Mongols 'were admitted to the Russian standard of common utilization of resources'. Although few countries could match the Soviet role in Asia this example demonstrated that if China was to extend her influence into the frontiers it must be upon a new basis, one consistent, Lattimore hazarded, only 'with far-reaching changes in the social fabric and political structure' of metropolitan China.[8]

In *Situation in Asia*, in addition to the recapitulation of the hypothesis of the Soviet 'power of attraction' over Asian peoples, these ideas form the basis for Lattimore's new analysis of the different types of empire to be found not only in Asia but in recent world history. According to his later recollection this position was first expounded in a lecture before a meeting of the American Historical Association in Washington in December 1948, a condensed version of which was published the following year.[9] In their respective geographical characters and methods of expansion the Russian empire was 'incorporative' and the Chinese empire was 'absorptive'; both were distinct from the 'accumulative' character of the British empire in Asia which had its origins in the military and economic command of the sea, and was conducted by an administrative and political élite who remained quite aloof from the conquered colonial subjects.[10] Lattimore's hostility towards imperialism, the major theme of the book, can thus be seen to derive from more than a naive Rooseveltian dislike of colonialism. On the one hand the age of maritime ascendancy was over, and thus the French and Dutch, as much as the British should not receive American support for an enterprise that could not be sustained. On the other, their empires were not of the kind that would permit the extension of 'the standard of utilization' already achieved in Soviet Asia to their colonial subjects. American trade and assistance alone might achieve this objective, but only if the United States took action in Asia for the right political reasons; military support for supposedly friendly despots would only recreate the conditions of the former empires and would be no match for the attractions of the Soviet example. In the Inner Asian frontier regions in particular, American civilisation was on its mettle to demonstrate the superiority of its values.

The New Power Alignment in Asia

In an important article published in 1953 Lattimore developed this analysis further to account for the historical geography of the frontiers of Inner Asia. The delimitation of these frontiers had the appearance of paradox for boundaries were drawn in a precise manner despite the fact that the areas in question were ethnographically and geographically mixed zones of sparse population. Between 1895 and 1907 the British and Russian Empires, having grown in the manner already described, came to a series of frontier agreements which reflected the diminished economic and administrative returns their expansion had by then encountered. The boundaries of Afghanistan were drawn so as to ensure that these empires had no common frontier, separate spheres of influence were agreed in Persia, and Britain's pre-eminence in Tibet found its equivalent in the Russian role in Outer Mongolia despite China's traditional suzerainty in those territories.[11]

This stabilisation, Lattimore points out, had been the basis of Mackinder's bold attempt to define the geographical foundations of the world balance of power. For Mackinder writing in 1904 the world was divided into two zones, the Eurasian land mass and the lands of the crescent around the rim of that mass. In recent times the supremacy of sea based power had extended the British Empire to dominate the lands of the crescent; now the construction of railways projected from newly industrialising Eastern Europe was resulting in a matching of this sea power by land based power. The age of Columbus had passed into history. Because the likely potential of the newly tapped resources of Asia (so remote as to be unaffected by the exertions of any sea power) was so great, if this territory fell to the possession of a single power naval forces could be constructed from this region large enough to overwhelm any power based on the crescent lands and thus rule the world. Mackinder's objective was to prevent military co-operation between Russia and Germany which would produce such a single power; to this end he advocated the maintenance of the balance of power through an Anglo-Russian alliance.[12]

Now in Lattimore's works there is a good deal of evidence that he was much influenced by the geopolitical school. The close of the era of the sea powers is a refrain in his writings first heard in his studies of Manchuria, and in 1943 he offered a trenchant critique of Nicholas Spykman (himself a critic of Mackinder's later work) on the grounds that Spykman's recommendation that the United States seek military control of the Eurasian rim was a mistaken attempt to recreate the vanished supremacy of 'Gunboat Policy'.[13] In his original analysis of 1904 Mackinder expressed the view that 'the pivot region of the world's politics' was the 'vast area of Euro-Asia which is inaccessible to ships, but in antiquity lay open to the horse riding nomads, and is to-day about to be covered with a network of railways'.[14] This statement, of course, was the inspiration for the title of Lattimore's book on Sinkiang. But it also prompted him to reconsider the geopolitics of Inner Asia in the light of the communist victory in China. The frontiers of this region, Lattimore avers, have been transformed. The old imperial powers no longer control the rim (the wars in Vietnam, Korea, and Malaya are at best holding operations) and far from the frontiers marking zones of diminishing returns they are now everywhere of vital interest to policy makers. Where communist and non-communist Asia face each other Soviet development exercises an undoubted and growing power of attraction. In the case of the Sino-Soviet frontier regions, these have become 'zones through which communication between China and Russia is imperatively necessary'. In the past the development of China took place, for the most part, near the coast. Now 'economically and strategically, China is making a right-angled turn away from the coast and toward Inner Asia' to develop the resources of the hinterland and link up with the Asian republics of the Soviet Union. Inner Asia is no longer peripheral to world politics: it is 'a frontier between revolutionary and evolutionary methods'. A new balance in Asian and world politics will only be struck if Western policy makers respond to this new situation by matching Soviet development initiatives:

> New processes of stabilization, to take the place of those that underlay the thinking of Mackinder, can only be created by deliberately initiating, on the non-Soviet side of the frontier, changes that match in their potential of growth the changes going on in Soviet territory. Only a counterbalance of change can satisfactorily replace the stabilization of inertia of half a century ago.[15]

It was this thinking which underlay Lattimore's insistence that the United States in pursuing military and strategic objectives was in danger of overlooking the more fundamental need to build friendships in Asia by encouraging and facilitating economic and social development.[16]

In one of his few writings directly concerned with policy making, Lattimore examined President Truman's 1949 'Point Four' proposal for the United States government to underwrite the investment of private capital in the underdeveloped countries. It was Truman's hope that such a scheme might perform for the Third World what the Marshall Plan aimed to provide for Europe, making American capital and technical expertise available to assist modernisation while winning influence in these countries for the West. Lattimore considered the likely political role of economic relationships with non-communist Asia, and with China. Although American prestige in Asia was high, colonialism had left a heritage of distrust of outside interference which would require careful political management to dispel. American investors, and American taxpayers, would have to accept that Point Four investment had to be directed towards those areas of the economy of the nation concerned that its government adjudged most in need of development. Investors also had to expect a time lag before they could repatriate profits, and they would have to resign themselves to eventual obsolescence as they were bought out or taken over when the nation or its capitalists were strong enough to do so. Anything less, however, would smack of the old colonialism, and it had to be the aim of the United States, thinking in terms of 'alliance' rather than 'control', to offer 'the sharing of sacrifices as well as the sharing of benefits' that an equal alliance implies. Lattimore was sure that the political benefits of enhanced world influence which would accrue to the United States would be worth the expense:

> The sacrifice, I am convinced, is worth making. Allies freely associated with the United States because they benefit by that association are worth having. Countries that are discontented with their association with the United States because they believe they are being controlled or exploited by the United States are undependable. Countries which, out of their association with the United States, develop an increasing class of modern-minded men running modern enterprises are the allies most worth having, because the most solid and sound democratic structures grow up where men who feel that they are free within their own country and independent of foreign rule join together to protect and promote their freedom by electing men of their own kind to represent them and their own government.[17]

In the case of China, the political function of economic relations presented a rather different problem to American policy makers. Although the communists were the masters of China they had drawn many others into support for their programme on the basis of their appeal to nationalist sentiment. Continued American support for the 'rump government' on Formosa, those remnants of Chiang Kai-shek's regime who had taken refuge on Taiwan, would not return the Kuomintang to the mainland but it would alienate that wide section of the population who had thrown in their lot with the communists, and provide an ideal excuse for the building of Soviet bases on the China coast. Setting aside the problem of direct diplomatic relations, which should only be resumed when it was possible to do so in a 'dignified and honorable' fashion, the United States should not obstruct the seating of Peking in the United Nations and should then open the way for 'two-way relations', economic and political, which would not drive the Chinese into a greater dependence on the Soviet Union. The ultimate aim would be to make China more like the 'third countries' of Asia, an outcome preferable from the point of view of the United States to the creation in China of reliable Soviet satellite.

Lattimore also entered a plea for the United States national effort to be co-ordinated with that of the United Nations. By the time this article was published, in July 1950, the outbreak of the Korean War in the preceding month had rendered many of these hopes politically impractical. President Truman had by then ordered (on 27 June) the United States Seventh Fleet into the Taiwan Strait to deter any attempt by the Chinese communist regime to expel Chiang Kai-shek. The entry of China into the war later that year guaranteed an American hostility towards China which was to last for twenty years, and the position taken in Washington on the third countries of Asia in the ensuing decade was to place the highest priority on enrolling them in treaty alliances aimed at the containment of communism.

The Historical Geography of Frontiers

These arguments are recapitulated and extended in two articles of the mid-1950s. Here Lattimore's project is nothing less than to develop an approach to historical geography in which the central role is accorded to the character and dynamics of the frontier.[18] In the circumstances of the time it is not surprising that this project was only sketched in the most general terms. Although Lattimore was reinstated at Johns Hopkins there was undoubted hostility towards him from some quarters in the university; others feared that too close an association with so controversial a figure would harm their careers, given the fate of many of those scholars who had originally worked with him on his Inner Asian project.

Discussing at this time the evolution of traditional China, Lattimore underlined the difference between the 'inclusive' southern frontier of the civilisation which permitted a more or less indefinite expansion of the civilisation, and the 'exclusive' northern frontier. The latter was more sharply delimited because the social and economic 'institutions' of the Chinese way of life 'were too strong to permit' adaptation towards forms of life which were more appropriate to the steppe. Lattimore offered an interpretation of the regional and frontier structure of the Chinese imperial state in terms of three contrasts of 'geographical range': the territorial limits for the state of military action, of centralised civil administration, and of economic integration. Lattimore found these to have been, in the Chinese case as in 'the whole of the Old World' prior to the fifteenth century, of progressively decreasing size. The radius of military action by the state was, at least potentially, very great, encompassing an area much larger than could be administered or was of vital importance for commerce. The ability of the state to administer an integrated empire was more limited due to the tendency towards regionalism which became manifest once a ruling dynasty had passed its early vigour. Economic integration had the shortest range for the sedentary empires, though nomads using camels grazed on the open steppe could trade profitably at considerable distances. Most commodities were produced locally, and long-distance trading though a feature of Chinese history was often political in motivation. With the differentiation of nomadic and agricultural populations in East Asia, a cycle of history began which was largely founded on these differences of range, and the fact that the former way of life permitted extensive 'lateral movement' whereby the nomads could if they wished maintain military pressure on China while eluding Chinese campaigns against them:

> For about two thousand years the rule of history was to be that great Chinese dynasties were formed in the heart of the country, moved up to the frontier with a strong momentum, enrolled nomad and semi-nomad auxiliaries, struck swiftly and at long range into the steppe, and paralyzed the nomadic society with such sudden defeats that the resulting Pax Sinica lasted for two generations or more; while the great nomad conquests were preceded by decades of gradual encroachment on the Chinese frontiers, accompanied by minor warfare among the tribes themselves and between rivals for supreme leadership.[19]

Lattimore found there to have been many parallels between the Roman and Chinese empires. Both aimed at ruling an *orbis terrarum* or *t'ien hsia* (*tian xia*) - terms 'semantically equivalent' to all of the civilised world - though ultimately from within boundaries fixed with the intention of defining a limit of expansion, with the Roman *limes* fulfilling the same functions as the Great Wall. And for the Romans the Mediterranean and Black Seas integrated their empire through water transport much as the Yangtze and Grand Canal did in imperial China. The activities of the various barbarians inhabiting the whole region between these empires exhibit many common characteristics.

European discoveries in navigation and armaments brought into being a new historical era with new types of frontiers and of colonies. In the second of these articles Lattimore again discussed the three types of empire to be found in Asia by the beginning of the present century.[20] The spread of maritime based imperialism to Asia produced rule at a distance by a small colonial élite who remained deliberately apart from the local population. Where, as in India, they became committed to economic development it was engineered so as to be integrated with British economic requirements.

Offering some prognosis on the future, given the relative decline of the maritime powers, Lattimore discerned both hopeful and worrying trends. There were now grounds for believing that some old antagonisms would disappear. Industrialisation had made feasible, for example, the economic integration of China and Mongolia, an impossibility while each relied upon the practice of a distinctive and exclusive way of life. On the other hand the strongest factor binding the Western nations together was a shared cultural identity (the strength of cultural continuities being often underrated), and as a result of the Second World War and its aftermath these nations now confronted the Soviet bloc in a geographical sense as well as in a competition for world hegemony. A third group or potential group of nations also existed in prototype of which India was the most prominent example. The frontiers between the two power blocs were unlike those of imperial China since each sought to remake the world in its image. Here the countries of the third group may yet act as mediators:

The frontiers between the American-Western and the Soviet-Chinese-Eastern groups are not of a Great Wall type for one very significant reason: each of these groups represents an institutional system of combined economic and social organization that is capable of taking over the entire world and making it an all inclusive *orbis terrarum*. The Indian type does not appear to have the capacity (or the desire) to take over the *orbis terrarum*, but it does appear to have the capacity to hold the other two groups apart, and if it should be able to do that long enough, perhaps an annealing process will become possible, integrating a world of different but reciprocating components.[21]

Once again, though for an additional reason, the countries of the Third World will have a vital role to play.

World Frontiers: a Later Exposition

The constancy of Lattimore's intellectual preoccupations may be judged by the fact that many of these historical ideas were restated twenty years later in a piece devoted to a discussion of the geography of the ancient empires. On several issues, however, Lattimore offered a more precise judgment. Within geographical parameters, we are told, human beings may choose a wide range of economic activities. Once a pattern was established 'vested interests' were created with the result that those social classes who derived most benefit from this pattern resisted its change and created institutions designed to perpetuate it. Thus the 'landlord class' of imperial China dominated the social and political institutions of the state, and resisted Chinese expansion into a terrain unsuited to intensive agriculture which would have led to 'a straining of the pattern of power in the hands of a small urban-landlord-bureaucratic élite'.[22] Again the comparison with Rome was pursued, though Lattimore pointed out that the greater diversity of the urban and rural units of the empire led to a greater diversity of trade in the Mediterranean and Black Sea arteries. The Roman empire did not possess a deep hinterland equivalent to the region south of the Yangtze and thus could not fall back when faced with barbarian onslaught.

Concerning the decline of empires Lattimore now maintained that both the Chinese and Roman empires fell to barbarian invasions 'because they could not establish mutually satisfactory balances of trade' with the nomadic confederations beyond their frontiers. Here Lattimore came close to accepting the idea that the emergence among the nomads of state forms could be explained in terms of the possibilities open to their leaderships of plunder. Barbarian chiefs could accumulate a surplus of goods not readily exchanged with their neighbours; they commanded followers whose everyday tools and skills could readily be turned to warlike purposes. In the case of China the

113

exchange of 'gifts' and 'tribute' with the nomads disguised the fact that 'barbarian chiefs used military pressure to obtain more trade than would have resulted from the ordinary operation of supply and demand'.[23]

China and the Chinese Revolution

In a number of writings of the early 1960s Lattimore set down his synoptic view of some of the major themes in Chinese history. For the most part this view was in accordance with his previous work,[24] though on several significant topics he introduced new arguments. In these writings he was particularly concerned to underscore the profound effects of imperialism on early modern China. In Lattimore's view imperialism biased development towards the coastal regions and foreign interests. In time, however, it generated a national reaction sufficiently strong as to embrace significant elements among the commercial classes; it also prompted the emergence of a communist movement whose prolonged contest with the bureaucratic and mercantile interests of the coast forced it to accommodate a variety of allies united under a predominantly nationalist platform. This unique Chinese path to communism explained the differences that had developed between the Chinese communists and their erstwhile brethren in Moscow. On the upheavals of the later Maoist period however, Lattimore - consistent with his views of the later 1940s - found continued American hostility to be the chief cause.

In his most considered piece on pre-revolutionary Chinese history Lattimore offered an account of the changes brought about by industrialism and the penetration of foreign capital.[25] There had been no indigenous development of industrialisation because of the particular social and political structure of traditional China in which the ethos and interests of 'the landlord class' prevailed. The spread of imperialism into China in the nineteenth century had consequences which obstructed modernisation and delayed the appearance of social and political forces with the inclination and power to harness modern industry to serve the cause of national independence. Foreign domination of Chinese railways tied development more to the needs of foreign trade than to domestic development. The Treaty Port system created a new middle class familiar with industry and trade but based for the most part in foreign concessions where they could play no political role. The Treaty Ports also offered refuge and immunity from Chinese justice for defeated warlords, and after the formation of the Nanking government provided a home for the 'bureaucratic monopolists' who were the chief beneficiaries of Kuomintang rule. When, after the Western hold on China had been weakened by the impact of the First World War, a 'national bourgeoisie' emerged to challenge their 'compradore' peers, the former had also to deal with the hostility of the foreign powers who policed the coastal enclaves:

Through the Treaty Ports, the industrial impact was concentrated on a tight geographical pattern of targets. Chinese who set out to master the industrial system found that in order to do so they had also to capture the politically fortified foreign positions of economic privilege in the Treaty Ports; but if, seeking a political support of their own, they appealed to Chinese nationalism, their demands were rejected by the foreigners as unjustifiably 'anti-foreign'. There followed a long chain of coalitions and splits. Businessmen and bankers of the new middle class and intellectuals of the new, Western-trained intelligentsia would shift to the Left. Later some of them, carrying in the Western press the label of 'dangerous radicals' would shift back to the Right - Chiang Kai-shek is an example, but always there would be a rallying of new 'moderate' recruits to the Left, as in the National Salvation Movement of the 1930s.[26]

In 1949 with the capture of the coastal cities by the communists a few capitalists fled, but the great bulk of the new classes and strata fostered by industrialisation stayed on to assist, for reasons of 'nationalistic pride', the new phase of modernisation that had begun.

In presenting this interpretation of the impact of foreign economic activity on the political and social fabric of China Lattimore was putting forward an argument which had long been popular with many Chinese intellectuals and which would soon be given greater currency in the 1960s by revisionist new left interpretations of the American role in world politics. Though such a broad hypothesis is difficult to test, the trend of much recent scholarship is to conclude, however, that imperialism as a force in Chinese history was neither as pervasive nor as deleterious as was once supposed. Historians have presented a good deal of evidence for the resilience of the traditional economy, and for the ability of the imperial government to ignore or obstruct foreign economic activity in Chinese domains. Indeed, some have even argued that the net effect of contact with world commerce was to transfer to China both capital and technology otherwise unobtainable.[27] Here it may be supposed that Lattimore was generalising from his former frontier experiences and his admitted dislike of the ethos of the Treaty Ports rather than submitting the evidence to any new scrutiny.

Chinese Communism

On the reasons for the communist victory in 1949 Lattimore argued in 1960 that the Chinese revolution was something of an exception to the pattern of revolutions in Asia and elsewhere. Rather than being the result largely of the weaknesses of the previous system, the triumph of the Communist Party was the product of a long struggle against a variety of opponents during which the leadership had to experiment with new state forms and mobilise new allies (particularly the peasantry), characteristics that set the Chinese revolution apart also from that in Soviet Russia and which explain the present divergence of view between the two communist states.[28] So far, then, it was Lattimore's view that the revolution in China was as much national as social, though the ideology of the Communist Party facilitated the recognition of peasant grievances thereby winning many of that class to the Party's programme.

With the advent of the Cultural Revolution, Lattimore, like many commentators on China sought, from the fragmentary evidences available, to offer an interpretation of these momentous events. It is not altogether surprising, given his personal experiences as much as his previous strictures on the conduct of the United States in Asia, that he should lay a good deal of the blame for this upheaval on the American government.

Lattimore stressed, in a series of lectures given in Sweden in 1968, the independent character of Chinese Marxism. The leaders of the revolution came to Marxism for their own reasons and not as surrogates of Moscow. They were therefore able to evolve their own method, harnessing the 'natural instinctive nationalism of the peasants in North China' in the fight with the Japanese. Lattimore offered an account of this method, Mao Tse-tung's 'mass line', which stressed its allegedly pragmatic and populist features:

[Mao's] conclusion is that if the communists wanted to put themselves at the head of a revolutionary movement in China, they must begin by following what the people wanted. Only after convincing the people that they were going in the direction that the people wanted could they put themselves at the head of the movement. This has remained characteristic of the revolutionary method of Mao Tse-tung. Throughout his career he seems to have had a conviction that the most downtrodden class in China, the peasantry, had an instinctive knowledge of what was in their own interest, the general direction in which they should move.[29]

It was the job of professional revolutionaries also, according to Mao's view, to refine and sophisticate the methods adopted by the peasants to achieve their ends. At several points Lattimore emphasised Mao's pragmatism, reflected in his belief that 'if the theories and the facts do not agree then it is probably the theory that needs some adjustment'. There is, of course, some irony in this claim. Although the post-Mao leadership in China now interpret their ideology in this spirit, claiming justification in Mao's dictum 'seek truth from facts', Mao himself is criticised for the dogmatic influence he exerted in the later years of his life.[30]

On the difficulties involved in making sense of the Cultural Revolution, Lattimore offered some caustic remarks on the pervasive influence of 'an American filter' on almost all expert and media opinion. He stated the view that the Cultural Revolution was not a chaotic aberration but was built on the previous experience of the communist movement in China and was addressed towards dealing with internal and external threats to the revolution and its goals. Public criticism of the Party, a practice which distinguished Chinese communism from the Soviet prototype, could be traced back to the techniques of mobilisation used at Yenan. The appearance of the Red Guards and the turmoil of the succeeding years could be understood as a response to the likelihood that, frustrated by the indecisive nature of the conflict in Vietnam, the United States would attack China. Lattimore linked the Sino-Soviet split to the different paths to victory taken by the Chinese and Russian revolutionaries. Whereas the Bolsheviks were only the beneficiaries of an unpopular war, the Chinese communists were patriotic participants in a long national struggle for survival. Echoes of this difference of historical experience could be detected in the internal political conflict between Mao and Liu Shao-ch'i (Liu Shaoqi) on the best means to respond to an inevitably aggressive imperialism. Whereas Liu favoured turning back to the Soviets for modern armaments (and accepting Soviet leadership as the political price), it was the view of Mao Tse-tung and Lin Piao (Lin Biao) that an American attack would force the revolution back to the Yenan stage: the country should therefore make itself ready for a decentralised struggle waged by an armed and mobilised population. The need perceived by the Maoists to preserve the gains of the revolution and fight the growth of bureaucracy was the background to the complementary great debate that was being conducted in education. The present preference given to students of worker and peasant origin was the result of the previous system of equal educational opportunities favouring the sons and daughters of 'the old bourgeoisie'. As Lattimore candidly observed in an article written at the same time, in view of the grave external threat confronting them, the Chinese could not afford to place the children of the old ruling classes in positions of power lest they prove unreliable followers of the new order:

> If there are to be any defectors or faint-hearted resisters, it is
> feared they will be of this origin. This is what lies behind the
> closing of schools and colleges for drastic reorganisation, which
> has accompanied the encouragement of revolutionary fervour,
> with its emphasis on youth, among the Red Guards.[31]

Where others saw chaos and disorder, Lattimore stressed the practical and indeed allegedly educational aspects of the Cultural Revolution:

> I suggest that often, by dropping such labels as marxism,
> communism and so on one can analyze a situation in a very
> practical way and show that the communist leadership in China, in
> spite of the disturbances we see in the Great Cultural Revolution,
> in the Red Guards, and in the reported controversies among
> leaders, are dealing more with hard facts and tough problems than
> with cloudy ideological obsessions; and the people themselves,
> through their mass organisations, are getting a political education.

This is more than being indoctrinated by a privileged élite. It is, in the newly fashionable phrase, 'participatory politics'.[32]

It should be noted also that Lattimore's assessment of the grounds for what he took to be the widespread peasant support for the communist regime underwent a significant change. Whereas in 1948 he understood the demands of the Chinese peasantry to be 'the private ownership of land and the right to be represented in government',[33] now he did not attribute the deficiencies of the programme of mass land collectivization in the commune movement - it 'fell short' of Chinese hopes but 'certainly was not a total collapse' - to the repression of those demands. Rather, the prestige of the communist cadres in the rural areas was apparently so high due to their role in the civil war with the Kuomintang that their peasant followers launched the communal experiment of 1958 and 1959 with an excess of zeal. The problems that resulted were 'not due to resistance but to over-enthusiasm'. In the long run important lessons were learned, just as in the contemporaneous Great Leap Forward concerning which movement Lattimore offers a similar assessment.[34] These sentiments run parallel, to a significant extent, with his view (to be considered in the next chapter) that the collectivisation programme mounted by the communists in Mongolia in the early 1930s failed due to a similar excess of indigenous zeal.

Although the historiography of the Cultural Revolution shows in retrospect that many who were at least as well acquainted with the country as Lattimore affirmed similar sentiments, his readiness to embrace what is now known to have been an episode characterised by chaos and blood letting is a measure of his deep disillusion with what he regarded as the wrong turn made in American Asian policy in the 1950s. What is most noteworthy in Lattimore's argument, from the point of view of his intellectual biography, is the vehemence with which America was blamed for precipitating the present crisis in Asia. Whereas Soviet expansion in the postwar era more or less matched 'the maximum frontiers of the old Tsarist empire', and the People's Republic of China conformed (with the exception of Mongolia) to the boundaries of the Manchu empire, the United States had enlarged the sphere of its control to the Pacific littoral of Asia. Showing in Vietnam that they intended to maintain their control of this sphere using war as a means if necessary, it was not surprising that China should conclude that a further 'escalation' may have brought United States forces to her territory. In Asia it was America rather than the communist bloc who had taken the initiative:

> Against [the] fact that both China and Russia represent on the whole the ... stable ... restoration of old frontiers there is the striking contrast that today, after World War II, the power of the USA is to be found in areas enormously distant from America, where it never existed before. We have US garrisons and US bases in South Korea, while neither Russians nor Chinese have troops in North Korea; US garrisons and bases in Japan and Okinawa (which has been in part detached from Japanese

118

sovereignty); in the Philippines; in Taiwan (where the Chinese are prevented from asserting their sovereignty, once promised to them by America); in South Vietnam, where there is a huge American army, while there are no Chinese troops in North Vietnam; in Thailand (actively used as a base for bombing Vietnam) - and so on. Where, then, is the expansionism, where is the 'domino effect'?[35]

Now, setting aside the question of Soviet dominance in Eastern Europe, this was a curious argument unless one accepts that the creation of the Tsarist empire was a largely benign exercise for the peoples of Asia thus encompassed and unless one maintains also that the American role in Asia has been played out despite the wishes of all the Asian peoples and governments concerned and against their interests. In fact Lattimore had accepted both of these premises for twenty years, though he had never stated the implications of this view in quite such forthright terms before. He had also long been persuaded that the American view of China had always been founded upon misunderstandings. The Americans imagined that their refusal to seek concessions on the China coast in the nineteenth century had won for them a special affection with the Chinese, whereas the Chinese knew that America was just as much as the European powers a beneficiary of the Treaty Port system, a hypocrisy compounded by American trade in strategic goods with Japan in the 1930s. From 'sentimentality' the American perception had veered to hostility when post-war hopes of China's role as the special friend of the United States in Asia had been dashed. Events since that time had only confirmed that these misunderstandings remained.[36]

Contemporary Chinese and Asian frontiers

The reappearance of frontier disputes in the later years of the People's Republic provided the occasion for comment from Lattimore on their basis in history. On the Sino-Soviet border clashes of 1969 he found that neither in the treaty of Nerchinsk of 1689 - 'the only equal, or non-unequal treaty signed by China' - nor in the later Russian annexation of the maritime region beyond the Ussuri River did the Russians acquire 'territory inhabited by Chinese or effectively ruled from Peking'. Rather, the present boundary between the two powers is largely the result of the mutual expansion of the Tsarist and Manchu empires in regions lightly populated by peoples of neither nation. On this frontier itself, therefore, 'there is no *casus belli*' and such incidents as there have been are more a reflection of the hostility between the two regimes.[37] This argument is certainly to give the Russians the benefit of the doubt for their acquisition in 1858 of all the territory north of the Amur River. As a result of the Taiping rebellion and the Arrow War the attention of the Chinese government was directed elsewhere, and there was little evidence of effective

Chinese control of those regions any distance from the bank of the river itself. Nevertheless this territory had been recognised as Chinese in 1689, and even in 1858 (as Lattimore pointed out) it was still proposed that the region south of the river and east of the Ussuri was to be held jointly by both empires. The weakness of the Russian position at that time and in 1969 is perhaps reflected in the recent Soviet proposal to allow the Chinese undisputed sovereignty over the islands on their side of the main channel of the Amur and Ussuri Rivers. It was a dispute over one of the largest of these islands - Chenpao (Zhenbao, Damansky) - which had precipitated the worst of the clashes in the latter year.[38]

In 1972, as part of efforts by the Chinese government to build bridges to the United States by inviting individuals thought to be 'old friends of China' for tours of their country, Lattimore spent two full months revisiting frontier regions from Manchuria to Sinkiang. For the most part his comments, in a lecture delivered to the Royal Geographical Society, on the economic and educational development of these areas were favourable. He also found the national minorities making significant progress in assuming positions of responsibility in the administration of their areas, and his mildly critical comments on the dismemberment of the Inner Mongolian Autonomous Region are balanced by the remark that the many changes experienced by the Mongols in China 'are definitely for the better'. But he did find fault with the official nationalities doctrine which claimed that China was and had always been a multi-nationality state. This would lead to what Lattimore regarded as the unlikely historical claim that the Mongol conquest of China was the result of a 'civil war'; it would also justify the charge that Russian and Soviet control of many North and East Asian peoples amounted to the imperialist annexation of regions that should be part of China. Lattimore's companion on the trip Fujiko Isono suggested to their Chinese hosts that instead of these inflated historical claims the present Chinese regime should begin with the conditions agreed under the 'equal' treaty of Nerchinsk, a suggestion approved at a dinner meeting, according to Lattimore's account, by Premier Chou En-lai (Zhou Enlai).[39]

Following the Chinese punitive invasion of Vietnam in 1979 Lattimore offered a more critical account of this nationalities doctrine. It was a fact that many of the northern peoples saw the Ch'ing empire as a Manchu rather than a Chinese entity, and owed their loyalty to its rulers rather than to a Chinese state. It was also true that the Great Wall frontier and the lack of Chinese cultural influence beyond it signified the superficiality of Chinese control of that portion of Inner Asia they held in the nineteenth century. In 1911, therefore, Tibetans and Mongols should have been permitted 'to go their own way'. This, of course, is in sharp contrast to the incorporative and non-racial character of imperial Russian expansion which was one of Lattimore's enduring themes. So too was the permeable and indefinite nature of China's southern boundary which was manifest in the strong cultural influence exerted on the lands of Indochina. This latter point, according to Lattimore, lay behind the current Chinese attempts to chastise Vietnam, for this region was taken to be within China's sphere:

> Although the Chinese did not claim the direct rule of Indochina, they were fully aware of the range and force of their prestige. They took it for granted that Indochina came within the sphere of their cultural and intellectual hegemony, and entitled them to ascendancy in judging questions of political philosophy.[40]

At least some of the old characteristics of the Chinese frontier were thus to be seen in events of the present.

Lattimore's more recent hostility towards China, at least regarding the question of the national minorities, can only be followed with reference to his contemporaneous work on and experiences in Mongolia (the subject of the following chapter). In the same article Lattimore had a few good words to say for those Cambodian communists who wished to return to the historical 'legacy' of Ho Chi Minh - the unity of the Indochinese peoples - and as might be expected attributed most of the blame for the Cambodian tragedy to the strategy of Nixon and Kissinger. The Pol Pot era was not the outcome of a communist revolution but a 'medieval *Jacquerie*'. And the savagery of a formerly gentle people was the product of 'an American-made situation'.[41] Such was the cost of American policy makers giving the highest priority to strategic and military objectives in Asia. Lattimore evidently felt that his warnings of thirty years previously, though ignored, had been well founded.

Notes to Chapter Six

1   *America and Asia*, pp 35 f.
2   'The Inland Crossroads of Asia', pp 122 f.
3   'Minorities in the Soviet Far East', p 158.
4   *Solution in Asia*, pp 134 f, 144.
5   The most important is *Pivot of Asia*. See also 'Sinkiang Survey'.
6   'Inner Asian Frontiers: Chinese and Russian Margins of Expansion', pp 134-59.
7   'Inner Asian Frontiers: Chinese and Russian Margins of Expansion', p 157.
8   'Inner Asian Frontiers: Chinese and Russian Margins of Expansion', p 159.
9   'The New Political Geography of Inner Asia' [1952/3], *Studies in Frontier History*, p 174 n. The published text is: 'The Opening of Asia', *Atlantic Monthly* 183 (March 1949), pp 29-33.
10 *Situation in Asia*, pp 14-19.
11 'The New Political Geography of Inner Asia', pp 165-79.
12 H J Mackinder, 'The Geographical Pivot of History', *The Geographical Journal* XXIII (1904), pp 421-44.
13 *America and Asia*, pp 35-8. Lattimore was commenting on: Nicholas J Spykman, *America's Strategy in World Politics* (New York: Harcourt, Brace and Co, 1942); see also his *The Geography of the Peace* (New York: Harcourt, Brace and Co, 1944).
14 Mackinder, 'The Geographical Pivot of History', p 434.
15 'The New Political Geography of Inner Asia', p 179.
16 'Battle of the Corridors', pp 70-1.
17 'Point Four and the Third Countries', *Annals of the American Academy of Political and Social Science* 270 (July 1950), pp 4-5.
18 'The Frontier in History' [1955/6], *Studies in Frontier History*, pp 469-91; 'Inner Asian Frontiers: Defensive Empires and Conquest Empires' [1957], *Studies in Frontier History*, pp 501-13.
19 'The Frontier in History', pp 485-6.
20 'Inner Asian Frontiers: Defensive Empires and Conquest Empires', pp 509-12. See also on the spread of the Chinese empire, 'An Inner Asian Approach to the Historical Geography of China' [1947/57], *Studies in Frontier History*, pp 492-500.
21 'The Frontier in History', p 491.
22 'Geography and the Ancient Empires', in M T Larsen (ed), *Power and Propaganda: A Symposium on Ancient Empires* (Copenhagen Studies in Assyriology vol 7, Copenhagen: Akademisk Forlag, 1979), p 37. These themes are also considered in a paper delivered in 1978 to a meeting in Birmingham of the Congress of Byzantinists: 'The Nomads and South Russia', *APXEION ΠΟΝΤΟΥ* (Athens, 1979), pp 193-200.

23   'Geography and the Ancient Empires', p 39.

24   In his inaugural lecture at Leeds, Lattimore records his agreement with the hypothesis of Joseph Needham that the development of Chinese science was retarded by the failure of the merchant class to prevail in developing capitalist economic relations against the strong hand of government: *From China Looking Outward* (Leeds; Leeds University Press, 1964), pp 13-14.

25   'The Industrial Impact on China, 1800-1950', *First International Conference of Economic History: Proceedings* (1960), pp 103-13.

26   'The Industrial Impact on China, 1800-1950', p 113.

27   For an excellent account of recent scholarship on imperialism in China, see: Paul A Cohen, *Discovering History in China. American Historical Writing on the Recent Chinese Past* (New York: Columbia University Press, 1984), pp 97-148.

28   *The Legacy of Empire in Asia*, Danforth Foundation Lectures no 9 (Greenville: East Carolina College, 1960).

29   *History and Revolution in China*, Scandinavian Institute of Asian Studies Monograph Series no 3 (Lund: Studentlitteratur, 1970), p 11.

30   See, Deng Xiaoping, 'Mao Zedong Thought must be correctly understood as an integral whole', *Selected Works of Deng Xiaoping* (Beijing: Foreign Languages Press, 1984), p 55-60. By the end of the following year, 1978, Deng's interpretation of Mao had won the day, as is indicated by the adoption of the slogan 'practice is the sole criterion for testing truth' at the Central Committee plenum of December: 'Communiqué of the Third Plenary Session of the 11th Central Committee', *Peking Review* 21(1978) no 52, p 15.

31   'China and the Ugly Americans', *New Statesman* 73(1967), 24 February, p 253.

32   *History and Revolution in China*, p 14.

33   'The Chessboard of Power and Politics', p 182.

34   *History and Revolution in China*, pp 31, 33.

35   *History and Revolution in China*, p 41.

36   'China: the American mystique', *The Listener* 72(1964), no 1853, 1 October, pp 491-4.

37   'Russo-Chinese Imperialism', *New Statesman* 77(1969), 21 March, pp 396-7. As John Stephan has pointed out, Chinese rule in these regions in the Yuan, Ming, and Ch'ing dynasties extended even as far as northern Sakhalin: J J Stephan, *Sakhalin. A History* (Oxford: Oxford University Press, 1971), pp 19-30.

38   'Mikhail Gorbachyov's speech at ceremony in Vladivostok', *Soviet News* no 6335, 30 July 1986, p 341.

39   'Return to China's Northern Frontier', *The Geographical Journal* CXXXIX(1973), pp 233-42.

40   'China's Historical Hegemony', *Nation* 108(1979), 17 March, p 276.

41   This interpretation of events in Cambodia is to be found in: William
     Shawcross, *Sideshow. Kissinger, Nixon and the Destruction of Cambodia*
     (New York: Simon and Schuster, 1979).

CHAPTER SEVEN

Mongol Civilisation, Past and Present

From the 1950s onwards Lattimore's chief preoccupation has been with the Mongols. Although he occupied a chair in Chinese studies at Leeds University from 1963 to 1970 his interest in the Mongols in no way diminished, indeed he was able to introduce a Mongolian studies programme into his new department, bringing to Britain one of his former collaborators at Johns Hopkins, Urgunge Onon, to assist with teaching. Even during the most difficult days of the McCarthy inspired persecution Lattimore found time to work (with Onon) on a translation of a Mongol biography of the first leader of socialist Mongolia, Sukebator (Süukhbaatar), publishing it with a lengthy introduction in 1955.[1] With the dismissal of the perjury charges against him, and the resumption of his teaching duties at Johns Hopkins, Lattimore undertook a fresh study of Western historical materials and commentary on the nomads in general and the Mongols in particular, the fruits of which he published in a series of articles over the next ten years.

In 1961 Lattimore's relationship with the Mongols took a new turn as a result of a visit he was able to make with his wife to the Mongolian People's Republic. The Lattimores had attended, in 1960, a gathering of the International Congress of Orientalists in Moscow. Among the Mongolian delegation was Natsagdorj (Nachukdorji), a member of the Mongolian Academy of Sciences and the author of the life of Sukebator Lattimore had previously translated. During the meeting the Mongolian delegation extended an invitation on behalf of the Academy of Sciences for Lattimore to visit their country, an invitation he was able to take up in the following year.[2] From that visit came a popular account of the history and present condition of the Mongols, *Nomads and Commissars*. This account evidently pleased his hosts for he was able to return on three further occasions in that decade, in 1969 being granted the rare honour of induction as a full member of the Academy of Sciences.[3] On the death of his wife, as they were travelling to the United States in 1970 to live in retirement, the solicitude of the Mongols was such that he was offered permanent residence anywhere in the country.[4] Though Lattimore did not accept this offer he returned to the Mongolian People's Republic on nine occasions in the 1970s, and was awarded the state decoration of the Order of the Golden Nail (the Polar Star) in 1979.

Though he laboured long and hard on the translation and editing of the political memoirs and autobiography of his saintly friend the Dilowa, a work eventually brought out with the assistance of Fujiko Isono in 1982, in this final phase of his career Lattimore devoted most of his time to teaching and to generating a wider popular and scholarly interest in Mongolia and Mongolian studies. He also devoted a good deal of time, through translations and commentary, to introducing to an international audience the best of contemporary Mongol scholarship. In time his reputation in America as a scholar outlasted and overcame his political denigration in the McCarthy era, and his pioneering role in his subject on both sides of the Atlantic was such that he eventually became Honorary President both of the Anglo-Mongolian Society and of the Mongolia Society of the United States.

In his writings of this time, though he repeats many of his ideas and arguments of former years, he does develop new understandings of historical and contemporary issues in Mongolian studies. Under the stimulus of Soviet and Mongol Marxist analyses he tackles the problem of 'feudalism' in Mongolian history, and the related question of the role of religion in late mediaeval times. He also devotes some attention to the course and character of the Mongolian revolution, and the relationship between the Mongols and Soviet Russia. In discussing these questions in more recent times he makes a point of introducing material from Mongol scholarship which, he complains, is too little known even by some of those writing on Mongolia.

Feudalism in Mongol History

Despite having been the recipient of criticism from Wittfogel for his use of the term 'feudal' - according to Wittfogel to describe Asiatic societies as feudal was to accept a key Marxist hypothesis against the evidence, and thus to signal theoretical subservience to Moscow - Lattimore offered his speculations on the applicability of the term to Inner Asian nomadic societies in a lengthy piece published in 1954. Here the influence of Russian and Soviet scholarship, particularly the work of Vladimirtsov and Yushkov is apparent. As has already been pointed out, Lattimore's reading of such sources had already led him to a reassessment of the differing characters of the nineteenth century empires in Asia. Regarding the Russian contribution to the study of feudalism, Lattimore remarked years later that he was sufficiently impressed by the attempt of Yushkov to develop a comparative study of feudal institutions to translate his article of 1946 while at Johns Hopkins.[5]

Lattimore postulates that for two thousand years steppe societies were subject to two feudalising tendencies. Although these for a period produced 'frontier feudalism' in those societies historical and geographical factors both prevented their transition to fully feudal social and economic formations and also ensured periodic partial regressions back towards tribalism.[6] The first tendency had its roots in the organisation adopted for expeditions to plunder the agricultural population of the neighbouring agricultural regions of China. The proceeds of plunder, in strengthening the nomads, made possible as well as attractive the formation of leagues larger than the traditional tribal or clan organisations of these peoples. Devices of fictive kinship enlarged the original clan, but the crucial device was the creation of the *nukur* (friend, or

126

companion) relationship through which a man could attach himself to a chief not his kinsman. Lattimore points out the etymological identity of this term with others found legitimising similar practices in contemporaneous feudalisms, though he does not find this in itself sufficient evidence for the interpretation of these leagues as feudal. The situation became transformed, he claims, upon the conquest of China (when it occurred) by one of these leagues.

Such a conquest led to the creation of truly feudal institutions. Some associates of the chieftain garrisoned the agricultural regions of China, their rule resting upon both their command of military levies supported by the peasant population, and the co-operation of tradition administrators and élites. Others in the border regions, entrusted with the command of nomadic military reserves, began to create feudal domains for themselves in the agricultural regions under their control. In the far steppe those of the original league who remained imitated as far as possible the new style of life of the conquering élite, importing where they could farmers and artisans and developing a taste for the commodities of advanced civilisation. None of these institutions, however, was stable. The original unity of the league evaporated with the passing of generations. Detached from their military levies on the borders the original conquerors in the metropolitan regions were unseated by rebellions or became absorbed by the original and far more numerous population. The border nobles took service under the new rulers, or abandoned their domains for the steppe. The more distant nomads reverted to the cycle of warfare and plunder which gave rise to the original conquest. As Lattimore points out, if this analysis is accepted then the chosen subject of Wittfogel's major contribution to Sinology - a discussion of the Liao, a dynasty of nomadic origins which ruled North China and adjacent parts of Inner Asia between 907 and 1125 - is one in which feudal relations should play a major part whereas for reasons of contemporary politics they are ignored.[7]

Feudal institutions were also created when a Chinese dynasty of sufficient vigour enrolled nomadic chieftains as feudatories in bordering regions in order to create a military shield round the core of the empire. In the long run these institutions were as unstable as those created by nomadic conquerors in China proper. The loyalty of the nomadic auxiliaries could not be guaranteed, and in periods of imperial turmoil they could turn against their overlord either on their own account or in the company of more distant tribesmen. If this did not occur there was, nevertheless, a constant temptation for such border feudatories to encourage agriculture and Chinese settlement in their domains in order to enjoy the greater revenues produced, thus destroying their military function.

From his writings of this period it is evident that Lattimore found the term 'feudalism' least applicable to the society of those nomads who had minimal contact with sedentary civilisations. The society of the pastoral nomads was one which exhibited an extreme of mobility in property and persons. Insofar as feudalism implies a foundation in landed property and the immobility of vassals enfeoffed with this property on condition of loyal service, such mobility would appear to preclude genuinely feudal relations. Lattimore therefore has little sympathy with the mainstream Soviet approach to this question:

> I have never been able to accept the Soviet model of 'nomadic feudalism', even when it is modified as 'patriarchal feudalism', mainly because the Soviet scholars are so much obsessed with working out theories of what the control of land must have been, asserting *a priori* that land is the determining kind of feudal property, that they neglect the significance of mobile four-footed property.[8]

In an important discussion published in 1961 of approaches to nomadic history, Lattimore offers further comment on the Soviet view that nomadic societies could exhibit feudal features.[9] Despite a renewed discussion in historical circles in the 1950s he finds there to have been little advance over the argument of Koz'min in the 1930s that the nobles in these societies controlled the territory and thus the common nomad was merely a peasant. But he is evidently in sympathy with the minority view of S E Tolybekov that under nomadic conditions the superfluity of land negates its usual role as a part of the means of production, and that such feudal tendencies as may appear in nomadic societies may be expected to derive from their relations with sedentary states rather than from their own internal dynamics. As to his own views, Lattimore offers a characterisation of nomadic societies which includes a discussion of the extent to which feudal relations may be found therein.

In this discussion, Lattimore advances the view that nomadic societies are set apart in history by the mobility of the population and the livestock upon which they primarily depend. Title to land may vary from common ownership and use through right only to passage of livestock to permanent division and possession. As to whether ownership of land or livestock is primary for the control of the society, this again (*contra* 'recent Marxist writers') is a question of period and circumstances. A given body of people may have so little connection with a piece of territory that they may prefer migration or flight to domination from outside. Relations with a sedentary empire whether through conquest or defeat may, conversely, lead to the according of exclusive rights of settlement to particular bodies of people under specified leaders on condition of loyal military service. Under these latter conditions 'we are certainly entitled to talk of feudalism, or of the beginnings of feudalism'. On relations between chiefs and subordinates, the factor of mobility led to certain unique features in nomadic societies. In periods of warfare the loyalty of retainers could not be ensured in the same way as in sedentary societies, though attempts were made by holding whole groups responsible for the conduct of their individual members. Attachment to a major empire transformed these relations which became more stratified. But such attachment was not likely to be an enduring phenomenon. Nomad history in sum is a series of cycles, 'alternating phases of centralization and decentralization', in which the forces within nomadic society interact with those of their sedentary neighbours.

In a work devoted to one of the 'centralizing' phases of Mongol history,[10] Lattimore explains how Chinggis Khan 'imposed a feudal unity on all the Mongol tribes'. Chinggis undermined the old practice of *anda*, the swearing of 'blood loyalty' to one putatively one's kinsman by a remote ancestor, a device appropriate to an era of clan warfare but one which obfuscated the issue of leadership, by substituting for it that of *nukur*, or allegiance to a superior not one's kinsman. He was able to use the long standing existence of tribes subordinate to his own for his new purposes, but he was forced to destroy the convention of the 'double tribe', a permanent alliance between different clans each with its own chiefs, which again was inconsistent with obedience to his leadership alone. From the beginning Chinggis was dedicated to the creation of 'a structure of power that would be capable of extension in both time and space', and with his growing success he brought into being other institutions which superseded the old tribal structure, including the creation of an élite imperial guard and the granting of 'appanages' or territories and populations to kinsmen on condition of loyal military service. The conquest of extensive sedentary states brought into being feudal relations both between conquerors and subjects and within Mongol society.

From his many comments on the Manchu period in Mongol history it is evident that here also Lattimore finds the term 'feudal' appropriate. After the submission of the principal Khalka (Khalkh, Outer Mongolian) leaders to the K'ang-hsi (Kang Xi) emperor at Dolonnor (Dolonnur) in 1691 the Mongols of both Inner and Outer Mongolia were settled in particular territories or 'banners' (*Khoshuu, ch'i*) ruled by hereditary Mongol princes or nobles usually of Chinggisid ancestry. These aristocrats, given new titles by the Manchus, held their lands on condition that they provide military levies in time of war. Those lands not held by the secular nobility were the property of the Buddhist church, also the object of Manchu patronage and control. The three classes of commoners (*arat, arad*) - ordinary bannermen, the personal retainers of particular nobles, and those settled on lands owned by the church - all owed service and tribute goods to their superiors.[11] Lattimore refers to this system of rule by secular and ecclesiastical notables holding particular lands as a 'dual feudalism'.[12]

Given the predominant Soviet view up to the 1960s, discussed earlier, that ownership or control of land is crucial for the character of the mode of production, it is noteworthy that Lattimore was able to find and make available through a translation a further work of Natsagdorj which, though it does not attempt to refute directly this assertion, approaches the question in a more empirical fashion.[13] Natsagdorj agrees that in the Manchu period the nobles were 'the owners, with full rights, of the territory' of their fiefs, and thus could 'appropriate any part' of it 'for their personal use'. Moreover the nobles and the monasteries possessed the best livestock which grazed on the most luxuriant pasture. But he finds also that commoners often did possess in small numbers their own animals, and that enough remained of the tradition of common land ownership that they could graze these animals in any locality on their banner. The full measure of feudalism in this period could only be taken thus, according to Natsagdorj, by considering the control of both land and animals, and by taking into account also the remnants which still existed of earlier practices. This leads Lattimore to remark, of another of Natsagdorj's writings, that there was evidence of a subtle but significant departure in his work from the hitherto rather narrow Marxist approach of Soviet scholarship.[14]

Feudalism and the State in the Marxist View of the Nomads

Given Lattimore's interest in Soviet and Mongol scholarship, and his criticism of some of the assumptions thereof, it is necessary to offer a brief account of the context of that scholarship. As has been shown Lattimore was long of the view that the Mongolian People's Republic was the first satellite state of the Soviet Union. In scholarship as much as in politics Mongolia has behaved as the most loyal and consistent of all the satellites, and thus the Marxist premises (and their transmutations as a result of political exigencies) that provide the foundation for scholarly enquiry in the Soviet Union fulfil the same function in Mongolia.

The study of nomadism and of the political entities which have been created from time to time by nomadic civilisations are, *prima facie*, difficult to reconcile with two propositions long taken as crucial assumptions in official Marxist scholarship. The first, based on an interpretation of some remarks of Marx in the 'preface' to *A Contribution to the Critique of Political Economy*, assumes a more-or-less linear progression of human societies from primitive communalism based upon the clan, through the intermediate stages of slave and feudal societies (characterised by the growth of class differentiation and the division of labour), to capitalism and thence socialism.[15] The dynamic for this progress is provided by the tensions that arise within each of these societies. At the beginning the 'production relations' (work and ownership relations) of a given society provide an appropriate means by which the 'productive forces' (labour, and its subject and instruments) are exploited, thus providing for the material needs of the society and for its reproduction. With the passage of time discoveries and inventions make new means of exploiting these productive forces possible, but the existing production relations obstruct and impede such advance. The tensions created fuel a social revolution which ultimately brings a new society into existence with production relations more appropriate for the accomplishment of these newly identified tasks. The second of these propositions advances the claim that the state is an epiphenomenon. According to Marx the form and character of the 'legal and political superstructure' is determined by the nature of the production relations; specifically, the class which controls property dominates the state.[16] Now it is true that both of these propositions insofar as they applied to Asia were somewhat modified in Marx's own view by the existence of a form of society ('the Asiatic mode of production') exemplified in the great civilisations of that continent. Though this in turn raises further questions regarding the coherence of Marx's social theory, the existence of such a uniquely Asian social formation was struck from the Marxist canon in 1931 as the result of political debates in the Soviet Union.[17]

As Ernest Gellner has pointed out,[18] pastoral nomadism, though a developed form of production with a long history, is something of an evolutionary cul-de-sac which changes only through contact (whether by way of conquest, trade, or colonisation) with other forms of society. In pastoral nomadism the division of labour is little developed, much property in land and livestock would seem to be communally owned, and clan ties are of great importance, all factors which would seem to be redolent of that primitive communal stage of social organisation allegedly found in greatest antiquity. On the other hand, from time to time for two millennia the pastoral nomads have produced large state formations even though there seems to have been little antecedent change in their way of life. The Mongol ruling class in particular, far from emerging to take charge of the state machine as a result of prior developments in the class structure seem themselves to have created that machine. Nomadism would appear, therefore, to challenge both of these essential Marxist propositions. Nomadism does not fit into the linear view of history, nor does it possess the internal dynamics necessary for its own transformation. Neither do the various political entities created by the nomads appear to be rooted in that which Marx takes to be fundamental and determinative of such innovations, that is, changes in the mode of exploitation of the productive forces.

In the period in which a relatively narrow Stalinist orthodoxy held sway, the Soviet and Mongol position was that the era from the appearance of 'the first states of the Huns to the empire of Genghis Khan' was the 'early period of feudalism'. Here it was claimed that class differentiation had emerged in Mongol society with the decay of primitive communalism, and that in the process the slave owning stage of society was simply omitted.[19] The foundations for this view insofar as they were scientific were provided by the eminent Russian scholar Vladimirtsov. In his posthumous work which appeared in the Soviet Union in 1934 Vladimirtsov claimed to have identified in 13th and 14th century Mongol society such essentials of feudalism as the fief (granted as a result of an act of homage to the ruler), an aristocracy, a retinue of the ruler's military followers, and a class of serfs.[20] Clearly, if

Mongol nomadism can be interpreted as feudal, Mongol civilisation can be appropriated into the linear Marxist schema of types of society. With even greater convenience the occasional efflorescence in nomadic societies of large state systems can as a consequence be grounded in the growth and permutation of feudal social relations.

In a critique of approaches to the phenomenon of feudalism Lawrence Krader argues that Vladimirtsov's analysis would appear to be invalidated by the presence of many features in the states of Chinggis and his immediate successors inconsistent with feudalism. Kinship relations remained important in the Chinggis era, with all Mongols claiming a common ancestry with the ruling clan and new allies enrolled often on the basis of fictive kinship bonds. Moreover, the law of Chinggis Khan (*yasa, jasag*) was absolute and recognised no mutual obligations but demanded only obedience from vassals and commoners alike. Here the ruler was recognised as master of all the territory of the empire, with the concept of the ownership of property in land little developed and many fiefs held over people rather than land. Far from the holders of territorial fiefs wielding any independent power over a distinct and separate subject population as in European feudalism, there seemed therefore to be few real obstacles to the absolute authority of the Mongol ruler. Indeed, Vladimirtsov himself concedes in another of his works that 'the power of a Mongol Khan, especially of such a one as Chingis, was in the strict sense unlimited'.[21] Insofar as the Mongol states were not based on and sustained by plunder, Krader concludes therefore that many of their features can best be interpreted as 'pale reflections' of those of their sedentary neighbours.[22]

Changes in Marxist scholarship in the last two decades have led to the re-examination of these arguments and the consequent appearance of a somewhat less dogmatic approach to the phenomenon of nomadism. Thus G E Markov, though he insists that class differentiation exists in nomadic societies through the individual ownership of livestock also maintains that private property in pasture land only comes into being with the decay and transformation of nomadism:

> The social structure of the nomads was determined by a lack of
> adequate development of productive forces and of division of
> labour, private property in cattle and communal property on
> pastures, and considerable social and proprietary stratification.[23]

In his view pastoral nomadism appears to be, despite its long history, a transitional form of society in which kinship ties and communal practices, both remnants of a former era, carry on an independent life for an extended period. As to the appearance of the nomadic states, Markov emphasises their transient and temporary character which is understood as a result of their lack of an 'economic and social base in the steppe'. Neither of these concessions would appear to square with the Marxist assumptions outlined previously, though these, of course, remain at the core of official Soviet Marxism. But they offer sufficient room for manoeuvre for Natsagdorj, as has been shown, to emphasise the communal elements of Mongol society as they may be seen even in the eighteenth century.

Anatoli Khazanov, though not in any way typical of recent Soviet scholarship, has insisted that one of the most common features of pastoral nomadic societies is communal ownership of land, with only the appearance of a 'tendency' towards other forms of ownership in particular examples.[24] So diverse are the practices, level of civilisation, and social and political organisation of nomadic societies that comparative analysis yields only the common feature of 'economic activity'. Moreover changes in nomadic societies appear to proceed, not from the internal dynamics thereof but as a consequence of contacts with other societies and civilisations.[25] Reviewing in particular the history of the political systems found from time to time in nomadic states Khazanov concludes that there is not one but three distinct types all of which may, though need not, proceed from an act of conquest.[26] Although the nomadic state based upon the payment of tribute by vassals inhabiting a separate ecological zone was a common form, some nomadic states have transformed themselves into sedentary agricultural and urban societies, and yet others have existed on the basis of a division of labour between steppe and sown. The empire of Chinggis was based upon the subjugation of sedentary populations who then paid tribute to their Mongol overlords. Khazanov evidently believes that to regard this empire or its immediate successors as transient is to understate their historical role, and to attribute the emergence of this empire to the growth of allegedly feudal social relations is to confuse cause and effect:

> Towards the beginning of the thirteenth century there emerged in
> Mongolia not nomadic feudalism which, according to the view of
> Vladimirtsov, differed little from feudalism in Western Europe,
> but a society of another type. In this society the main differences
> between the different strata and classes consisted not in their
> relation to key resources, but in their relation to power and
> government. Those direct obligations which the rulers imposed on
> the ruled were not the cause, but the consequence of the
> emergence of the rulers.[27]

Here it should be pointed out that, in his discussion of the applicability of the term 'feudal' to nomadic states, Khazanov has perforce to take into account the fact that in Soviet (and Mongol) scholarship feudalism is more than a set of institutions. It is, rather, one of the fundamental forms of human society given its identity by unique 'production relations', specifically the control of agricultural land, the chief 'productive force' and source of surplus, by a class of nobles who extract by threat of force an agricultural surplus from the producing class of serfs. In this view, feudal institutions of a political character - homage, fiefs, an aristocracy, and so on - will only appear after the emergence of these 'production relations'. And these production relations will themselves develop only with advances in the mode of exploitation of the 'productive forces'. Khazanov's remarks are principally directed, therefore, against a major supposition of Soviet Marxist scholarship, that is the supposition that politics cannot be an independent variable.

Lattimore, of course, is under no constraints with regard to his treatment of politics. It is clear in his account of Chinggis, and in his more general work on the feudalising tendencies present in the border regions of Inner Asia, that Lattimore has derived much information from Soviet (and latterly Mongol) scholars and indeed may have come to understand these historical issues in a new light as a result. He nevertheless interprets the construction of 'feudal' institutions during the rise of the Mongol world empire and later in the Mongol regions of the Manchu empire as acts of political will. As we have seen, Lattimore believes that the creation in Chinese history of tribal 'reservoirs' and the rule by dynasties of nomadic origin of states of mixed ecological character was a response to military and political imperatives. It would seem that Lattimore's analysis of the nature of the institutions established by Chinggis to supplant those that had prevailed amongst the Mongols previously is incorrect, though some scholars would still regard the Mongol polity in this period as an example of 'nomadic quasi-feudalism'.[28] If Lattimore is in error, however, this follows from his neglect of the fundamentally absolutist features of the institutions of Chinggis and not from any conceptual mistake. On the other hand his account of the Manchu period in which deliberately designed feudal political institutions coexisted with various older communal practices and conventions (notably the common ownership of pasture) would seem to be accurate.

Looking at this later work in the light of his historical writings of the later 1930s it is clear that Lattimore is still developing ideas given their fullest expression in *Inner Asian Frontiers of China*. Although they spring from different geographical bases for the last two millennia the cycles of nomadic and sedentary human history in Inner and East Asia have constantly intersected yet without adopting a stable relationship. Even the careful creation of feudal institutions by an energetic dynasty can only bring a temporary stability, though a different and possibly mutually beneficial relationship may come with the industrial age.

Buddhism in Mongolia

Lattimore is also concerned in his later writings to comment on the introduction into Mongol society of other institutions interpreted by some to perform a feudal role, namely, the institutions of Tibetan style lama Buddhism. Here too while he praises the contribution of (Marxist) Mongolian scholars to an understanding of the complex of historical issues involved, Lattimore again develops an account in which political motives are pre-eminent.

The rise of the influence of lama Buddhism among the Mongols in the later sixteenth century, and particularly the role of Altan Khan (1507-1582) as its principal patron and promoter, should be understood according to Lattimore in relation to the decline of Chinese power beyond the Great Wall at that time. This decline had opened the possibility for the emergence of a marginal state or states of a mixed character co-existing and trading with China or even capable, in the long term, of conquests inside the Great Wall. Such a state would only develop and grow in power if it incorporated agricultural areas to provide 'storable cereal foods', urban centres to furnish a regular supply of sophisticated arms, and regular administrators to order these non-nomadic activities and populations. In the event the Manchu Nurhaci (1559-1626) was to found such a state at the eastern end of the Great Wall, but the ambitions and methods of the Mongol Altan were similar. Altan had the additional objective of establishing a 'moral superiority' over those Mongols not directly subject to him, an objective forced on him by the endemic conflicts amongst the various Chinggisid rulers of a people who had become increasingly divided since the expulsion in 1368 of the Yuan dynasty from China.

In endeavouring to realise his ambition Altan sought to avoid that ensnarement of his state which would follow his reliance upon Chinese administrators. For his literate administrators and clerks he turned therefore to Tibet, seeking also to use the Tibetan religion to legitimise his claim to be the pre-eminent Mongol ruler. As Lattimore puts it, the 'monastery-building, account-keeping, establishment-minded Tibetans were the answer to his problem'.29 And here Mongol and Tibetan interests coincided since the followers of the reformer Tsong-kha-pa (Tsongkaba) required at that time a secular patron in order to assert their control over the Tibetan church hierarchy. Their leader, bSod-nams rgya-mtsho, met Altan in 1578, at which meeting Altan was recognised as a reincarnation of Khobilai Khan while the Tibetan pontiff received the title of Dalai Lama. It was not piety, therefore, but statecraft which led to Altan's acceptance of the Buddhist faith and the consequent conversion of many Mongols to Buddhism. Similar motives may be detected in patronage of the church in the following century by the Mongol Khans Ligdan and Abdai. Indeed, the greatgrandson of the latter became the first Jebtsundamba (Javzandamba), or principal Mongol Buddhist reincarnation, in 1639, being confirmed in the title by the then Dalai Lama.

By this time, though, hopes of uniting the Mongols by political or religious means were fading with the rise of the Manchus. The emerging institutions of the Mongol church, now claiming the allegiance of the majority of the Mongols, were put to other uses by their new overlords. According to Lattimore Manchu patronage of the Buddhist faith was used to prevent any resurgence of Mongol (and also Tibetan) unity. By encouraging the growth of extensive monastic estates with their control of considerable revenues, and by enhancing the prestige of the religious leadership the Manchus ensured that the now enfeoffed Mongol nobles would have priestly rivals. The chances of any single Mongol noble coming to control a dangerously large and potentially disloyal fiefdom were reduced in a system of control which might be characterised as a 'dual feudalism'.30 Constraints were placed on the contact between the secular and religious worlds by the Manchu insistence after 1757 that reincarnations of the Jebtsundamba could no longer be found among the Chinggisid families of Mongolia, but only in Tibet. And patronage of more than one reincarnation among both the Mongols and the Tibetans gave the Manchus the option of dividing further the loyalties of these subject peoples. As Lattimore points out, the Manchus were careful to balance the authority of the Jebtsundamba with an Inner Mongolian reincarnation, the lCan skya (Changchia):

> The *Changchia* Reincarnation ... completed a triangle within which Manchu policy could manoeuvre: the Dalai and Panchan Lamas in Tibet, the Jebtsundamba Khutukhtu in Outer Mongolia, and the Changchia Khutukhtu in Peking and Inner Mongolia.31

From this account it can be seen that Lattimore is very much concerned to interpret the spread of lama Buddhism in Mongolia as a political phenomenon. In his work on Mongol religion Walther Heissig similarly emphasises the importance of political factors, as does Larry Moses in his standard account of the social role of the church.32 Both authorities, however, understand the political dimension in terms of Altan's search for legitimation, rather than his conscious wish to design a border state free from the enervating effects of Chinese culture. Moses also makes the point that Buddhism only became the faith of the Mongols after a long struggle with Shamanism during which it absorbed certain of the forms and features of the vanquished religion.

Moses claims that there is some evidence that Buddhism did not entirely disappear in Mongolia between the expulsion of the Yuan rulers from China in 1368 and the meeting of Altan and bSod-nams rgya-mtsho two centuries later. In this period, moreover, there is to be found a prior example of an ambitious Mongol ruler seeking Buddhist legitimation for his ambitions. Esen, in 1446 and again in 1452 sought religious articles and instruction from the Buddhist church, though he turned to China rather than Tibet (where the religion was then in profound disorder). To understand this development it must be pointed out that the Mongols by this time were divided (as a consequence of Mongol inheritance rules) by the rivalries of various Chinggisid families, despite the continued existence of a Yuan ruler in the steppe. Esen's need was much the same as Altan's, except that he was not even a member of the Chinggisid clan (the Borjigin) whereas Altan was a member thereof, though not of the pre-eminent lineage. Esen's attempt to overthrow the inheritance of Chinggis on the basis of a new religious legitimation came to nothing with his murder by one of his erstwhile followers. Altan's attempt to create a new Mongol empire was threatened, after his initial military successes and the granting of titles to him by the Ming rulers of China, by the Yuan claimant and by disloyalty among his own kinsmen. The conquests of Altan's nephew had put him in contact with Tibet and had brought Tibetan Lamas to his court. It was to this quarter that Altan turned:

> The line of Borjigin Chinggisids who could propose re-unification cloaked in the mantle of the Great Conqueror never acquired the necessary military power to force its acceptance by the collateral tribes. Here is perhaps the single most important reason for Altan's systematic overtures to the leader of the new Yellow sect [bSod-nams rgya-mtsho] of Tibet, which was by 1570 AD a powerful force in Tibet and Northwest China.[33]

Altan had sent to the Chinese also for a Tibetan cleric, and here it is clear that the attraction of Tibetan church figures was not that their culture was not Chinese, but that Tibetan support recalled the role of the 'Phags-pa Lama, the Tibetan preceptor of Khobilai who had seen his overlord as a *Chakravartin*, or lordly Buddhist ruler. Thus it is no accident that Altan at the meeting of 1578 was recognised as an incarnation of Khobilai at the same time as his Tibetan adviser identified himself as the 'Phags-pa Lama.[34] At a stroke this stratagem recalled the greatness of that era while setting aside the strict rules of inheritance that were its legacy in Altan's time. It is a tribute to Altan's statecraft that in the years immediately following other Mongol leaders sought to emulate him. From the account offered by Moses, then, it may be concluded that it was Altan's search for legitimation rather than for administrators which led him to turn to Tibet, although Moses agrees that the subsequent divisions imposed on the Mongols by the lama church prevented the reemergence of a unified Mongol nation.

The Mongolian Revolution and Satellitism

In a great variety of writings Lattimore repeatedly considered and reconsidered a further complex of themes - the nature of the Mongolian revolution and the Soviet role therein. Throughout he was concerned to emphasise the relative autonomy of the Mongolian revolutionary movement and the benign character of Soviet assistance. Here there may be detected echoes of that stark choice Lattimore perceived in 1935 in the predicament of the Mongols of China: social revolution or ethnic obliteration. For whatever could be said of the social or political character of the Mongolian People's Republic it has permitted the continued existence of the Mongols as a people, a cause to which Lattimore had long been attached. It will be maintained here that this perspective often dominated Lattimore's view of recent Mongolian history.

Writing in 1949 Lattimore detected in Soviet initiatives in Mongolia a continuation of the Tsarist policy of using the country as a buffer or screen, except that the Soviets also 'encouraged the Mongols to become able to look after themselves'.[35] The position of the Mongols had always rendered relations with Russia a crucial issue of foreign policy. They had never been able, in Lattimore's view, to play off the neighbouring powers against each other since the sorry fate of their kinsmen in Inner Mongolia demonstrated that close relations with China would bring extinction. Here it should be noted that Russian patronage after 1911 played a major part in allowing the Mongols to maintain their detachment from the new Chinese Republic. In the period of autonomy (1911-1919) the fear of reabsorption into China and the consequent loss of national and ethnic identity was the major preoccupation of the government of the Jebtsundamba, who combined religious and secular authority in these years. The reassertion of Chinese control enforced by the army of Hsu Shu-cheng (Xu Shujeng) in November 1919 stimulated the growth of nationalist feeling, such figures as Sukebator turning inevitably to the Russians for support.

Lattimore compared the role of Sukebator in the Mongolian revolution to that of Sun Yat-sen in the Chinese. Referring to the biography by Natsagdorj which he was later to publish in translation, Lattimore described Sukebator as the leader of a nationalist group of diverse composition, some of whom sought merely the restoration of autonomy while others had more far reaching social and political objectives. They came into contact with a more radical group led by Choibalsang (Choibalsan) who had already formed an association with Russian revolutionaries. With Russian encouragement the two factions merged in much the same way as the Kuomintang and the Communist Party in China formed an alliance in 1923, and thereafter both leaders were to depend on assistance from the Soviets. Unlike the protracted history of the Chinese revolution, the Mongolian revolutionaries were able to set up a government by 1921, and though they co-existed for a time with the remnants of the old regime of the Jebtsundamba, by 1925 they were able to declare their ultimate goal to be 'the attainment of communism'.

Although Lattimore believed that a policy of seeking Russian assistance 'would have been a necessity for any Mongol government' determined to achieve complete independence from China, he did not believe that this by itself made the particular form of the close association that followed between the Russian and Mongolian regimes and parties inevitable. Indeed, the subsequent political history of Mongolia may be interpreted, in Lattimore's view, as the result of a struggle between factions with different attitudes towards the link with the Soviets:

> The record shows ... that Mongol politics have largely taken the form of competition between men who placed unquestioning confidence in Russia and men who, while recognizing the necessity of association with Russia, have attempted to avoid both complete integration with the policies of Russia and involvement with the policies of any country not friendly to Russia. For this second type of policy, which falls between conventional

classifications and is hard to define, there has until recently been
no convenient term; but a term has recently come into use which
describes it well: it is Titoism.[36]

Accordingly, Lattimore interprets the history of inner party conflict in
Mongolia, particularly in the crises of 1924 and 1930-32, as a manifestation of
this competition, although competition seems a somewhat jejune term for a
process which resulted in the physical extinction of the losers. Thus the latter,
in which a rapid and ill-planned attempt at the collectivisation of the chief
economic resource of the population, their flocks and herds, brought economic
and political disaster should not be seen as a result of misguided Soviet
interference or the overspill of similar attempts in the Soviet Union. The lurch
to the left in this period was, rather, the outcome of an endeavour to
demonstrate, by Mongolian Titoists, 'leftist independence of Russia'.
Lattimore was in no doubt that the dominant trend in Mongolian politics had
been both nationalist and Marxist, such differences as there had been relating
to the degree of independent development Mongolia should exhibit. In the
event the winning faction was content with a great degree of reliance on
Soviet guidance. This reliance produced, insofar as sound evidence is
available, a positive balance sheet, with the prosperity of traditional herding
activities being maintained while financing a 'gradual industrialization,
accompanied step by step by the technological training of Mongols to man
industry as it expands'. As to the degree of 'independence' of Mongolia as a
nation, this is a question which must be 'judged on the total evidence', by
which Lattimore meant that in view of the pervasiveness of power bloc
politics and the dependence of smaller countries on the great powers the
sovereignty of such nations is a fiction.[37] All that can be said is that, relative
to other small and under-developed countries, and to the position of the
Mongols of Inner Mongolia, the loyalty of the Mongolian People's Republic
to the Soviet alliance is evidence of the positive nature of that alliance.

In his introduction to the translation of the life of Sukebator by Natsagdorj
Lattimore enlarged upon this view of the Mongolian revolution. As he had
come to regard the Mongolian People's Republic as a satellite of Soviet Russia
but believed that this did not transform the Mongols into puppets he took his
analysis further by offering a general account of the phenomenon of
'satellitism'; he also commented on those characteristics of Soviet policy that
appeared to govern the Soviet approach towards countries in that third zone
that Lattimore had long maintained would play an important role in world
politics.

Soviet conduct in the Third World seemed to follow a role Lattimore
proposed to term the 'doctrine of the irreversible minimum'. The Soviets
were prepared to give some measure of support to the regime of a Third World
country provided that regime had made efforts to free its nation permanently
from capitalist domination. Thus the Soviets had assisted the Ataturk regime
in Turkey and the Nanking regime of Chiang Kai-shek in China not because

they expected to enlist these nations as client states but because long term Soviet policy had been advanced with the rebuffs these nations had offered to Western trading and diplomatic privileges. In Mongolia in the early years of the revolution Soviet interests had been sufficiently served by the stabilisation of the Siberian frontier and the exclusion of Chinese and Japanese interests that had followed the 1921 revolution. Taking the longer view here also, the Soviets had refrained from annexation of Mongolia despite its occupation by the Red Army in 1921; they were also content in the years that followed 'to go slowly in pressing internal Sovietization of the country'.[38]

Going back to a distinction Lattimore first developed in 1936, because the Soviets had abstained from annexation of Mongolia despite the presence there of a regime well disposed towards them, Mongolia was not a puppet state (a term which was then applicable to Manchukuo) but a satellite.[39] Lattimore then offered a definition of the anatomy of satellitism as distinct from the 'feudal' form of dependence, the crucial features of which are the character and aims of the satellite regime. Such a regime comes to power with the assistance of the regime of the patron state, depends upon it for its continuing existence, and seeks to emulate it in internal policy. Within the satellite state there is a hostile opposition or potential opposition which, should it supplant the ruling regime, would create the conditions for the gravitation of the state 'into the orbit of some country other than, and probably hostile to, the country protecting the actual regime'. Given the closeness of patron and client 'any variations within the dominant state are promptly reflected within the satellite state'.[40]

By viewing Mongolia as an example of satellite dependence, Lattimore believed that many otherwise puzzling episodes in modern Mongolian history became explicable. These included the rapid development of the revolution in Mongolia, the 'genuine warmth' of Mongolian references to Soviet example and assistance - in this 'Choibalsang was no sycophant' - and the alleged absence of 'conflicting nationalisms' in the record of Soviet-Mongolian relations. On this latter point Lattimore put in the mouth of a hypothetical Mongol commoner as eloquent a case as might be presented for internal class warfare (though he believed this analysis 'is entirely independent of Marxist terms'). Alleging that the educated classes wished only to maintain their own privileges, and were compromised by their manifest willingness to rely upon Chinese and Japanese 'protectors' no case could be made according to this spokesman for an overriding national and class solidarity:

> Our only defense against the kind of outside protectors ... [the 'privileged classes'] will try to call in is to find outside protectors of our own. There is only one answer: the revolutionary Russians. We must rely upon them while we gain time to train up a new generation of Mongols to run things in a new way. These new men we must, for our own safety, find to the maximum possible extent in families that have no ties with the old privileged classes,

and that will increase the antagonism between us and the right-wing nationalists. In order to get the Russian help - which is the only thing that will pull us through - the Russians, too, must feel they are getting something out of it. That is going to mean ... they will take the lead ... in international policy ... [and in] economic development.[41]

Co-operation with the Russians was therefore the only alternative for such people, which explains the reason why, even given the extent of Russian penetration of Mongolia, there was 'never ... a really dangerous revolt in Outer Mongolia' in the 1930s despite the close proximity of potential Japanese patrons of an alternative regime.

In 1956, as a result of the publication by Nicholas Poppe of a very different account of the Mongolian satellite regime as well as of some direct criticism of Lattimore's approach thereto, Lattimore offered some significant amendments to his view of satellitism. He now wished to emphasise the fact that, though the regime and its supporters in a satellite state are a minority, they have a 'disproportionate influence'. This is so:

because the moment of decision arises when other groups, which taken together are in fact the majority, are more afraid of some other country or countries than they are of the one into whose orbit the conscious minority wants to bring them as a satellite.[42]

In the case of Mongolia it was Lattimore's opinion that a satellite regime came into being principally through the fear of the majority of the threat posed by China and Japan. The Mongolian revolution was thus an illustration of a principle Lattimore found to be common in history, though little noticed by historians, that of a people marching backward into a future they little anticipated or understood through dislike and fear of the known. Lattimore was prepared to acknowledge that once this regime was securely in power 'cruel things were done' in order to prepare against the danger of Japanese attack and in order to ensure continuing Russian support. But, repeating a point he had made on many occasions before, at that time 'Mongolia had a vital interest in supporting the Soviet Union', as was shown by the repulse by Soviet and Mongolian forces of a major Japanese invading force on the Mongolian border at Khalkhyn Gol (Chalchyn Gol) in May-June 1939.[43]

In *Nomads and Commissars*, written following his 1961 visit to Mongolia, Lattimore restated many of these judgments on the Mongolian revolution. He emphasised the independent but emulatory development of the political and economic strategy of the revolutionary regime, arguing at one point that the very extremism of the forced collectivisation policies of 1929-31 was evidence that neither Soviet nor Comintern advice was the cause, though the Soviets had the power to intervene if they had so chosen. Because Mongol-Soviet relations were so intimate 'the Russians must have known all about the policies while they were being debated and passed, and could have caused them to be modified if they had considered them wrong'.[44] But as a result of his experiences in 1961 Lattimore was now of the opinion that his definition of the term 'satellite' would need to be 'modified' to fit the present reality of the Mongolian People's Republic. The precise nature of the necessary modification was not specified, but Lattimore adverted to the unique circumstances of the country and the knowledge Mongols evidently had of the inapplicability of many Soviet policies as a solution to these problems.[45]

So far Lattimore's treatment of the connection between the Mongolian revolution and the Soviet Union had followed that of Mongolian sources. In the year that *Nomads and Commissars* was published, the Mongolian People's Revolutionary Party (MPRP) made public criticism of the personality cult that had developed around the Mongolian leader Choibalsang. There can be little doubt that Stalin was the original for the cult of his Mongolian contemporary, just as Krushchev's denunciation of Stalin began the reinterpretation, initially within the Party, of Choibalsang's historical role. At first Choibalsang's critics had in mind his purge (again in emulation of Stalin) of many senior political and military figures between 1937 and 1939,[46] but in time their actions opened the way for an official reexamination of other issues in the history of the revolution. In his later work Lattimore amended his interpretation of some particular episodes accordingly, though he stuck doggedly to most of his earlier assertions including his view that the revolution of 1921 was not simply imposed by the Soviet Red Army, and that the collectivisation fiasco of 1929-31 was the result of misplaced Mongolian zealotry.[47] On the unrest generated by the latter movement, Lattimore now acknowledges that it was sufficiently widespread and serious that Soviet forces were called in to repress it, though this apparently at the request of the regime in Ulan Bator.[48] Concerning the changes in the leadership of the regime in 1928 which closed off any other alternative than the status for Mongolia of a Soviet client, Lattimore now follows the most recent historical account published in Mongolia. This acknowledges that when the 'Rightists' (including the Central Committee Chairman Dambadorji [Dambadorj]) refused at the Seventh Party Congress in 1928 to modify their tolerance of private trading in the economy in line with the changes then being made in the Soviet Union they were purged on the orders of a commission dispatched by the Comintern.[49] But even the abandonment in 1932 of the extreme policies that had prevailed up until that time in favour of 'the new turn' Lattimore still regarded as being the result of the Mongolian Party, after an extensive debate, taking good advice, rather than 'the response of "satellites" who meekly obey foreign orders'.[50]

The Historiography of the Mongolian Revolution

It is evident that in this final stage of his career Lattimore had become quite deeply attached to a conception of the Mongolian revolution as an autonomous though externally inspired movement which rescued a previously declining people from national and ethnic oblivion. The reasons for this attachment will be speculated upon in the concluding section of this work, but the importance of this conception for Lattimore was such that it must be discussed in the light of the historical record.

Up until the 1950s the obscurity of Mongolia, its lack of any international ties except with the Soviet Union, and the paucity of historical materials available from Ulan Bator, rendered serious work on the country very difficult. Lattimore had visited the capital with Vice-President Wallace in 1944 for three days but such materials as he had been able to gather (including Natsagdorj's life of Sukebator) reflected the personality cult and the Stalinist distortion of the historical record then as prevalent in Mongolia as in the Soviet Union.

Many of the points made in Lattimore's writings of the 1950s accept the basic account offered by the regime of itself at least regarding the personal role of various members of the leadership and the nature and extent of Russian intervention and control in Mongolia. At the same time a school of Western scholars evidently writing with the experience of post-war Eastern Europe in mind interpreted the creation of a Soviet satellite in Mongolia as following the same pattern as in Europe. These scholars emphasised the organisation of the Party on Soviet territory in 1921 after revolutionary Mongols had travelled to the Soviet Union in the previous year to seek Russian aid against the Chinese occupiers of their country, and the subsequent installation of the regime as a consequence of Soviet military occupation. The period since 1921, or 1924 when the last Jebtsundamba died and the Party was reorganised (and shortly thereafter renamed the Mongolian People's Revolutionary Party) to accept a specifically revolutionary programme on the instructions of the local representatives of the Comintern, was seen as one in which the Soviet Union dominated political affairs in the Mongolian People's Republic. Thus from that time the hapless Mongols experienced all the vicissitudes of their Soviet brethren, being encouraged to 'enrich' themselves when the equivalent of the New Economic Policy prevailed in Mongolia, then being thrown into a disastrous and bloody collectivisation campaign in 1929, and suffering purges of leading personnel after 1936.[51]

There is a good deal of evidence for many of the contentions made by members of this school. Thus, to take some examples, at the third Party Congress which began its deliberations on 4 August 1924, the representative of the Comintern, the Buryat-Mongol from the Soviet Union Rinchino (Rinchin), distributed a pamphlet setting out the case for Mongolia now choosing the socialist road under Soviet tutelage. When he was opposed in this by the local revolutionary Danzan as too advanced for the concrete conditions of Mongolia, Rinchino riposted with the charge that Danzan wished to deliver Mongolia to the Chinese. With the help of members of the League of Revolutionary Youth, the youth wing of the Party, Rinchino and his

Mongol allies turned the Congress into an *ad hoc* court which declared Danzan and others guilty of treason and had them summarily executed. The Soviet Minister to Mongolia, Vasiliev, then turned up to comfort the delegates with the observation that they had done the correct thing as this was also the practice in the Soviet Union.[52] In his account of a visit to Ulan Bator in early 1927 as a representative of the Kuomintang (then still in alliance with the Communist party in China, and recognised as a 'fraternal party' by the Comintern) Ma Ho-t'ien (Ma Hetian) observed that the various organs of the government were dominated by Soviet advisers.[53] And, as has been shown, Lattimore himself now accepts that the purge at the seventh Party Congress in 1928 of those 'Rightists' (including Dambadorji) who had pursued an 'anti-Party opportunist policy' was carried out on the instructions of a commission despatched to Ulan Bator by the Comintern. This work being done, the Congress then 'underlined the importance of strengthening the bonds between the MPRP and the Comintern, making the advice given by Comintern instructions the guidelines for operations, solidifying the friendly relations established between Mongolia and the Soviet Union, and remaining boundlessly loyal to them'.[54] The introduction of the 'New Turn' in 1932 was also a result of direct Soviet intervention. In accordance with a joint resolution of the Comintern Executive Committee and the Central Committee of the Soviet Communist Party of 29 March 1932 the former policy of rapid collectivisation was abandoned at a meeting of the Central Committee of the Mongolian Party the following month. A number of prominent leaders were purged at this meeting, the Mongolian comrades taking note of the Soviet view of 'the serious mistakes committed by the majority of the leaders of the MPRP' and the 'concrete ways of correcting them'.[55]

But the authors of the school who see Mongolia as an early prototype of the form of regime later created in Eastern Europe tend to telescope periods, and take it as almost self-evident that the Soviet Union in 1921 was as much disposed to acquire new dependencies as was Stalin in 1945. With the revisions that have occurred in recent Mongolian and Soviet scholarship on the evolution of the Mongolian revolution a definitive account of the later 1920s and events thereafter remains to be written, though many old judgments have been overturned. Several authors, however, have offered new interpretations of the origins and turning points of the revolutionary regime, and its relationship with the Soviet Union.

According to T E Ewing, there is something to Lattimore's contention that there were important differences between the two groups who came together to form the nucleus of the Mongolian People's Party. The 'Consular Hill' group who included Choibalsang seems to have been more inclined to seek revolutionary solutions to the Mongol predicament and numbered among its members individuals who by the standards of the time and place might be termed radical intellectuals. The 'East Urga' group, of which Sukebator was a member, had the more limited aim of promoting Mongol independence, perhaps because it included men who were or had been state and military functionaries. But the leaders, respectively, of these groups were, contrary to later accounts, Bodoo and Danzan.[56] Bodoo went on to be the chairman of the revolutionary government while it was still established on Soviet territory in April 1921, though he was purged in an obscure episode in 1922, Danzan suffering the same fate in 1924. Sukebator's prominence at this time derived (as befitted a person of military training and experience) from his leadership in military affairs; the later cult of Sukebator evidently has more than a little to do with the fact that as he died in 1923 his reputation was not sullied in the subsequent political struggles. Similarly the dominant role accorded to Choibalsang in later Mongol accounts of these years is a reflection of his predominance after 1936.

Encouraged by a visit from I A Sorokovikov, who came to Mongolia in March 1920 to assess for the Comintern reports he had received of a revolutionary movement among the Mongols, and two further clandestine Soviet missions, Danzan and Choibalsang travelled to Verkhneudinsk (Ulan Ude) in July in the hope of securing Soviet help against the occupation of their country by the Chinese. The initial response of the Soviets, however, was extremely cautious, no doubt because they were endeavouring to avoid further military entanglements with the Civil War not yet won. The Japanese had only begun the withdrawal of their troops from the Russian Far East which had been reconstituted as the buffer Far Eastern Republic. The Soviets also had to deal with the activities of hostile White forces, particularly those led by Semenov. It should be noted that, in view of their later role, it was at the suggestion of the Mongols themselves at this time that Buryats including Rinchino should be recruited to assist in their revolutionary plans. In the following month further members of the incipient revolutionary regime travelled from Urga to join their colleagues Danzan and Choibalsang. This group has come to be known to historians collectively as the Khalkha Seven, and it is significant that all apart from Sukebator and Choibalsang died in purges between 1922 and 1939. Although some members of the group had disdained contact with the Jebtsundamba it was the Soviets who had insisted from the first that an appeal from the former head of state would help to legitimise a Soviet role in Mongolian attempts to expel the Chinese.[57]

The Mongols travelled on to Soviet territory in Irkutsk in August, a group led by Danzan finally making its way to Moscow probably in late September 1920. Here the Soviets finally offered the Mongols some money and weapons, though it is apparent that they did so because Mongolia had in the meantime been invaded by a White force led by Baron Ungern-Sternberg who intended to turn the country into a base for the reconquest of Russia. Even at this point the Soviet commitment to the revolutionary group remained limited. Two further developments, however, changed this policy abruptly. Repeated overtures to China failed to secure the permission of the government in Peking for the Soviets to intervene in Mongolia with the objective of expelling

Ungern-Sternberg. When Urga fell to his forces on 3 February 1921 the Chinese showed no inclination to do the job themselves, with or without Soviet co-operation. This tipped the balance, and the Soviets resolved to back whatever revolutionary force could be fostered among the Mongols. The first congress of the Mongolian People's Party was held accordingly on Soviet soil at Kyakhta from 1-3 March 1921, and on 13 March a provisional government was established there by the new Party. The way was thus opened for military action by revolutionary partisans against the Chinese still in occupation of parts of Mongolia and against Ungern-Sternberg, and for the intervention of the Soviet Red Army which entered Urga on 6 July.[58] The formation of the new revolutionary government though it was brought into being by Soviet intervention may thus be interpreted as a result of the Soviet resolve to protect their Far Eastern borders rather than of an incipient Soviet imperialism.

Thereafter, though there was a whole series of changes of tactics and personnel, the Soviets seem to have exercised a strong influence on Mongolian affairs. But Charles Bawden disputes the Soviet and Mongol claim that with the death of the Jebtsundamba in 1924 a 'general line' was laid down that ensured that henceforth Mongolia would follow the socialist road, 'bypassing capitalism', with the assistance of the Soviet Union. It is Bawden's contention, as against both Soviet scholars and those who would interpret Mongolian history as an early example of what befell the states of Eastern Europe after 1945, that the real turning point was 1928.[59] Until that time though the power of the old nobility had been undermined and a start had been made in the modernisation of education and other aspects of society, the policies followed in Ulan Bator neither tied the country economically to the Soviet Union nor destroyed the religion which was the centrepiece of the old culture. But in 1928 direct Soviet intervention eradicated a political leadership which was showing signs of independence, and launched Mongolia irrevocably upon a course of social and economic transformation closely modelled after that of the Soviet Union. Though Bawden's assertion that Mongolia might in other circumstances have become a 'liberal democracy' seems far-fetched, it appears incontrovertible that from that time any other course of development for the country was closed off. This is confirmed by the resolution of the 1928 Party Congress:

> Unless we implement such things as directly opposing the feudalists and *lamas*, and more especially the new rich - a newly emergent force which will tie up the revolution - develop and improve the livelihood of the poor and middle *ards* [commoners] and co-operativize, there is no way we can develop outside the capitalist road.[60]

'Satellitism' and Lattimore's Assumptions

Although the historical record would now appear to support the view that the formation of the original revolutionary circles in Mongolia was an autonomous and local reaction to a national crisis, and that Soviet military intervention in 1921 was a reluctant response to the threat posed by Ungern-Sternberg rather than a ploy to introduce a socialist regime in Ulan Bator, what is known about events thereafter provides little foundation for Lattimore's interpretation of the Mongolian revolution. Without Soviet support and armed intervention the original revolutionary regime would never have been placed in power. As early as 1924 Soviet intervention kept the revolutionaries on the path approved by Moscow, and the purge of the 'Rightists' in 1928 and the subsequent lurch to the left ensured that from that time the revolution would proceed at the pace and in the direction required by the Soviet elder brother.

As the principal American specialist on modern Mongolia Lattimore ought to have been aware even in the 1950s of some of the inadequacies of his view of the communist regime. While it is true that after 1950 many aspects of his scholarly routine (not to mention his intellectual assumptions) were disrupted by his political and legal ordeal, he had already defended this interpretation for a decade. That he was not so aware, at least on the evidence of his published writings, may perhaps be understood by a reconsideration of the assumptions underlying his analysis of Mongolian 'satellitism'. While conceding that the very existence and programme of the satellite regime depends upon the actions of the patron state, and describing the regime and its supporters as a minority, Lattimore then reduces 'Mongol politics' to a struggle between factions both equally Marxist but divided on the amount of emphasis to be placed on the national aspects of the revolution. In the event the 'Titoists' lost, which would seem to indicate that what little capacity the Mongols had for independent development was destroyed, but what Lattimore ignores is the opinion of those groups he collectively identifies as the 'majority' who apparently had no particular wish to live under a Marxist government at all. It is no wonder that there was little capacity for 'conflicting nationalisms' in relations between patron and client if one restricts one's analysis solely to the ruling Marxist factions. Of course Marxist regimes, in a tradition which has its origins in Marx's own rejection of the opinions of the European peasantry, have customarily accorded political status only to those groups thought favourable to the rulers and their programme. For an external analyst to fall in with this practice while claiming objectivity is indicative of irresponsibility.

A further assumption of Lattimore's argument is that any other course would result in the alternative national leadership selling out to the Chinese, thereby presiding over the collective obliteration of the Mongols as a distinct people. This, as Charles Bawden has pointed out, is to underrate the potential shown in those beginnings of contacts between Mongolia and Western Europe in the 1920s. These resulted in the dispatch of students to France and to

Germany and of a trade mission to and quasi-diplomatic relations with the latter country. All these contacts were evidently broken off at Soviet insistence in 1929, though those trained personnel who returned to their country and survived the purges of the 1930s have made important scientific and social contributions to national development.[61]

This argument is also to impute a consistency of opinion to this majority for which there is little evidence. In the Mongolia of the 1920s there were no doubt atavistic lamas and lay nobles who could see no further than the restoration of the autonomous regime. But there were also those in the church who were strongly critical of its role, and there were yet others who looked to a transformation of the old order short of ideological and political subservience to Moscow. Even the new socialist administration had sought to open contacts with the United States, and right through the 1920s despite their intentions and the many advantages that they enjoyed the Soviets were unable to displace China as Mongolia's dominant trading partner until 1929 when a vigorous anti-Chinese campaign effectively severed these trading links by political means.[62] It is as well to recall also that the sentiments of the non-political majority were undoubtedly influenced by the conduct of the Marxist regime. If this majority had come to take on a real identity by 1932 (when the regime was threatened by major rebellions) then it may be surmised this was because they did not agree with the attacks on religion and personal property which were threatening the existence of both of these apparently cherished institutions.[63] If by then assistance was sought by members or groups within this majority from the Chinese and Japanese this is not to be thought surprising since the regime in Ulan Bator had made it plain it ruled by force and therefore nothing less than force would destroy it.

Whether, in fact, anything short of Soviet satellite status would have delivered the country to either the Chinese or the Japanese is a moot point. From the collapse of the Manchu empire to the communist victory of 1949 neither Tibet nor Sinkiang was ruled from Peking (or Nanking). In the latter region a considerable number of Chinese colonists sustained a Chinese administration with which the young Lattimore was impressed. Soviet trade penetrated the region, and Soviet military assistance was crucial in putting down a major internal rebellion, but Sinkiang became neither a Soviet satellite nor Soviet territory. When the Chinese warlords had attempted to bring Mongolia under their control their efforts had ended in ignominious failure since their energies were principally directed towards conquest of ethnic China and control of the capital. An independent Mongolia might have fallen to a resolute Chinese attack by a united government, but, after 1916, it is not really possible to talk at all of a single national government, though this fiction was maintained for external purposes. Indeed, an independent Mongolia might have provided just the right stimulus for a more equitable policy on the part of the Chinese towards the Mongols of Inner Mongolia, those people whose plight had awakened Lattimore's interest and concern in the first place.

As it was, at the critical time energies within the Mongolian People's Republic were absorbed in an internecine conflict, and this and the dictates of Comintern and Soviet policy prevented Ulan Bator from playing an active or interested role.

It remains to account for Lattimore's lack of interest in the views and aspirations of the Mongolian majority, something of the explanation of which should now be visible. The Dilowa who was evidently a shrewd judge of character once remarked that as Lattimore 'had no vocation for religion' there was no point in his trying to explain Buddhism to him.[64] Consider now Lattimore's treatment of Altan Khan's conversion to Buddhism. Lattimore regarded even Altan's quest for a legitimising theory for his imperial ambitions as too ethereal a purpose. Consequently he hypothesised a materialist interpretation of the spread of the Tibetan religion among the Mongols. Consider also the nub of Lattimore's analysis of Buddhism in the Manchu period. Whatever its beliefs and social practices it was essentially a form of feudalism, and an obstacle as well to national unity. It can be concluded that, having no patience with religion himself Lattimore had little concern for the religion of others. The religious and other beliefs of the Mongols, insofar as they did not advance the social revolution he had come by 1935 to regard as necessary for the survival of the Mongols as a people, were of as little interest politically as those of their ancestors were historically. It is but a short step to denying their existence.

Notes to Chapter Seven

1   *Nationalism and Revolution in Mongolia. With a translation from the Mongol of Sh. Nachukdorji's 'Life of Sukebatur'* (Leiden: E J Brill, 1955).

2   *Nomads and Commissars. Mongolia Revisited* (New York: Oxford University Press, 1962), p xvii.

3   'Mongolia once more', *Mongolia Society Bulletin* 9(1970), no 1, pp 1-4.

4   John Gombojab Hangin, 'The Second International Congress of Mongolists, Ulan Bator, 1970', *The Mongolia Society Bulletin* 9(1970), no 2, p 3.

5   *Leeds Lectures* (Leeds University: Chinese Studies Department, 1969), 1/4. These are a verbatim typescript of lectures delivered by Lattimore in Leeds in 1968-69. They are numbered here according to folder (1-13, there is no no 6) and page. I am indebted to Mr Urgunge Onon for drawing them to my attention. The original article in question is: S Yushkov, 'K voprosu o dofeodal'nom ("varvarskom") gosudarstve' [On the question of the pre-feudal ('barbarian') state], *Voprosy Istorii* 7(1946), pp 45-65.

6   'Frontier Feudalism' [1954], 'Feudalism in History' [1957], *Studies in Frontier History*, pp 514-41, 542-51. Lattimore discusses Russian scholarship in the following bibliographical essay: 'Introduction to second edition', *Inner Asian Frontiers of China* (New York: Capitol Publishing & American Geographical Society, 1951), pp xxxvii f. These essays also reflect in part the stimulus provided by Eberhard, who maintained in the first edition of his book published in 1952 that all instances of feudalism followed the conquest of sedentary societies by nomads which then resulted in the creation of 'ethnic superstratification', that is rule by an aristocracy of the conquerors. W Eberhard, *Conquerors and Rulers. Social Forces in Medieval China*, second edition (Leiden: E J Brill, 1970), p 58.

7   K A Wittfogel and Feng Chia-sheng, *History of Chinese Society. Liao*; 'Frontier Feudalism', p 530 n 29.

8   'Feudalism in History', p 550.

9   'The Social History of Mongol Nomadism', W G Beasley and E G Pulleybank (eds), *Historians of China and Japan* (London: Oxford University Press, 1961), pp 328-43. On Russian scholarship, see pp 333 f.

10 'Chingis Khan and the Mongol Conquests', *Scientific American* 209(August 1963), pp 54-68.

11 A M Pozdneyev, *Mongolia and the Mongols*, J R Krueger (ed), (Bloomington: Indiana University Press, 1971); C R Bawden, *The Modern History of Mongolia* (London: Weidenfeld and Nicolson, 1968), pp 82 f; T E Ewing, *Between the Hammer and the Anvil? Chinese and*

Russian Policies in Outer Mongolia 1911-1921, Indiana University Uralic and Altaic Series vol 138 (Bloomington: Indiana University, 1980), pp 7 f.

12   'From Serf to Sage. The Life and Work of Jamsrangiin Sambuu', *Journal of the Anglo-Mongolian Society* 3(1976) no 1, p 2; cf *Nomads and Commissars*, pp 55 f, *Nationalism and Revolution in Mongolia*, pp 15 f.

13   Sh Natsagdorj, trans O Lattimore, 'The Economic Basis of Feudalism in Mongolia', *Modern Asian Studies* 1(1967), pp 265-81.

14   *Leeds Lectures*, 9/17. The essay in question was later translated by Urgunge Onon: Sh Natsagdorj, 'Arad Ayush the Commoner', *Mongolian Heroes of the Twentieth Century*, trans and ed Urgunge Onon, introduction by Owen Lattimore (New York: AMS Press, 1976), pp 1-42. On Mongol views of the Manchu period see also: M Sanjdorj, *Manchu Chinese Colonial Rule in Northern Mongolia*, trans Urgunge Onon, preface by Owen Lattimore (London: Hurst, 1980). On the policy of the Manchus towards the Mongols, see D M Farquhar, 'The Origins of the Manchus' Mongolian Policy', J K Fairbank (ed), *The Chinese World Order* (Cambridge, Mass: Harvard University Press, 1968), pp 198-205.

15   Karl Marx, *A Contribution to the Critique of Political Economy* (Moscow: Progress Publishers, 1970), pp 20-1; cf J Stalin, 'Dialectical and historical materialism', *Problems of Leninism* (Moscow: Foreign Languages Publishing House, 1953), pp 730-45.

16   Any summary discussion of these issues cannot reflect the variety of positions taken by exegetes of Marx. See M Evans, *Karl Marx* (London: Allen & Unwin, 1975), pp 61-78; W H Shaw, *Marx's Theory of History* (Stanford: Stanford University Press, 1978).

17   M Sawer, *Marxism and the question of the Asiatic mode of production*, pp 80 f.

18   E Gellner, 'Foreword', A M Khazanov, *Nomads and the Outside World*, pp ix-xxv.

19   Sh Sandag, *The Mongolian People's Struggle for National Independence and the Building of a New Life* (Ulan Bator: State Publishing House, 1966), p 15; cf USSR & MPR Academies of Science, *History of the Mongolian People's Republic* (Moscow: Nauka, 1973), pp 104 f. The latter work, which is a translation of the second edition of a Russian and Mongolian work of 1967, is authored by the most senior Soviet and Mongolian scholars including the Mongols B Shirendyb, Sh Natsagdorj and Sh Bira, and the Russian I Ya Zlatkin. An earlier Mongol account traces the emergence of feudalism to the Liao dynasty, Chinggis Khan bringing this development to its maturity: N Zhagvaral (ed), *The Mongolian People's Republic* (Ulan Bator: The Committee of Sciences of the MPR, 1956), pp 28-33.

20 B Ya Vladimirtsov, *Le Régime Social des Mongols: le Féodalisme Nomade*, trad M Carsow (Paris: du Musée Guimet Bibliothèque d'études, Libraire d'Amérique et d'Orient Adrien-Maisonneuve, 1948).

21 B Ya Vladimirtsov, *The Life of Chingis-Khan*, trans D S Mirsky (London: Routledge, 1930), 118.

22 L Krader, 'Feudalism and the Tatar Polity of the Middle Ages', *Comparative Studies in Society and History* 1(1959), pp 76-99. In the more recent of his writings Krader, for no apparent reason, has claimed that despite these facts the Mongol polity was feudal: cf L Krader, 'The Origin of the State Among the Nomads of Asia', H J M Claessen and P Skalnik (eds), *The Early State* (The Hague: Mouton, 1978), pp 93-107.

23 G E Markov, 'Problems of Social Change Among the Asiatic Nomads', W Weissleder (ed), *The Nomadic Alternative*, p 311.

24 A M Khazanov, *Nomads and the Outside World*, pp 123 f.

25 A M Khazanov, *Nomads and the Outside World*, pp 192 f.

26 A M Khazanov, *Nomads and the Outside World*, pp 231-3.

27 A M Khazanov, *Nomads and the Outside World*, p 240.

28 Sechin Jagchid and P Hyer, *Mongolia's Culture and Society* (Boulder, Col: Westview, 1979), pp 263 f.

29 'Religion and Revolution in Mongolia', *Modern Asian Studies* 1(1967), p 85.

30 'Frontier Feudalism', p 527; 'From Serf to Sage', pp 2 f.

31 'A Treasury of Inner Asian History and Culture', *Pacific Affairs* 50(1977), p 437.

32 L W Moses, *The Political Role of Mongol Buddhism*; W Heissig, *The Religions of Mongolia* (London: Routledge, 1980), pp 24 f.

33 L W Moses, *The Political Role of Mongol Buddhism*, pp 92-3.

34 L W Moses, *The Political Role of Mongol Buddhism*, pp 95 f.

35 'Mongolia's Place in the World' [1949], *Studies in Frontier History*, pp 270-95. Similar points are made in 'The Outer Mongolian Horizon' [1946], *Studies in Frontier History*, pp 259-69.

36 'Mongolia's Place in the World', p 288.

37 'Mongolia's Place in the World', pp 290 f.

38 *Nationalism and Revolution in Mongolia*, p 45.

39 'The Historical Setting of Inner Mongolian Nationalism', p 454.

40 *Nationalism and Revolution in Mongolia*, p 42.

41 *Nationalism and Revolution in Mongolia*, p 39.

42 'Satellite Politics: the Mongolian Prototype' [1936], *Studies in Frontier History*, p 297. See the review by Poppe which criticises 'Mongolia's Place in the World', *The Yale Review* 39(1949-50), pp 565-7.

43 A D Coox, *Nomonhan: Japan Against Russia, 1939*, 2 vols (Stanford: Stanford University Press, 1985).

44 *Nomads and Commissars*, p 128. On the independence of Mongolian political developments from direct Soviet interference, see pp 98-9, 118 f, 122 f.

45 *Nomads and Commissars*, p 157.

46 On the criticism of Choibalsang, see 'Resolution of the Second Plenum of the Mongolian People's Revolutionary Party, 29th January 1962', *Mongolian Heroes of the Twentieth Century*, trans and ed Urgunge Onon, pp 213-5.

47 *Leeds Lectures*, 5/18 f, 8/34 f.

48 *Leeds Lectures*, 5/19-20.

49 'The Collectivization of the Mongolian Herding Economy', *Marxist Perspectives* 9(1980), p 119; cf *Nomads and Commissars*, pp 119-20.

50 'The Collectivization of the Mongolian Herding Economy', pp 120-1.

51 Representatives of this school (which shows the influence of the point of view of Nicholas Poppe) include W B Ballis, 'The Political Evolution of a Soviet Satellite: the Mongolian People's Republic', *The Western Political Quarterly* 9(1956), pp 293-328; George G S Murphy, *Soviet Mongolia. A Study of the Oldest Political Satellite* (Berkeley: University of California Press, 1966); R A Rupen, *Mongols of the Twentieth Century*, Indiana University Ural & Altaic Series vol 37 (Bloomington: Indiana University, 1964); R A Rupen, *The Mongolian Peoples's Republic* (Stanford: The Hoover Institution, 1966); R A Rupen, *How Mongolia is Really Ruled*; a late example of this approach is T T Hammond, 'The Communist Takeover of Outer Mongolia: Model for Eastern Europe?', T T Hammond (ed), *The Anatomy of Communist Takeovers* (New Haven: Yale University Press, 1971), pp 107-44.

52 E H Carr, *Socialism in One Country 1924-1926*, vol 3 (Harmondsworth: Penguin, 1972), pp 845 f. Carr offers an extensive if uncritical summary of Party and Comintern documents of this period.

53 Ma Ho-t'ien, *Chinese Agent in Mongolia*, trans J De Francis (Baltimore: Johns Hopkins Press, 1949), pp 94-5.

54 W A Brown and Urgunge Onon (trans and ed), B Shirendev et al, *History of the Mongolian People's Republic* (Cambridge, Mass: Harvard University Press, 1976), p 238. This is a translation of the final part of a three volume work on Mongolian history by a committee of senior scholars from the Mongolian People's Republic which appeared in 1969.

55 *History of the Mongolian People's Republic*, pp 333-4; Brown and Onon, *History of the Mongolian People's Republic*, 277 f.

56 T E Ewing, *Between the Hammer and the Anvil?*, pp 159 f.

57 T E Ewing, *Between the Hammer and the Anvil?*, pp 171 f; Fujiko Isono, 'Soviet Russia and the Mongolian Revolution of 1921', *Past and Present* 83(May 1979), pp 116-40.

58 T E Ewing, *Between the Hammer and the Anvil?*, pp 201 f; C R Bawden, *The Modern History of Mongolia*, pp 209 f.

59   C R Bawden, *The Modern History of Mongolia*, pp 282-9; cf *History of the Mongolian People's Republic*, pp 315 f; B Shirendyb, *By-Passing Capitalism* (Ulan Bator: Mongolian People's Republic State Publishers, 1968).

60   Brown and Onon, *History of the Mongolian People's Republic*, p 238.

61   C R Bawden, *The Modern History of Mongolia*, pp 282 f.

62   G M Friters, *Outer Mongolia And Its International Position*, ed E Lattimore, Introduction by O Lattimore (London: Allen & Unwin, 1951), pp 136-9.

63   For a discussion of the difficulties that confronted the regime in their campaign to destroy the church see L W Moses, *The Political Role of Mongol Buddhism*, pp 188 f.

64   'Introduction', *The Diluv Khutagt*, p 15.

Conclusions

From this account of the intellectual biography of Owen Lattimore it can be seen that he has been concerned in a long life with many ideas and issues. From an interest in the political geography of frontiers, he developed a then novel approach to Chinese history which stressed the role of the frontier in the making of that history. From an interest in the situation and plight of Chinese frontier peoples, he came to champion the cause of the Mongols, first those within the Chinese Republic and later those in independent Mongolia. An early observer of the emergence into world politics of a third bloc or Third World of nations, he came to advocate an American foreign policy which would recognise the aspirations of those nations for development and national sovereignty.

Throughout his life the greatest continuity that can be discerned is his intellectual and emotional commitment to the Mongols, the former to their historical role, the latter to their right to a separate national and cultural existence. In his lectures at Leeds Lattimore once observed that in the 1930s he had been 'sentimentally [and] romantically aroused by the Inner Mongolian nationalist movement'.[1] It would not be too extreme to claim that this statement describes not a fleeting phase of his intellectual development but an enduring feature of his world view. It has been the purpose of this study to show how this commitment came about, and how it affected his approach to historical and contemporary issues.

Lattimore's original interest had been in long distance trade and trade-routes. This interest had provided the impetus for his first travels into the interior of China, travels which stimulated an enduring curiosity concerning frontier regions and peoples. Up to this point Lattimore had been most influenced by the extensive literature already available on exploring and travel in the interior of Asia, a literature in which remarks on topography and history are often juxtaposed with comments on folkways and the local manifestations of 'The Great Game' of Anglo-Russian rivalry. To an extent this literature has always been for Lattimore a model, since he has been concerned most often to understand any given phenomenon in its widest geographical and historical context even if this led to the broadest of speculations. Probably the most uniform feature of this otherwise diverse literature is its concern with the influence of geography and climate on these regions. The desiccation hypothesis of Huntington was then in vogue as an explanation for the disappearance of formerly thriving civilisations particularly in the Taklamakan basin. In this way Lattimore was introduced to the notion of geographical determinism, and to the ideas of Huntington in particular.

In the Chinese frontier regions Lattimore was confronted with a series of puzzles. Although modern means of transport were facilitating the expansion of Chinese civilisation, and drawing even the most remote areas into economic intercourse with the world market, the Chinese in these regions were apparently reluctant to adopt ways of life more suited to their new habitat. They were also contemptuous of those frontier peoples unwilling to seek incorporation into that civilisation. At this point during his travels in Manchuria in 1930 conclusions formed from personal observation and intellectual discovery appeared for Lattimore to coincide. Although in a frontier region, the Chinese in Manchuria did not behave like the pioneering frontier populations of Western literature. At the same time they were determined to reduce to subservience those of the indigenous inhabitants (the most numerous of whom were the Mongols) who showed any wish to remain in these regions, an intention often abetted by the conduct of the local traditional élites. In short both Chinese and frontier peoples seemed to evince the characteristics ascribed by Spengler, the first volume of whose *Decline of the West* accompanied Lattimore on his travels,2 to 'late' or moribund civilisations.

By this time Lattimore had resolved to make the Mongols an object of special study. Both Huntington and Spengler as well as his desire to understand the mainsprings of Mongol civilisation led him to Toynbee, Huntington because he is the source of the desiccation hypothesis Toynbee applied in order to explain the occasional but spectacular contributions of the pastoral nomads to world history, Spengler because Toynbee seemed to be engaged in a similar project though from a more empirical standpoint. But greater familiarity with the nomads led Lattimore to reject Toynbee's assertion that their way of life, and consequently their contribution to world history, simply reflected the limited possibilities of their habitat. Pastoral nomadism for Lattimore is a stage of civilisation which in part represents an historically late choice or range of choices for those practising it. As for the contribution of the nomads to world history, further research led Lattimore to the view that interactions between nomads and sedentary civilisations were more continuous and complex than Toynbee had allowed. In the later 1930s Lattimore formulated his definitive interpretation of nomad-Chinese interactions. Rather than, with Toynbee, the nomads playing a limited and essentially ahistorical role, being 'pushed' by climatic fluctuations and 'pulled' by the commodities of the sedentary civilisations, in the East Asian case it is the sedentary civilisation which is itself locked in a cycle of production and reproduction of its fundamentals which remains unchanged despite political and dynastic fluctuations. Here the influence of Wittfogel's characterisation of the pattern of Chinese history was an undoubted influence, though there are also echoes of Spengler and Toynbee in the apparent inability of Chinese civilisation to divert its energies into different channels.

Meanwhile, the contemporary predicament of the Mongols became for Lattimore a major preoccupation. For some time he held the hope that the Inner Mongolian nationalist movement would force the Chinese authorities to recognise the just claims and redress the grievances of their frontier inhabitants. Here the ideology of Sun Yat-sen would seem to hold out such a possibility, though in practice the Kuomintang regime in Nanking (to the extent that it took an interest in the problems of the Mongols) proved incapable of controlling the regional warlords who effectively dominated Inner Mongolia. However the ultimate inability of the old secular and ecclesiastical élites to protect the Mongols from national oblivion eventually brought Lattimore round to the view that only a social revolution would preserve them as a distinct people.

Having by this time written up in definitive form his interpretation of the history of nomad-Chinese interactions, Lattimore's appointment in Chungking led him to ponder the prospects for China. Whereas in earlier days Lattimore had been something of a critic of the Kuomintang, he now formed the view that in coalition (since 1936) with the Communist Party, Chiang Kai-shek's regime could successfully tackle the social and economic crises before which previous reformers had been impotent. There is no doubt that though Spengler and Toynbee were now distant influences in his thinking, Lattimore was as convinced of the need for a fundamental renovation in Chinese society as he was regarding the society of the Mongols. In 1941, for example, he emphasised the domestic problems the remedying of which would be crucial if the regime in Chungking was to continue to exist. Foreign assistance might help this regime in the fight against the Japanese for a time, but ultimately 'it must get on with the revolution or it will find that the revolution can get on without it'.[3] In his remarks on the communists it appears that he viewed them as principally nationalist articulators of peasant interests whose activities were largely independent of Soviet Russian direction. When, by 1947, he had lost his confidence in Chiang's ability to lead a reforming administration, Lattimore came to regard the communists as most likely (given their experiences and programme) to carry out the reforms China so urgently needed. His later writings on China suggest that he found this expectation confirmed.

Lattimore's growing stature as a public commentator and his sporadic contacts with government led him to offer a series of proposals regarding the best course for American policy in the aftermath of the war. Although his experience and knowledge of Asia were largely confined to China, Lattimore was confident that he detected across the whole continent the same forces at work: a desire for national sovereignty and material improvement coupled with a conviction that the old economic and political order was no longer acceptable. If the United States chose to ignore or repress those forces, as much present in the communist movements of Asia as elsewhere, American prestige and influence would suffer and the appeal of the Soviet Union would be enhanced. Soviet-American rivalry in Asia was acute at the frontiers of their respective zones, which for the US included South Korea, Taiwan, and Japan. In Asia the Soviet Union, in Lattimore's view, exerted a powerful force of attraction. A successful United States policy in Asia would need to match that power of attraction, economically by sharing the bounty of US resources and technological accomplishments, politically by backing reforming national governments against either old or new reactionaries. In the event not only was Lattimore's advice not followed, but he and others were called to account for the consequences for American power in Asia they had feared and predicted.

In his work from the 1950s onwards two further themes have been prominent. In some respects his somewhat speculative writings on the world history of frontiers are a generalising of his previous insights. In an important sense Lattimore has judged Chinese and Russian, and later American society by their respective treatment of the peoples on their frontiers or peripheries, this being a further example of the persisting influence of his early frontier experiences. As he was to observe in his retrospective judgment in 1962 of the central thesis of his many writings up to that date, 'every society tries to establish frontiers that conform to its own characteristics'.[4] The second theme, and the one which has dominated his life, has been the history and contemporary civilisation of the Mongols, his preoccupation with which will be considered in connection with his views on the Soviet Union and world politics.

In retrospect, the latter half of the twentieth century, though it has seen a struggle between the two great power blocs in Asia as elsewhere, has not been one in which the countries of the Third World have played as much of a mediating role as Lattimore had anticipated. And the socialist regimes of Asia, though they have all been responsible for great internal upheavals in their societies have not brought forth that marked improvement in material conditions that Lattimore thought would be forthcoming from the new era in that continent. Undoubtedly the greatest testimony to the failure of communist style modernisation to make a real difference to mass conditions of living has been the major shift in development strategy in China after 1978. Lattimore was correct, however, in predicting that communism in Asia would manifest as time went on a strongly nationalist character. The only and supremely ironical exception has been the Mongolian People's Republic which has followed doggedly behind the Soviet elder brother through all the vicissitudes of the world communist movement. As Lattimore feared, American intervention in Asia has, in some localities, helped keep in power authoritarian regimes. But far from being the prisoners of old interests and classes these regimes have often carried through social transformations as extensive as those seen in socialist political systems; in the cases of Taiwan, South Korea and Japan they have brought about economic changes for which the present era will be remembered.

How are Lattimore's expectations of the socialist bloc to be explained? The 1930s and 1940s of this century are littered with the misplaced hopes of

Western intellectuals in the mission and promise of the Soviet Union. The most common origins of these hopes were either disillusion with liberal and parliamentary systems in their own countries, or an identification of the Soviet Union with the achievement of socialism as it is prescribed in Marxian doctrine. Now it is clear that from about 1936 Lattimore was wont to voice uncritical opinions on the Soviet Union. These were usually concerned with matters related to his special interests - with Soviet policy in East Asia or the position of the peoples of the Far Eastern regions of the Soviet Union - but he nevertheless felt sufficiently well informed to describe, in a phrase often discussed before the US Senate Committees in the early 1950s, Stalin's show trials as 'a triumph for democracy'.[5] Indeed, Lattimore's interest in the USSR was sufficiently aroused by his trip through the country in 1936 for him to take a short course in the Russian language in London in the winter of that year. In 1940 Lattimore characterised Soviet policy in Mongolia as 'in the interests of the Mongol people as a whole',[6] and in his work in the 1950s on the original pattern of colonisation in the Russian Far East he went so far as to accept the then current Soviet position[7] that Tsarist expansion by (in his terms) progressive 'incorporation' was altogether more benign to the peoples concerned despite its imperialist impulse as compared with the activities of the other colonial powers. In the 1960s he had nothing but praise for Soviet conduct towards Mongolia, and for the internal policy of the Mongolian People's Republic which was and is closely modelled on Soviet precedents and guided by Soviet instructions. Lattimore's intellectual route to this uncritical approach towards the Soviet Union was not, however, either of those commonly taken by Western intellectuals of that era.

Spengler and Toynbee rather than Marx and Lenin seem to be the origins of Lattimore's belief that the present century was one of conflict between civilisations in which the peoples of Asia, if they were not to be overwhelmed by external force, would need to initiate and undergo fundamental social renovation. Already in his remarks of 1931 on the struggle of civilisations in Manchuria, Lattimore described Soviet Russia as a 'young' culture, and to that extent a model for the regeneration of Asian peoples. Lattimore's further work on frontier peoples, and in particular his close personal involvement with the predicament of the Mongols reinforced these notions. It is evident, thus, that his subsequent favourable assessment of the Soviet Union derived in part from Soviet sponsorship of Mongolia which not only kept the Mongols alive as a separate people with their own national identity but apparently admitted them to a share of the resources created by Soviet industrialisation. It also derived in part from the political and social progress of Soviet border areas which was a marked contrast, in Lattimore's opinion, with the sorry tale of Chinese frontier regions. There is also a geopolitical current in Lattimore's ideas which again goes back to his earlier intellectual preoccupations. If Asia was to be a theatre of struggle between the two major powers, Soviet power would inevitably be land based whereas American power would need to take on a maritime form. For some time Lattimore had believed that the era of maritime empire was at an end. He had also formed the opinion that the success of the Soviet Union in Asia could be traced to its progressive treatment of its Asian population. This was to be contrasted with the logic of maritime empires which dictated clinging onto beachheads and latter day Treaty Ports in the interests of trade and profit. Therefore a direct contest in Asia between the great powers could not be won by the United States. When these realities were ignored by American policy makers Lattimore could regard the United States as pursuing an imperialist strategy as against the progressive stance of the Soviet Union, a position he openly affirmed by the late 1960s.

It may be surmised that Lattimore's renewed enthusiasm from 1960 onwards for the Mongolian People's Republic and all its works has at its root (in addition to the continuation of his earlier interest) a further cause. Although the perjury charges against him were finally dismissed in 1955, Lattimore's career in the United States was then effectively at an end. Formerly a man who had moved in the highest academic and political circles, he now found himself an outcast, his institute liquidated and many scholars fearful of contact with him lest they suffer a similar fate. His ordeal had also exacted a considerable physical toll, as individuals who knew him in those years will testify. When he was greeted with such enthusiasm by the delegation of Mongol scholars in Moscow in 1960, and treated to an extensive trip in the Mongolian People's Republic (a country he had made so many efforts to visit in the past) subsequently, his reception must have seemed to him a contrast in every sense with the treatment he had received in his native country. Once again, intellectual conviction and personal experience combined to have a powerful impact on his world view. Long convinced that only a fundamental social renovation would save the Mongols as a people, Lattimore was now being given the rare honour, bearing in mind Mongolia's then remoteness and inaccessibility, of being able to view at first hand that social renovation in action. From that time Lattimore's completely uncritical attitude towards the Mongolian People's Republic (though not necessarily to Mongolian Marxist scholarship) flowed from these two intellectual and emotional springs. Thus, despite having pioneered (with Mongolia in mind) the use of the term 'satellite' to refer to a political and ideological dependent state, Lattimore abandoned it in 1962 as no longer appropriate to the Mongolian People's Republic. It is an ironic comment on his life's work that Lattimore will be remembered much longer for this contribution to the modern political vocabulary than for his contentions regarding the independent status of contemporary Mongolia.

Notes on Conclusions

1   *Leeds Lectures*, 8/7.
2   'Preface', *Studies in Frontier History*, pp 27-8.
3   'After Four Years', p 152.
4   'Preface', *Studies in Frontier History*, p 29.
5   *Pacific Affairs* XI(1938), pp 371-2.
6   *Inner Asian Frontiers of China*, p 199.
7   Michael Rywkin, *Moscow's Muslim Challenge. Soviet Central Asia* (Armonk, New York: M E Sharpe, 1982), pp 100 f.

Bibliography

Partial bibliographies of Owen Lattimore's writings may be found in the following:

Owen Lattimore, *Studies in Frontier History. Collected Papers 1928-58* (London: Oxford University Press, 1962), pp 553-61.

Stephan A Halkovic, 'Professor Owen Lattimore - A Bibliography', *The Mongolia Society. Occasional Papers*, 8(1972), pp 123-42.

Books

Dmitri Alioshin, *Asian Odyssey* (London: Cassell, 1941).

Thurman Arnold, *Fair Fights and Foul* (New York: Harcourt, Brace and Co, 1961).

S Avineri (ed), *Karl Marx on Colonialism and Modernization* (New York: Anchor Books, 1969).

Stanley D Bachrack, *The Committee of One Million: 'China Lobby' Politics 1953-1971* (New York: Columbia University Press, 1976).

Alexandre Barmine:

> *Memoirs of a Soviet Diplomat* (London: Lovat Dickson, 1938).
>
> *One Who Survived* (New York: Putnam, 1945).

Joseph Barnes (ed), *Empire in the East* (London: Kegan Paul, 1934).

W Barthold, *Turkestan Down to the Mongol Invasion* (London: Oxford University Press/Luzac & Co, 1928).

C R Bawden, *The Modern History of Mongolia* (London: Weidenfeld and Nicolson, 1968).

T A Bisson, *Yenan in 1937: Talks with the Communist Leaders*, University of California China Research Monograph (Berkeley: University of California Press, 1973).

J M Blum (ed), *The Price of Vision: The Diary of Henry A Wallace 1942-1946* (Boston: Houghton Mifflin, 1973).

George Boas and Harvey Wheeler, *Lattimore the Scholar* (Baltimore: Boas and Wheeler, 1953).

H L Boorman and R C Howard, *Biographical Dictionary of Republican China* (New York: Columbia University Press, 1967), vol I.

W A Brown and Urgunge Onon (trans and ed), B Shirendev et al, *History of the Mongolian People's Republic* (Cambridge, Mass: Harvard University Press, 1976).

E H Carr, *Socialism in One Country 1924-1926*, vol 3 (Harmondsworth: Penguin, 1972).

Robert K Carr, *The House Committee on Un-American Activities 1945-1950* (Ithaca: Cornell University Press, 1952).

Douglas Carruthers, *Unknown Mongolia. A Record of Travel and Exploration in North-West Mongolia and Dzungaria*, 2 vols (London: Hutchinson, 1913).

David Caute, *The Fellow-Travellers. A Postscript to the Enlightenment* (London: Weidenfeld and Nicolson, 1973).

Hok-lam Chan and W T deBary (eds), *Yüan Thought. Chinese Thought and Religion Under the Mongols* (New York: Columbia University Press, 1982).

Chang Mu (Zhang Mu) *Meng-ku Yu-mu Chi* (Menggu Yumu Ji) (Changsha: Basic Sinological Series, 1938).

Chang Yin-t'ang, *The Economic Development and Prospects of Inner Mongolia* (Shanghai: The Commercial Press, 1933).

Chi Ch'ao-ting, *Key Economic Areas in Chinese History. As revealed in the development of public works for water-control* (London: Allen and Unwin, 1936).

Hsi-sheng Chi, *Nationalist China at War. Military Defeats and Political collapse, 1937-45* (Ann Arbor: University of Michigan Press, 1982).

Henri J M Claessen and P Skalnik (eds):
> *The Early State* (The Hague: Mouton, 1978).
> *The Study of the State* (The Hague: Mouton, 1981).

F W Cleaves (trans and ed), *The Secret History of the Mongols* (Cambridge, Mass: Harvard University Press, 1982).

O Edmund Clubb, *The Witness and I* (New York: Columbia University Press, 1975).

Paul A Cohen, *Discovering History in China. American Historical Writing on the Recent Chinese Past* (New York: Columbia University Press, 1984).

Warren I Cohen, *The Chinese Connection. Roger S Greene, Thomas W Lamont, George E Sokolsky and American-East Asian Relations* (New York: Columbia University Press, 1978).

R Conquest:
> *The Great Terror. Stalin's Purge of the Thirties* (London: Macmillan, 1968).
> *Kolyma. The Arctic Death Camps* (New York: Viking Press, 1978).

A D Coox, *Nomonhan: Japan Against Russia, 1939*, 2 vols (Stanford: Stanford University Press, 1985).

H G Creel, *Studies in Early Chinese Culture* (Philadelphia: Porcupine Press, 1978 [1937]).

W T deBary, *Neo-Confucian Orthodoxy and the Learning of the Mind-and-Heart* (New York: Columbia University Press, 1981).

Lloyd E Eastman, *The Abortive Revolution: China under Nationalist Rule, 1927-1937* (Cambridge, Mass: Harvard University Press, 1974).

W Eberhard:
> *Conquerors and Rulers. Social Forces in Medieval China*, second edition (Leiden: E J Brill, 1970).
> *China's Minorities: Yesterday and Today* (Belmont: Wadsworth, 1982).

Bibliography

Robert B Ekvall, *Fields on the Hoof. Nexus of Tibetan Nomadic Pastoralism* (Prospect Heights, Illinois: Waveland Press, 1983).

Mark Elvin, *The Pattern of the Chinese Past* (Stanford: Stanford University Press, 1973).

Joseph W Esherick, *Lost Chance in China. The World War II Despatches of John S Service* (New York: Random House, 1974).

M Evans, *Karl Marx* (London: Allen & Unwin, 1975).

T E Ewing, *Between the Hammer and the Anvil? Chinese and Russian Policies in Outer Mongolia 1911-1921*, Indiana University Uralic and Altaic Series vol 138 (Bloomington: Indiana University, 1980).

J K Fairbank:

> (ed), *The Chinese World Order* (Cambridge, Mass: Harvard University Press, 1968).
>
> *Chinabound: A Fifty-Year Memoir* (New York: Harper & Row, 1982).
>
> *The United States and China*, third edition - first published 1948 (Cambridge, Mass: Harvard University Press, 1971).

J K Fairbank et al, *East Asia. Tradition and Transformation* (Boston: Houghton Mifflin, 1973).

Herbert Feis, *The China Tangle* (Princeton: Princeton University Press, 1953).

Frederick V Field, *From Right to Left. An Autobiography* (Westport, Conn: Lawrence Hill, 1983).

Peter Fleming, *News from Tartary* (London: Jonathan Cape, 1936).

John T Flynn, *The Lattimore Story* [1953], revised edition (New York: Devin-Adair, 1962).

Andrew D W Forbes, *Warlords and Muslims in Chinese Central Asia: A Political History of Republican Sinkiang 1911-1949* (Cambridge: Cambridge University Press, 1986).

Richard M Fried, *Men Against McCarthy* (New York: Columbia University Press, 1976).

G M Friters, *Outer Mongolia And Its International Position*, ed E Lattimore, Introduction by O Lattimore (London: Allen & Unwin, 1951).

John Lewis Gaddis, *Strategies of Containment. A Critical Appraisal of Postwar American National Security Policy* (New York: Oxford University Press, 1982).

Joseph Geleta (with Ladislaus Forbath), *The New Mongolia* (London: Heinemann, 1936).

Donald G Gillin, *Warlord, Yen Hsi-shan in Shansi Province 1911-1949* (Princeton: Princeton University Press, 1967).

James Gilmour, *Among the Mongols* (London: The Religious Tract Society, nd).

Henning Haslund:

> *Tents in Mongolia (Yabonah)* (London: Kegan Paul, 1934).
>
> *Men and Gods in Mongolia (Zayagan)* (London: Kegan Paul, 1935).

W Heissig:

A Lost Civilization. The Mongols Rediscovered (London: Thames & Hudson, 1966).

The Religions of Mongolia (London: Routledge, 1980).

Ping-ti Ho, *The Cradle of the East. An Inquiry into the Indigenous Origins of Techniques and Ideas of Neolithic and Early Historic China, 5000-1000 BC* (Hong Kong: Chinese University of Hong Kong Press, 1975).

I C Y Hsu, *The Rise of Modern China*, third edition ((New York: Oxford University Press, 1983).

Ellsworth Huntington, *The Pulse of Asia* (Boston: Houghton Mifflin, 1907).

Paul Hyer and Sechin Jagchid (eds), *A Mongolian Living Buddha: Biography of the Kanjurwa Khutughtu* (Albany: State University of New York Press, 1982).

Harold R Isaacs, *Re-encounters in China. Notes of a Journey in a Time Capsule* (Armonk, New York: M E Sharpe, 1985).

Philip J Jaffe, *The Rise and Fall of American Communism* (New York: Horizon Press, 1975).

Sechin Jagchid and P Hyer, *Mongolia's Culture and Society* (Boulder, Col: Westview, 1979).

J S Kahn and J R Llobera (eds), *The Anthropology of Pre-Capitalist Societies* (London: Macmillan, 1981).

A M Khazanov, *Nomads and the Outside World* (Cambridge: Cambridge University Press, 1984).

Lawrence Krader, *Social Organization of the Mongol-Turkic Pastoral Nomads*, Indiana University Uralic and Altaic Series vol 20 (The Hague: Mouton, 1963).

Anthony Kubek, *How the Far East was Lost: American Policy and the Creation of Communist China*, 1941-1949 (Chicago: Regnery, 1963).

Stanley I Kutler, *The American Inquisition. Justice and Injustice in the Cold War* (New York: Hill and Wang, 1982).

Luc Kwanten, *Imperial Nomads. A History of Central Asia, 500-1500* (Leicester: Leicester University Press, 1979).

Earl Latham, *The Communist Controversy in Washington. From the New Deal to McCarthy* (Cambridge, Mass: Harvard University Press, 1966).

Owen Lattimore:

> *America and Asia. Problems of Today's War and the Peace of Tomorrow* (Claremont: Claremont Colleges, 1943).
>
> *The Desert Road to Turkestan* (London: Methuen, 1928).
>
> (and Fujiko Isono), *The Diluv Khutagt, Memoirs and Autobiography of a Mongol Buddhist Reincarnation in Religion and Revolution*, Asiatische Forschungen, 74 (Wiesbaden: Harrassowitz, 1982).
>
> *From China Looking Outward* (Leeds; Leeds University Press, 1964).
>
> *High Tartary* (Boston: Little Brown, 1930).
>
> *History and Revolution in China*, Scandinavian Institute of Asian Studies Monograph Series no 3 (Lund: Studentlitteratur, 1970).

Bibliography

Inner Asian Frontiers of China (London: Oxford University Press, 1940).
The Legacy of Empire in Asia, Danforth Foundation Lectures no 9 (Greenville: East Carolina College, 1960).
The Making of Modern China. A Short History [1944] (London: Allen and Unwin, 1945).
Manchuria, cradle of conflict, revised edition [1935] (New York: AMS Press reprint, 1975).
Mongol Journeys (London: Jonathan Cape, 1941).
The Mongols of Manchuria (New York: Macmillan, 1934).
Nationalism and Revolution in Mongolia. With a translation from the Mongol of Sh Nachukdorji's 'Life of Sukebatur' (Leiden: E J Brill, 1955).
Nomads and Commissars. Mongolia Revisited (New York: Oxford University Press, 1962).
Ordeal by Slander (New York: Greenwood reprint of Little, Brown 1950 edition, 1971).
Pivot of Asia. Sinkiang and the Inner Asian Frontiers of China and Russia (Boston: Little, Brown, 1950; New York: AMS reprint, 1975).
The Situation in Asia (Boston: Little, Brown, 1949).
Solution in Asia (New York: AMS reprint of Little, Brown edition of 1945, 1975).
Studies in Frontier History, (London: Oxford University Press, 1962).
Robert H G Lee, *The Manchurian Frontier in Ch'ing History* (Cambridge, Mass: Harvard University Press, 1970).
C Lefèbure, Walter Goldshmidt et al, *L'Equipe écologie et anthroplogie des sociétés pastorales*, *Pastoral Production and Society* (Cambridge: Cambridge University Press, 1979).
Ma Ho-t'ien, *Chinese Agent in Mongolia*, trans J De Francis (Baltimore: Johns Hopkins Press, 1949).
Andrew L March, *The Idea of China* (Newton Abbott: David & Charles, 1974).
Karl Marx, *A Contribution to the Critique of Political Economy* (Moscow: Progress Publishers, 1970).
Gary May, *China Scapegoat. The Diplomatic Ordeal of John Carter Vincent* (Washington: New Republic Books, 1979).
Yasuo Misshima and Tomio Goto (trans and ed A Gradjdanzev), *A Japanese View of Outer Mongolia* (New York: International Secretariat, Institute of Pacific Relations, 1942).
Ivor Montagu, *Land of Blue Sky. A Portrait of Modern Mongolia* (London: Dobson, 1956).
James W Morley, *The China Quagmire. Japan's Expansion on the Asian Continent 1933-41* (New York: Columbia University Press, 1983).
L W Moses, *The Political Role of Mongol Buddhism* (Bloomington: Indiana University Asian Research Institute, Uralic Altaic Series no 133, 1977).

George G S Murphy, *Soviet Mongolia. A Study of the Oldest Political Satellite* (Berkeley: University of California Press, 1966).

Joseph Needham, *The Grand Titration. Science and Society in East and West* (London: Allen and Unwin, 1969).

V A Obruchev, *Kukushkin. A Geographer's Tales* (London: Constable, 1961).

Urgunge Onon (trans and ed), *Mongolian Heroes of the Twentieth Century* (New York: AMS Press, 1976).

Ferdinand Ossendowski, *Beasts, Men and Gods* (London: Edward Arnold, 1923).

David M Oshinsky, *A Conspiracy So Immense. The World of Joe McCarthy* (New York: The Free Press, 1983).

Herbert L Packer, *Ex-Communist Witnesses* (Stanford: Stanford University Press, 1962).

N Poppe, *Reminiscences* (Bellingham: Western Washington University, 1983).

A M Pozdneyev, *Mongolia and the Mongols*, J R Krueger (ed), (Bloomington: Indiana University Press, 1971).

N Prejevalsky:

    Mongolia, The Tangut Country, and the Solitudes of Northern Tibet, 2 vols, (London: Samson Low, 1876).

    From Kulja, Across the Tian Shan to Lob Nor (London: Sampson Low, 1879).

J R V Prescott, *Boundaries and Frontiers* (London: Croom Helm, 1978).

Richard H Rovere, *Senator Joe McCarthy* (New York: Harcourt, Brace, Jovanovich, 1959).

Winwood Reade, *The Martyrdom of Man* (London: Watts & Co, 1948).

Morris Rossabi:

    China and Inner Asia. From 1368 to the Present Day (London: Thames & Hudson, 1975).

    (ed), *China among Equals. The Middle Kingdom and its Neighbours, 10th-14th Centuries* (Berkeley: University of California Press, 1983).

Andrew Roth, *Dilemma in Japan* (London: Gollancz, 1945).

R A Rupen:

    How Mongolia Is Really Ruled (Stanford: Hoover Institute Press, 1979).

    The Mongolian Peoples's Republic (Stanford: The Hoover Institution, 1966).

    Mongols of the Twentieth Century, Indiana University Ural & Altaic Series vol 37 (Bloomington: Indiana University, 1964).

M Rywkin, *Moscow's Muslim Challenge. Soviet Central Asia* (Armonk, New York: M E Sharpe, 1982).

Sh Sandag, *The Mongolian People's Struggle for National Independence and the Building of a New Life* (Ulan Bator: State Publishing House, 1966).

M Sanjdorj, *Manchu Chinese Colonial Rule in Northern Mongolia*, trans Urgunge Onon, preface by Owen Lattimore (London: Hurst, 1980).

M Sawer, *Marxism and the Question of the Asiatic Mode of Production* (The Hague: Martinus Nijhoff, 1977).

Michael Schaller, *The US Crusade in China, 1938-1945* (New York: Columbia University Press, 1979).

H G Schwarz (ed), *Studies on Mongolia*, Proceedings of the First North American Conference on Mongolian Studies (Bellingham: West Washington University, 1979).

H Serruys, *Sino-Mongol Relations During the Ming, II. The Tribute System and Diplomatic Missions (1400-1600)*, *Mélanges Chinois et Boudhiques* vol XIV (Brussels: Institut Belge Des Hautes Etudes Chinoises, 1967).

John S Service, *The Amerasia Papers: Some Problems in the History of US-China Relations* (Berkeley: University of California China Research Monograph no 7, 1971).

W H Shaw, *Marx's Theory of History* (Stanford: Stanford University Press, 1978).

William Shawcross, *Sideshow. Kissinger, Nixon and the Destruction of Cambodia* (New York: Simon and Schuster, 1979).

James E Sheridan:
    Chinese Warlord: The career of Feng Yü-hsiang (Stanford: Stanford University Press, 1966).
    China in Disintegration. The Republican Era in Chinese History 1912-1949 (New York: The Free Press, 1975).

B Shirendyb, *By-Passing Capitalism* (Ulan Bator: Mongolian People's Republic State Publishing House, 1968).

Oswald Spengler (trans C A Atkinson), *The Decline of the West. Form and Actuality* (London: Allen and Unwin, 1926).

Nicholas J Spykman:
    America's Strategy in World Politics (New York: Harcourt, Brace and Co, 1942).
    The Geography of the Peace (New York: Harcourt, Brace and Co, 1944).

J J Stephan, *Sakhalin. A History* (Oxford: Oxford University Press, 1971).

Joseph W Stilwell, *The Stilwell Papers*, (ed) T H White (London: MacDonald, 1949).

Jing-shan Tao, *The Jurchen in Twelfth-Century China. A Study of Sinicization* (Seattle: University of Washington Press, 1976).

J N Thomas, *The Institute of Pacific Relations. Asian Scholars and American Politics* (Seattle: University of Washington Press, 1974).

Christopher Thorne, *Allies of a Kind. The United States, Britain, and the War Against Japan, 1941-1945* (Oxford: Oxford University Press, 1978).

James Thorp, *Geography of the Soils of China* (Nanking: National Geological Survey of China, 1936).

Arnold Toynbee:
    A Study of History vol III, 2nd edition (Oxford: Oxford University Press, 1935).

Arnold Toynbee: A Selection from his Works, E W F Tomlin (ed) (Oxford: Oxford University Press, 1978).

Tang Tsou, *America's Failure in China 1941-50* (Chicago: University of Chicago Press, 1963).

Barbara W Tuchman, *Sand Against the Wind: Stilwell and the American Experience in China 1911-45* (New York: Macmillan, 1970).

G L Ulmen, *The Science of Society. Toward an Understanding of the Life and Work of Karl August Wittfogel* (The Hague: Mouton, 1978).

UNESCO, *International Symposium on the Role of Nomadic Peoples in Central Asian Civilizations* (Paris: UNESCO, 1973).

US Congress: Senate, *Hearings on State Department Loyalty. Hearings before a subcommittee of the Committee on Foreign Relations* (Washington: US Government Printing Office, 1950).

US Congress: Senate, *Hearings on State Department Loyalty: Report* (Washington: US Government Printing Office, report no 2108, 1950).

US Congress: Senate, Committee on the Judiciary, Subcommittee to Investigate ... Internal Security ..., *The Amerasia Papers: A Clue to the Catastrophe of China* (Washington: US Government Printing Office, 1970).

US Congress: Senate, *Institute of Pacific Relations. Hearings before the Subcommittee ... of the Committee on the Judiciary* (Washington: US Government Printing Office, 1951-2).

US Congress: Senate, *Report of the Committee on the Judiciary. Hearings held ... by the Internal Security Subcommittee* (Washington: US Government Printing Office, report no 2050, 1952).

US Department of State, *Foreign Relations of the United States. 1941*. vol IV. The Far East (Washington: US Government Printing Office, 1956), 362.

US Department of State, *Foreign Relations of the United States. 1942*. China, (Washington: US Government Printing Office, 1956).

USSR & MPR Academies of Science, *History of the Mongolian People's Republic* (Moscow: Nauka, 1973).

Freda Utley, *The China Story* (Chicago: Regnery, 1951).

Sevyan Vainshtein (Caroline Humphrey ed), *Nomads of South Siberia: The Pastoral Economies of Tuva* (Cambridge: Cambridge University Press, 1980).

B Ya Vladimirtsov:

   The Life of Chingis-Khan, trans D S Mirsky (London: Routledge, 1930).

   Le Régime Social des Mongols: le Féodalisme Nomade, trad M Carsow (Paris: du Musée Guimet Bibliothèque d'études, Libraire d'Amérique et d'Orient Adrien-Maisonneuve, 1948).

H H Vreeland III, *Mongol Community and Kinship Structure* (New Haven: Human Relations Area Files, 1954).

Arthur Waley, *The Travels of an Alchemist* (London: Routledge, 1931).

Richard L Walker, *The Multi-State System of Ancient China* (Hamden, Conn: Shoe String Press, 1953).

William Watson, *Cultural Frontiers in Ancient East Asia* (Edinburgh: Edinburgh University Press, 1971).

Hans W Weigert and Vilhjalmur Stefansson (eds), *Compass of the World. A Symposium on Political Geography* (London: George Harrap, nd).

Wolfgang Weissleder (ed), *The Nomadic Alternative. Modes and Models of Interaction in the African-Asian Deserts and Steppes* (The Hague: Mouton, 1978).

T H White, *In Search of History* (London: Jonathan Cape, 1979).

Allan M Winkler, *The Politics of Propaganda. The Office of War Information 1942-1945* (New Haven: Yale University Press, 1978).

Allen S Whiting and Sheng Shih-ts'ai, *Sinkiang: Pawn or Pivot?* (East Lansing: Michigan State University Press, 1958).

K A Wittfogel and Feng Chia-sheng, *History of Chinese Society. Liao. Transactions of the American Philosophical Society* n s 36(1946) (Philadelphia: American Philosophical Society, 1949).

K A Wittfogel, *Oriental Despotism. A Comparative Study of Total Power* (New Haven: Yale University Press, 1957).

Francis E Younghusband, *The Heart of a Continent*, 4th edition (London: John Murray, 1904).

Sir Henry Yule, *Cathay and the Way Thither. Being a Collection of Medieval Notices of China*, new edition, 4 vols (London: The Hakluyt Society, 1913-16).

N Zhagvaral (ed), *The Mongolian People's Republic* (Ulan Bator: The Committee of Sciences of the MPR, 1956).

Articles

W B Ballis, 'The Political Evolution of a Soviet Satellite: the Mongolian People's Republic', *The Western Political Quarterly* 9(1956), pp 293-328.

G B Barbour, 'Recent Observations on the Loess of North China', *The Geographical Journal* LXXXVI(1935), pp 52-64.

Thomas J Barfield, 'The Hsiung-nu Imperial Confederacy: Organization and Foreign Policy', *Journal of Asian Studies* XLI(1981-2), pp 45-61.

G C Binstead, 'The Tribal and Administrative System of Mongolia' *Far Eastern Review* X (1913-14), no 2, pp 41-8, 70.

C W Bishop:

> 'The Beginnings of North and South in China', *Pacific Affairs* VII(1934), pp 297-325.
>
> 'The Rise of Civilization in China with reference to its Geographical Aspects', *The Geographical Review* 22(1932), pp 617-31.
>
> 'The Chronology of Ancient China', *Journal of the American Oriental Society* 52(1932), pp 232-47.

'Origin and Early Diffusion of the Traction Plow', *Antiquity* X(1936), pp 261-81.

Paul D Buell, 'The Role of the Sino-Mongolian Frontier Zone in the Rise of Cinggis-Qan', Henry G Schwarz (ed), *Studies on Mongolia. Proceedings of the First North American Conference on Mongolian Studies* (Bellingham: Western Washington University, 1979), pp 63-76.

Warren I Cohen, 'Acheson, His Advisers, and China, 1949-1950', Dorothy Borg and Waldo Heinrichs (eds), *Uncertain Years. Chinese-American Relations, 1949-1950* (New York: Columbia University Press, 1980), pp 13-52.

'Communiqué of the Third Plenary Session of the 11th Central Committee', *Peking Review* 21(1978) no 52.

Deng Xiaoping, 'Mao Zedong Thought must be correctly understood as an integral whole', *Selected Works of Deng Xiaoping* (Beijing: Foreign Languages Press, 1984), pp 55-60.

N Dyson-Hudson, 'The Study of Nomads', *Journal of Asian and African Studies* VII(1972), pp 2-29.

Max Eastman and J B Powell, 'The Fate of the World is at Stake in China', *Readers' Digest* 46(1945), June, pp 13-22.

Ney Elias, 'Narrative of a Journey through Western Mongolia, July 1872 to January 1873', *Journal of the Royal Geographical Society* XLIII(1873), pp 108-56.

T E Ewing:

'The Origin of the Mongolian People's Revolutionary Party: 1920', *Mongolian Studies* V(1978-79), pp 79-105.

'Russia, China, and the Origins of the Mongolian Peoples's Republic, 1911-1921: A Reappraisal', *The Slavonic and East European Review* 58(1980), pp 399-421.

'The Mongolian People's Republic Today', *Asian Affairs* XI(1980), pp 309-21.

'Mongolia's Mess', *The Guardian*, 21 January 1980.

D M Farquhar, 'The Origins of the Manchu's Mongolian Policy', J K Fairbank (ed), *The Chinese World Order* (Cambridge, Mass: Harvard University Press, 1968), pp 198-205.

Joseph Fletcher, 'A Brief History of the Chinese Northwestern Frontier' in M Alonso (ed), *China's Inner Asian Frontier* (Cambridge, Mass: Harvard University Press, 1979), pp 21-52.

J L Gaddis, 'The Strategic Perspective: The Rise and Fall of the "Defensive Perimeter" Concept, 1947-1951', Dorothy Borg and Waldo Heinrichs (eds), *Uncertain Years. Chinese-American Relations, 1949-1950* (New York: Columbia University Press, 1980), pp 61-118.

Brian Gilbert [pseud], 'New Light on the Lattimore Case', *The New Republic* 131(1954), 27 December, pp 7-12.

Bibliography

'Mikhail Gorbachyov's speech at ceremony in Vladivostok', *Soviet News* no 6335, 30 July 1986, p 341.

John Gross, 'The Years of the Purges', *New Statesman* 76(1968), 27 September, pp 397-8.

T T Hammond, 'The Communist Takeover of Outer Mongolia: Model for Eastern Europe?', T T Hammond (ed), *The Anatomy of Communist Takeovers* (New Haven: Yale University Press, 1971), pp107-44.

John Gombojab Hangin:

'The Second International Congress of Mongolists, Ulan Bator, 1970', *The Mongolia Society Bulletin* 9(1970), no 2, pp 1-9.

and Urgunge Onon, 'Professor Owen Lattimore - A Biographical Sketch', *The Mongolia Society. Occasional Papers* 8(1972), pp 7-9.

David Harvey, 'Owen Lattimore. A Memoire', *Antipode* 15(1984), no 3, pp 3-11.

William L Holland, 'Source Materials on the Institute of Pacific Relations', *Pacific Affairs* 58(1985-86), pp 91-7.

Caroline Humphrey, 'The Role of Herdsmen's Co-operatives in the National Economy', *Development and Change* 9(1978), pp 133-60.

Fujiko Isono:

'The Mongolian Revolution of 1921', *Modern Asian Studies* X(1976), pp 375-94.

'Soviet Russia and the Mongolian Revolution of 1921', *Past and Present* 83(May 1979), pp 116-40.

Sechin Jagchid:

'Mongolian Nationalism in Response to Great Power Rivalry 1900-1950', *Plural Societies* 5(1974), part 4, pp 43-57.

'Patterns of Trade and Conflict Between China and the Nomads of Mongolia', *Zentralasiatische Studien* 11(1977), pp 177-204.

'Prince Gungsangnorbu, Forerunner of Inner Mongolian Modernization', *Zentralasiatische Studien* 12 (1978), pp 147-58.

'The Failure of a Self-Determination Movement: The Inner Mongolian Case', W O McCagg and B D Silver (eds), *Soviet Asian Ethnic Frontiers* (New York: Pergamon Press, 1979), pp 229-45.

'Kitan Struggle Against Jurchen Oppression - Nomadism versus Sinicization', *Zentralasiatische Studien* 16(1982), pp 165-85.

Gareth Jenkins, 'A Note on Climatic Cycles and the Rise of Chinggis Khan', *Central Asiatic Journal* 18(1974), pp 217-26.

Stephen B Jones, 'Boundary Concepts in the Setting of Place and Time', *Annals of the Association of American Geographers* 49(1959), pp 241-55.

Journal of the Anglo-Mongolian Society.

Alfred Kohlberg:

'Owen Lattimore: "Expert's Expert"', *China Monthly* 6(October 1945), 10-12.

'Stupidity and/or Treason', *China Monthly* 9(June 1948), pp 151-2.

L Krader:

'Feudalism and the Tatar Polity of the Middle Ages', *Comparative Studies in Society and History* 1(1959), pp 76-99.

'The Ecology of Nomadic Pastoralism', *International Social Science Journal* 11(1959), pp 499-510.

'The Origin of the State Among the Nomads of Asia', H J M Claessen and P Skalnik (eds), *The Early State* (The Hague: Mouton, 1978), pp 93-107.

Ladis K D Kristof, 'The Nature of Frontiers and Boundaries', *Annals of the Association of American Geographers* 49(1959), pp 269-82.

Owen Lattimore:

'Gosforth Cross', *The Mitre* (St Bees School) vol 1, no 9 (July 1919).

'Now the Mongols are Pawns in a Game', *New York Times Magazine* 2 September 1928, pp 4-5.

'Strife over the Last Forbidden Land', *New York Times Magazine* 23 September 1928, pp 10-11.

'Mongolia Enters World Affairs' *Pacific Affairs* VII (1934), pp 14-28.

'Prince, Priest and Herdsman in Mongolia', *Pacific Affairs* VIII (1935), pp 35-47.

'The Inland Gates of China', *Pacific Affairs* VIII (1935), pp 463-73.

'Russo-Japanese Relations', *International Affairs* 15 (1936), pp 525-42.

'Land and Sea in the destiny of Japan', *Pacific Affairs* IX (1936), pp 586-9.

'Inner Mongolia - Chinese, Japanese or Mongol?', *Pacific Affairs* X (1937), pp 64-71.

'The Lines of Cleavage in Inner Mongolia', *Pacific Affairs* X (1937), pp 196-201.

'Japan Hung Up on the Hypotenuse', *Amerasia* 2 (1938), pp 475-80.

'The Moscow Trials: Comment', *Pacific Affairs* XI(1938), pp 370-2.

'Siberia seals Japan's fate' *Amerasia* 2 (1938), pp 380-4.

'American Responsibilities in the Far East', *Virginia Quarterly Review* 16(1940), pp 161-74.

'As China Goes, so Goes Asia', *Amerasia* 4(1940), pp 253-7.

'China's Turkestan - Siberian Supply Road', *Pacific Affairs* XIII (1940), pp 393-412.

'Not China's Lifeline, But America's', *The China Monthly* (November 1940), p 8.

'America and the Future of China', *Amerasia* 5(1941), pp 296-7.

'After Four Years', *Pacific Affairs* XIV(1941), pp 141-53.

'Stalemate in China', *Foreign Affairs* 19(1941), pp 621-32.

'The Fight for Democracy in Asia', *Foreign Affairs* 20(1942), pp 694-704.

'Yunnan, Pivot of Southeast Asia', *Foreign Affairs* 21(1943), pp 476-93.

Bibliography

'Minorities in the Soviet Far East', *Far Eastern Survey* XIII(1944), pp 156-8.

'New Road to Asia', *The National Geographic Magazine* LXXXVI(1944), pp 641-76.

'Reply to Mr Kohlberg', *China Monthly* 6(December 1945), pp 15-17.

'The Czech Exception Disproves the Rules', *The New Republic* 117(1947), 22 September, pp 6-7.

'The Chessboard of Power and Politics', *Virginia Quarterly Review* 24(1948), pp 174-86.

'Sinkiang Survey', *Far Eastern Survey* XVII(1948), no 5, pp 56-63.

'Spengler and Toynbee', *Atlantic Monthly* 181 (April 1948), pp 104-5.

'Opening of Asia', *Atlantic Monthly* 183 (March 1949), pp 29-33.

'Point Four and the Third Countries', *Annals of the American Academy of Political and Social Science* 270 (July 1950), pp 1-7.

'We Need Asia', *Nation* 171(1950), 16 December, pp 556-9.

'Korea: We Win a Round', *Nation*, 173(1951), p 44.

'When Japan Has a Treaty', *Nation*, 173(1951), 4 August, pp 88-9.

'Safeguard Democracy!', *Nation* 174(1952), 9 February, p 134.

'Battle of the Corridors', *Nation*, 178(1954), 23 January, pp 69-71.

'The Industrial Impact on China, 1800-1950', *First International Conference of Economic History: Proceedings* (1960), pp 103-13.

'The Social History of Mongol Nomadism', W G Beasley and E G Pulleybank (eds), *Historians of China and Japan* (London: Oxford University Press, 1961), 328-43.

'Chingis Khan and the Mongol Conquests', *Scientific American* 209(August 1963), pp 54-68.

'China: the American mystique', *The Listener* 72(1964), no 1853, 1 October, pp 491-4.

'China and the Ugly Americans', *New Statesman* 73(1967), 24 February, p 253.

'Religion and Revolution in Mongolia', *Modern Asian Studies* 1(1967), pp 81-94.

'Left-Wing Consciences', *New Statesman* 76(1968), 11 October, p 461.

Leeds Lectures (Leeds University: Chinese Studies department, 1969).

'Russo-Chinese Imperialism', *New Statesman* 77(1969), 21 March, pp 396-7.

'Mongolia once more', *Mongolia Society Bulletin* 9(1970), no 1, pp 1-4.

'Unpublished Report from Yenan 1937', J Ch'en and N Tarling (eds), *Studies in the Social History of China and South East Asia* (Cambridge: Cambridge University Press, 1970), pp 153-63.

'Return to China's Northern Frontier', *The Geographical Journal* CXXXIX(1973), pp 233-42.

'From Serf to Sage. The Life and Work of Jamsrangiin Sambuu', *Journal of the Anglo-Mongolian Society* 3(1976) no 1, pp 1-23.

'A Treasury of Inner Asian History and Culture', *Pacific Affairs* 50(1977), pp 426-44.

'Geography and the Ancient Empires', in M T Larsen (ed), *Power and Propaganda: A Symposium on Ancient Empires* (Copenhagen Studies in Assyriology vol 7, Copenhagen: Akademisk Forlag, 1979), pp 35-40.

'China's Historical Hegemony', *Nation* 108(1979), 17 March, p 276.

'The Nomads and South Russia', *APXEION ΠΟΝΤΟΥ* (Athens, 1979), pp 193-200.

'The Failure of a Self-Determination Movement: The Inner Mongolian Case' in W O McCagg and B D Silver (eds), *Soviet Asian Ethnic Frontiers* (New York: Pergamon Press, 1979), pp 229-245.

'Inner Mongolian Nationalism and the Pan-Mongolian Idea: Recollections and Reflections', *Journal of the Anglo-Mongolian Society* VI (1980), no 1, pp 5-21.

'The Collectivization of the Mongolian Herding Economy', *Marxist Perspectives* 9(1980), pp 116-27.

G Lichtheim, 'Oriental Despotism', *The Concept of Ideology and Other Essays* (New York: Vintage Books, 1967), pp 62-93.

H J Mackinder, 'The Geographical Pivot of History', *The Geographical Journal* XXIII (1904), pp 421-44.

G E Markov, 'Problems of Social Change Among the Asiatic Nomads', W Weissleder (ed), *The Nomadic Alternative* (The Hague: Mouton, 1978), pp 305-11.

Marvin W Mikesell, 'Comparative Studies in Frontier History', *Annals of the Association of American Geographers* 50(1960), pp 62-74.

Julian V Minghi, 'Boundary Studies in Political Geography', Roger E Kasperson and J V Minghi (eds), *The Structure of Political Geography* (London: University of London Press, 1970), pp 140-60.

Mongolia Society Newsletter.

Mongolia Society Bulletin.

Sh Natsagdorj:

(trans O Lattimore), 'The Economic Basis of Feudalism in Mongolia', *Modern Asian Studies* 1(1967), pp 265-81.

'Arad Ayush the Commoner', *Mongolian Heroes of the Twentieth Century*, trans and ed Urgunge Onon, introduction by Owen Lattimore (New York: AMS Press, 1976), pp 1-42.

Robert P Newman:

'Bureaucrats As Heroes. The FBI In The Age Of McCarthy', *Pitt - Supplement*, February 1982, pp 14-19.

'The Self-Inflicted Wound: The China White Paper of 1949', *Prologue* 14(1982), pp 141-56.

'Lattimore and His Enemies', *Antipode* 15(1983), no 3, pp 12-26.

'Clandestine Chinese Nationalist Efforts To Punish Their American Detractors', *Diplomatic History* 7(1983), no 3, pp 205-22.

Bibliography

'Red Scare in Seattle, 1952: the FBI, the CIA, and Owen Lattimore's "Escape"', *The Historian* XLVIII(1985), pp 61-81.

N Poppe, 'Central Asia', *The Yale Review* 39(1949-50), pp 565-7.

Friederich Ratzel, 'The Laws of the Spatial Growth of States', Roger E Kasperson and J V Minghi (eds), *The Structure of Political Geography* (London: University of London Press, 1970), pp 17-28.

Wolf Schenke, 'Vast Area as an Instrument of War', *Amerasia* 3(1939), pp 539-44.

Amnon Sella, 'Khalkhin-Gol: The Forgotten War', *Journal of Contemporary History* 18(1983), pp 651-87.

Lawrence N Shyu, 'China's "Wartime Parliament": The People's Political Council, 1938-1945', in Paul K T Sih (ed), *Nationalist China During the Sino-Japanese War, 1937-1945* (Hicksville, New York: Exposition Press, 1977), pp 280-1.

J Stalin, 'Dialectical and historical materialism', *Problems of Leninism* (Moscow: Foreign Languages Publishing House, 1953), pp 730-45.

Sir Aurel Stein, 'Innermost Asia: Its Geography as a Factor in History', *The Geographical Journal* LXV(1925), pp 377-403, 473-501.

[Arnold Toynbee], 'Europe in the Valley of Death', *Times Literary Supplement* no 926, 24 June 1920, p 390.

U Vogel, 'K A Wittfogel's Marxist Studies on China, 1926-1939', *Bulletin of Concerned Asian Scholars* 11(1979) no 4, pp 30-7.

Arthur N Waldron, 'The Problem of the Great Wall of China', *Harvard Journal of Asiatic Studies* 43(1983), pp 643-63.

Wang Yü-ch'üan, 'The Rise of Land Tax and the Fall of Dynasties in Chinese History', *Pacific Affairs* IX(1936), pp 201-20.

William Watson, 'The Chinese Contribution to Eastern nomad culture in the pre-Han and early Han periods', *World Archaeology* 4(1972), pp 139-49.

W Weissleder, 'The Promotion of Suzerainty Between Sedentary and Nomadic Populations in Eastern Ethiopia' in: W Weissleder (ed), *The Nomadic Alternative. Modes and Models of Interaction in the African-Asian Deserts and Steppes* (The Hague: Mouton, 1978), pp 275-88.

Ian Whitaker, 'Tuvan Reindeer Husbandry in the Early 20th century', *Polar Record* 20(1981), pp 337-51.

K A Wittfogel:

   'The Foundations and Stages of Chinese Economic History', *Zeitschrift Für Sozialforschung* IV(1935), pp 26-60.

   'Die Theorie der orientalischen Gesellschaft', *Zeitschrift Für Sozialforschung*, VII(1938), pp 109-14.

   'Meteorological Records from the Divination Inscriptions of Shang', *The Geographical Review* 30(1940), pp 110-31.

   'Chinese Society and the Dynasties of Conquest', H F MacNair (ed), *China* (Berkeley: University of California Press, 1946), pp 112-26.

Victor A Yakhontoff, 'Mongolia: Target or Screen?', *Pacific Affairs* IX(1936), pp 13-23.

S Yushkov, 'K voprosu o dofeodal'nom ("varvarskom") gosudarstve' [On the question of the pre-feudal ('barbarian') state], *Voprosy Istorii* 7(1946), pp 45-65.

Index

Index